Principles of human resource management

Principles of human resource management provides an excellent introduction to key issues in the field of human resource management. Avoiding the prescriptive approach, David Goss identifies a number of underlying assumptions and principles associated with developments in human resource management and explores the implications of these in a manner which encourages a critical attitude in his readers.

The chapters provide analyses of key areas of human resource policy both in terms of internal developments and relevance to wider HRM projects. Issues covered include new developments in human resource planning and performance management, assessment, training and development, reward, commitment and employee involvement, welfare, trade unions and equal opportunities. The book concludes with a discussion of the prospects for a European human resource management.

David Goss is Senior Lecturer in the Department of Human Resource Management, University of Portsmouth Business School, where he teaches HRM, Research Methodology and Business Environment on the MBA course. He is the author of a book on employment relations in small firms and has also published a number of articles on various aspects of human resource management. He is currently researching in the area of AIDS/HIV and employment.

Routledge series in the principles of management
Edited by Joseph G. Nellis

The Routledge series in the principles of management offers stimulating approaches to the core topics of management. The books relate the key areas to strategic issues in order to help managers solve problems and take control. By encouraging readers to apply their own experiences, the books are designed to develop the skills of the all-round manager.

Principles of marketing
G. Randall

Principles of financial management
Keith Ward and Keith Parker

Principles of information systems management
John Ward

Principles of law
A. Ruff

Principles of applied statistics
M. Fleming and J. Nellis

Principles of accounting and finance
P. Sneyd

Principles of operations management
R. L. Galloway

Principles of service operations management
Colin Armistead and Graham Clark

Principles of human resource management

David Goss

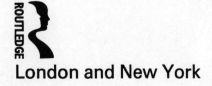

London and New York

First published 1994
by Routledge
11 New Fetter Lane, London EC4P 4EE

Simultaneously published in the USA and Canada
by Routledge
29 West 35th Street, New York, NY 10001

Typeset in Times by Michael Mepham, Frome, Somerset
Printed and bound in Great Britain by
Mackays of Chatham PLC, Chatham, Kent

British Library Cataloguing in Publication Data
A catalogue record for this book is available from the British Library.

Library of Congress Cataloging-in-Publication Data has been applied for

ISBN 0–415–09188–8

Contents

List of figures   vi
List of tables   vii
Series editor's preface   viii
Preface   x
Acknowledgements   xii

1 **HRM: a new trajectory?**   1

2 **Human resourcing: planning and performance**   19

3 **Assessment: judging people and performance**   39

4 **Training and development: building bridges?**   62

5 **Reward: motivation and control**   83

6 **Commitment and employee involvement: HRM's Holy Grail?**   101

7 **Welfare: health and efficiency?**   122

8 **Trade unions and the New Industrial Relations**   140

9 **Equal opportunities: challenge and change**   156

10 **Towards a European HRM?**   175

References   183
Index   192

Figures

1.1 Strategic change and HRM   15

1.2 Elements of a HRM network   16

1.3 Tightly coupled HRM network   17

1.4 Loosely coupled 'string' network   17

2.1 Molecular CPIS structure   23

2.2 The flexible firm   31

2.3 Risk assessment model of flexible working patterns   35

4.1 A Kolb-type learning cycle   74

5.1 Types of reward   87

5.2 Maps of different reward systems   88

6.1 Organizational commitments   109

7.1 Work-related stress   136

9.1 Equal opportunities agendas   157

Tables

1.1 Twenty-seven points of difference   3

3.1 Characteristics of assessment functions   40

3.2 Most important selection methods   43

3.3 Numbers of interviews and interviewers   44

3.4 Use of selection tests by employee groups   46

4.1 Evaluation table   81

5.1 Types of PRP scheme   92

6.1 The impact of team briefing on employees   113

9.1 Monitoring equal opportunities   162

10.1 HRM in Europe   176

Series editor's preface

In recent years there has been a dramatic increase in management development activity in most western countries, especially in Europe. This activity has extended across a wide spectrum of training initiatives, from continuing studies programmes of varying durations for practising managers to the provision of courses leading to the award of professional and academic qualifications. With regard to the latter the most prominent developments have been in terms of the Master of Business Administration (MBA) and Diploma in Management (DMS) programmes, particularly in the UK where virtually every university now offers some form of post-graduate and/or post-experience management qualification.

However, the explosion of formal management training programmes such as the MBA and DMS has tended to be in advance of suitably tailored management textbooks. Many of the core functional areas of these programmes have had to rely on some of the more specialized and thus more narrowly focused textbooks, which are more appropriate for undergraduate requirements. They have generally not provided a suitable balance between academic rigour and practical, business-related relevance. The Routledge series covering the principles of management has been specifically developed to service the needs of an expanding management audience. The series deals with the full range of core subjects as well as many of the more popular elective courses that one would expect to find in most MBA and DMS programmes. Many of the books will also be attractive to those students taking professional exams, for example in accountancy, banking, etc., as well as managers attending a wide range of development courses. Each book in the series is written in a concise format covering the key principles of each topic in a pragmatic style which emphasizes the balance between theory and application. Case studies, exercises, and references for further reading are provided where appropriate.

It gives me pleasure to express my thanks to the staff of Routledge for the commitment and energy which they have devoted to the development of this series, and in particular to Francesca Weaver who has skilfully steered each book through the minefield of production from beginning to end. I would also like to express my gratitude to my secretary Christine Williams for maintaining her joviality throughout the development of the 'Principles' series.

Joseph G. Nellis
Cranfield School of Management

Preface

The intention of this book is to provide an introduction to key issues in the field of human resource management. In doing this I have tried not to adopt a prescriptive approach which advocates one particular model of HRM to which all organizations must aspire. Rather I have sought to give readers access to some of the different perspectives which exist in this field and to encourage them to evaluate these against their own experiences of work organizations. What I have tried to do, therefore, is to identify a number of important underlying assumptions and principles associated with a variety of developments in HRM and to explore the implications of these in a manner which encourages critique and challenge, rather than passive acceptance.

How and to what extent HRM constitutes a 'strategic management' discipline remains a subject of some debate. However, rather than get bogged down in semantic arguments over what is or is not to be defined as 'strategic', I have taken the view that strategy cannot be treated as a purely 'top-down' exercise, one step removed from operational procedures, but must be premised on an understanding of the component processes that it seeks to manipulate and control. For this reason I feel that it is important to examine the functional areas upon which any form of strategic HRM must depend. Put metaphorically, it is my view that to build a decent wall one must not only have an eye for the aesthetic, but also a rudimentary understanding of the properties of bricks and mortar for, ultimately, it is upon these that the integrity of the structure will rest. However, I have also tried to avoid treating these areas simply as discrete units, as operations to be mastered in relative isolation, in favour of an approach which explores them in terms of underlying principles and the options to which these give rise.

Thus, Chapter 1 is an account of the emergence of the HRM debate and the perspectives to which it has given rise. The emphasis is upon developing an understanding of HRM in terms of 'content' and 'form', the former being constituted by the policy levers and 'tools' of contemporary personnel practice, and the latter by the way in which these 'unit ideas' can be combined to meet the strategic intentions and environmental/organizational constraints faced by specific organizations in particular situations. Subsequent chapters develop this notion by providing analyses of key areas of human resource policy in terms of their internal developments and their relevance to wider HRM projects. These chapters cover new developments in human resource planning and performance management, assessment, training and development, reward, commitment and employee involvement, welfare, trade unions and equal opportunities. The book concludes with a discussion of the prospects for a European approach to HRM.

I do not see it as the role of the academic to provide neatly packaged, predetermined answers: at best, managers can be encouraged to ask questions about their own organizations and provided with the analytical skills and techniques to develop their own solutions, appropriate to their own organizations. As such this is not a 'how to do it' book; rather it looks at how things have been done and why they may have turned out the way they did; the emphasis is on a mixture of theory and practical example which it is hoped will encourage and enable readers to develop their own approaches to HRM through criticism and evaluation, rather than by blindly following prescription.

David Goss

Acknowledgements

Many people have contributed to the writing of this book. First and foremost are Fiona, Sophie, Charlotte, Michael, Betty and Jean, without whose support, tolerance and sacrifice the long hours at the word processor would not have been possible. Also I owe a great deal to colleagues at Portsmouth Business School and, in particular, to my MBA students who have been a constant source of ideas and constructive criticism. Finally I must thank Francesca Weaver of Routledge and Joe Nellis of Cranfield for their editorial assistance and advice.

Acknowledgement is made to the following sources for their kind permission to reproduce the following figures and tables: Blackwell Publishers and John Storey for Table 1.1; Institute of Manpower Studies/Institute of Personnel Management for Figure 2.1, *Personnel Management*, the monthly magazine of the Institute of Personnel Management, for Figure 2.3; Controller of Her Majesty's Stationery Office for Table 6.1; Macmillan Publishers for Figure 7.1.

Chapter 1

HRM

A new trajectory?

THE CONTEMPORARY SIGNIFICANCE OF HRM

Human resource management (HRM) is a term which, throughout the 1980s and into the 1990s, has become increasingly familiar to managers and management students. But a decade of familiarization has done little to clarify exactly what HRM is, where it differs from traditional personnel management, and how important it will be for the future. In this book, HRM will be treated as a diverse body of thought and practice, loosely unified by a concern to integrate the management of personnel more closely with the core management activity of organizations. There is, however, little agreement among HRM theorists or practitioners as to how this project should best be accomplished. As such, the thrust of this book is to offer accessible accounts of the key debates, in the hope that by laying bare some fundamental principles, readers will be able to assess for themselves the options available and the implications of different approaches for their own organizations.

> **The development of HRM as a body of management thought in the 1980s can be linked to a conjunction of socio-economic factors – in particular, changes in international competition, the restructuring of industrial sectors and organizations, and the rise of a renewed confidence in the power of managers to manage.**

Under these conditions the contribution of human resources to the success of organizations has been emphasized through the championing of doctrines of 'excellence', 'quality', 'innovation' and 'entrepreneurship'. These developments placed the management of people firmly on the agenda and created the conditions for the emergence of a new-style theory of personnel management, bearing the label HRM. Krulis-Randa (1990:136) provides a good example. According to this writer, HRM involves the following characteristics:

- A focus on horizontal authority and reduced hierarchy; a blurring of the rigid distinction between management and non-management.
- Wherever possible, responsibility for people-management is devolved to line

managers; the role of personnel professionals is to support and facilitate line management in this task, not to control it.

- Human resource planning is proactive and fused with corporate level planning; human resource issues are treated strategically in an integrated manner.
- Employees are viewed as subjects with the potential for growth and development; the purpose of human resource management is to identify this potential and develop it in line with the adaptive needs of the organization.
- HRM suggests that management and non-management have a common interest in the success of the organization. Its purpose is to ensure that all employees are aware of this and committed to common goals.

Unfortunately, many of those taking this 'path-breaking' road promised more in theory than could be delivered in practice. As a result, arguments about a 'new HRM' have often been met with scepticism and sometimes hostility on account of their apparent idealism, naive oversimplification and remoteness from everyday practice. In many ways this is unfortunate. As this book will suggest, there is much to be gained from a re-examination of personnel practice, albeit not necessarily in terms of proselytizing a wholly new paradigm that must replace everything that has gone before. In this respect, HRM may be more useful if it is seen to have more modest aims – in particular, the development of a better understanding of the holistic nature of organizational practices (Evans *et al.* 1989), the interrelation between different personnel policies, their relevance to other management activity, and the development of tools for the analysis and evaluation of human resource requirements in specific organizational settings.

Even this less ambitious project, however, requires a model of HRM to give its content a structure and focus. One solution would seem to be the construction of a model with a very clear theoretical status. This has been undertaken to good effect by Storey (1992) in the form of an 'ideal type', the function of which is to provide an analytical construction of a situation which *might* exist if the appropriate conditions are present (see Table 1.1). Using this type of model the task of the analyst is to explore if, how, and to what extent, this 'ideal' is realizable in practice. Whether or not organizations are adopting HRM is thus a matter for investigation, rather than prescription. In this respect, therefore, the clear distinction between HRM and other forms of people-management is very much a caricature developed for the purpose of analysis, and we should expect there to be debate about both the extent to which any large-scale transformation of traditional personnel management into HRM has actually taken place (Storey 1992; Guest 1992), and the exact nature of specific HRM regimes.

For the purpose of subsequent exposition, the final section of this chapter will introduce a simplified model of HRM based on a variant of this 'ideal type' approach. But before turning to this, it is first necessary to understand more fully the factors which led to the emergence of the HRM debate and the key ideas which this has involved, as these will have a bearing on subsequent investigations.

Table 1.1 Twenty-seven points of difference

Dimension	Personnel and IR	HRM
Beliefs and assumptions		
1 Contract	Careful delineation of written contracts	Aim to go 'beyond contract'
2 Rules	Importance of devising clear rules/mutuality	'Can-do' outlook: impatience with 'rules'
3 Guide to management action	Procedures	'Business-need'
4 Behaviour referent	Norms/custom and practice	Values/mission
5 Managerial task *vis-à-vis* labour	Monitoring	Nurturing
6 Nature of relations	Pluralist	Unitarist
7 Conflict	Institutionalized	De-emphasized
Strategic aspects		
8 Key relations	Labour–management	Customer
9 Initiatives	Piecemeal	Integrated
10 Corporate plan	Marginal to	Central to
11 Speed of decision	Slow	Fast
Line management		
12 Management role	Transactional	Transformational leadership
13 Key managers	Personnel/IR specialists	General/business/line managers
14 Communication	Indirect	Direct
15 Standardization	High (e.g. 'parity' an issue)	Low (e.g. 'parity' not seen as relevant)
16 Prized management skills	Negotiation	Facilitation
Key levers		
17 Selection	Separate, marginal task	Integrated, key task
18 Pay	Job evaluation (fixed grades)	Performance-related
19 Conditions	Separately negotiated	Harmonization
20 Labour-management	Collective bargaining contracts	Towards individual contracts
21 Thrust of relations with stewards	Regularized through facilities and training	Marginalized (with exception of some bargaining for change models)
22 Job categories and grades	Many	Few
23 Communication	Restricted flow	Increased flow
24 Job design	Division of labour	Teamwork
25 Conflict handling	Reach temporary truces	Manage climate and culture
26 Training and development	Controlled access to courses	Learning companies
27 Focus of attention for interventions	Personnel procedures	Wide-ranging cultural, structural and personnel strategies

Source: Storey (1992: 37)

International competition

During the 1970s and early 1980s it became increasingly apparent that US and UK industry was failing to compete effectively at an international level, evidenced by the seemingly unstoppable market penetration of Japanese manufacturers, growing trade deficits and international debt, declining productivity and increasingly severe recessions. Not surprisingly, faced with such obvious decline, many western managers looked to Japan for inspiration. What they saw, and were told, was that Japanese manufacturing success was rooted in its people and the way in which they were managed. As one widely quoted Japanese executive put it:

> We will win and you will lose. You cannot do anything about it because your failure is an internal disease. Your companies are based on Taylor's [scientific management] principles. Worse, your heads are Taylorized too. You firmly believe that sound management means executives on the one side and workers on the other, on the one side men who think and on the other side men who can only work. For you, management is the art of smoothly transferring the executives' idea to the workers' hands.

> (Quoted in Best 1990:4)

The result of this analysis of Japanese industry was the belief that success stemmed from extensive employee involvement in the business and resulting high levels of commitment, the *leitmotif* of this being the quality circle.

What the Japanese lesson suggested was that people were indeed the key asset of the business and that the management of people was a central strategic issue, rather than a necessary inconvenience.

A similar but weaker message was also culled from the experience of West Germany, the one notable success story of western industrial nations, where attention was drawn to forms of worker participation and involvement through mechanisms such as works councils and board level representation (Beer *et al*. 1984:45). Such ideas were readily accepted in the US, where the Japanese example provided the proof that proponents of the Human Relations style of management had long sought to convince sceptical corporate leaders of the value of 'treating people right'. This enhanced credibility gave a new impetus to Human Relations ideas which now form a key plank in many aspects of HRM.

In short, then, diminishing international competitiveness in most western industrial nations forced managers to reassess their methods. The glowing examples of Japanese and German industrial success all appeared to point to the need to bring people back into the equation; to think of them as a resource to be valued, developed and actively managed – a potential for competitive advantage (Porter 1990). This insight opened the way for the development of HRM as a body of theory geared to promoting the management of people as a strategic resource.

Industrial and organizational restructuring

Coupled to the challenge of international competition was the effect of recession and trade crises. In the UK and USA these reached a peak in the early 1980s and resulted in the significant restructuring of industries and organizations. In particular, there was an emphasis on the need drastically to improve competitiveness by developing 'leaner and fitter' organizations. This generally meant shedding labour, rationalizing production processes and tightening managerial control. In both the US and the UK this shake-out of private industry was matched in the public sector by governments which were committed to reducing public spending and getting better 'value for money', by attacking what they perceived as excessive bureaucracy.

The result has been a growing interest in 'flatter', i.e. less hierarchical, structures, a greater concern with flexibility, adaptiveness and change, and with decentralization and the devolution of responsibility to cost and profit centres as a means of exposing strengths and weaknesses in organizational effectiveness.

Because these initiatives were seen as representing a break with bureaucratic control, they also raised questions about the management of people. Again the conclusions pointed towards greater participation and commitment (to encourage flexibility and adaptability), a greater reliance on self-discipline (to allow the 'thinning' of supervisory levels), and the development of more effective systems for measuring and rewarding individual contributions to the organization.

Once more these developments created a space within which the emerging HRM approach could develop, calling for a fresh perspective on people-management and forcing the connection between this and other central organizational concerns.

The new managerialism

A final factor contributing to the emergence of HRM was a change in the power and confidence of management, especially the reassertion of the 'right to manage'. This was facilitated by a combination of economic and social factors. The recession of the early 1980s resulted in widespread job loss and, in consequence, a drastic undermining of trade union power, giving management an opportunity to push through radical changes in working practices with minimal resistance. In addition, however, the political ideologies of Thatcherism and Reaganism exhorted management to 'regain control' of industry, reinforcing this message with legislation aimed at curbing what were regarded as excessive union powers (see Chapter 8 below). By the mid-1980s the role of the manager had risen considerably in social and academic esteem and, spurred on by business schools and management gurus, there was a greater confidence and willingness to experiment with new ideas and approaches in the years of economic boom which followed the recession.

In this climate of change the emerging notion of HRM, itself stimulated by this transition, had a topical novelty, capturing the spirit of the times by seeming to address what was hailed in many circles as a key reason for economic decline: the failure to manage labour effectively. Thus, while HRM had a general appeal to management, it held out even greater promise to personnel professionals. Within the profession there seems to have been a widespread fear that the tough recession years were speeding a noticeable decline in its status within the ranks of management. According to Storey (1989:5) personnel management had long been 'dogged by problems of credibility, marginality, ambiguity and a "trash-can" labelling' which had reduced it to a relatively disconnected set of duties tainted with low status and a 'soft' image. HRM, therefore, offered both a 'disciplinary base' and a rationale for incorporating this into top-level strategic decision-making. It is perhaps not surprising that the personnel profession has generally supported (implicitly, if not always explicitly) the dissemination of HRM ideas and identities. Despite the charge of 'old wine in new bottles', the willingness with which many organizations have supported the change of title from 'personnel management' to 'human resource management' does seem to suggest a high level of managerial receptiveness to the notion.

In summary, then, HRM fulfilled two needs of a newly confident managerial 'profession': it offered the promise of a solution to the problem of labour management, and it provided a large group of 'threatened' management specialists with the opportunity to revitalize their flagging fortunes. In these respects it was clearly an idea whose time had come.

To draw these threads together, therefore, it can be said that the 'unit ideas' of HRM, while not in themselves new, were galvanized together as a body of theory and given a heightened priority by the historical coincidence of a variety of factors associated with the economic and political environment of the 1980s.

HRM: KEY THEMES

With some understanding of why HRM has risen to prominence, a more detailed examination of its nature and substance can be undertaken. Although an issue on which opinion differs, it is possible to isolate three key themes which inform, in some measure, most approaches which go under the name HRM:

- human relations psychology;
- strategic management theory;
- doctrines of flexibility and quality management.

These provide a convenient framework within which different 'schools' of HRM can be located.

Human relations psychology

The origins and development of the Human Relations school have been fully described elsewhere (e.g. Rose 1975; Hollway 1991) and it is necessary only to consider here those ideas which have contributed to contemporary HRM thinking. In particular these include the concepts of motivation, group dynamics, and commitment. In line with much of the Quality of Work Life (QWL) theory fashionable in the 1960s and 70s, Human Relations asserts that individuals are motivated not merely by financial returns (or fear of punishment), but by 'psychological' rewards such as recognition, and the opportunity to contribute to decision-making and take responsibility. The notion of 'commitment' has particular relevance as a unifying concept in this respect (see Chapter 6 below). According to Neale and Northcraft (1991), for instance:

> Organizational commitment is the relative strength of an individual's identification with and involvement in a particular organization. It usually includes three factors: (1) a strong belief in the organization's goals and values; (2) a willingness to exert considerable effort on behalf of the organization; and (3) a strong desire to continue as an organization member. Organizational commitment, then, is not simply loyalty to an organization. Rather it is an ongoing process through which organizational actors express their concern for the organization and its continued success and well-being.
>
> (Ibid. :290)

This, in turn, involves the design of jobs in such a way as to allow discretion in the work task and the opportunity for individual development and progression within the organization (the possibility of 'self-actualization', in Maslow's terminology). For example:

> jobs are designed to be broader than before, to combine planning and implementation, and include efforts to upgrade operations, not just maintain them. Individual responsibilities are expected to change as conditions change, and teams, not individuals, often are the organizational units accountable for performance. With management hierarchies relatively flat and differences in status minimised, control and lateral coordination depend on shared goals, and expertise rather than formal position determines influence.
>
> (Walton 1991:447)

The emphasis is firmly on commitment rather than traditional (Taylorist) forms of supervisory control; upon 'partnership' and team spirit rather than autocratic hierarchy. Indeed, the emphasis on team working which now plays an important part in most HRM approaches (Lawler and Mohrman 1991) has a long tradition, dating back to the Hawthorn experiments of the 1930s. Elton Mayo in particular attributed many benefits to team-based work:

> [The work group was] At first shy and uneasy, silent and perhaps somewhat suspicious of the company's intention, later their attitude is marked by con-

fidence and candour. Before every change of program the group is consulted. Their comments are listened to and discussed; sometimes their objections are allowed to negate a suggestion. The group unquestionably develops a sense of participation in the critical determinations and becomes something of a social unit.

(Cited in Grenier 1988: 56)

The attraction of Human Relations ideas for HRM is the insights it provides into motivation and commitment and how these can be fostered to build a sense of 'mutuality' within the organization, to generate high levels of trust and to encourage flexible, adaptive and innovative behaviour. These, it will be recalled, are the qualities claimed to be needed to fight industrial decline and uncompetitiveness. If, however, HRM were based only on Human Relations theory, it would certainly be difficult to regard it as being in any way novel. What is significant is that these ideas have been combined with other strands of management theory, giving them a renewed lease of life.

Strategic management theory

Of these other strands, strategic management theory has played a key role. As a distinct body of thought, strategic management emerged in the 1970s from the combination of long-range planning and 'research proven' strategic success analysis (Ansoff and McDonnel 1990; Chandler 1962). The result of this synthesis was a set of propositions, aimed at senior management, according to which resources could be allocated rationally, relative to environmental conditions, to secure competitive advantage.

However, the exact nature of this 'rationality' is subject to debate. At one extreme there is an emphasis on strategy as a discipline designed to determine the outcomes which an organization wants to achieve and to secure the best possible 'fit' between that organization and its environment. This type of 'outcome analysis' is most apparent in areas such as portfolio planning. The Boston Consulting Group Matrix (which uses the well-known expressions 'Question Mark', 'Star', 'Dog', and 'Cash Cow') provides an example of this, focusing on two variables: the rate of growth of the product market area and the market share in that area held by the firm relative to that of its largest competitor. These measures give an indication of the attractiveness of the market and the overall strength of the firm in that market relative to its competitors (Howe 1986:67). Thus, according to Pettigrew:

The rational approach describes and prescribes techniques for identifying current strategy, analysing environments, resources and gaps, revealing and assessing strategic alternatives and choosing and implementing carefully analysed and well thought through outcomes. This rational picture of business problem-solving has as its concern the content or 'what' of strategy – the outcome which is sought – and has nothing to say at an explicit level of how to achieve that outcome. In other words, it has no process theory within it of how and why to create the strategic outcomes so perceptively and logically derived from the analysis of competitive forces.

(Pettigrew 1985:19)

As an alternative to this 'rational-outcome' view, therefore, other writers have shifted attention towards the rationality of the 'process', i.e., how outcomes are actually achieved. Thus, strategy is defined as a process of calculated decision making intended to guide the direction in which organizational effort is directed (e.g. Mintzberg et al. 1976; Butler 1991). This involves the logical sequencing of successive stages of strategic activity which act as filters, progressively reducing uncertainty and imposing meaning upon environmental and organizational data. Strategy, it is claimed, should be seen as the outcome of a complex of more or less calculative decisions which do not necessarily reflect the most technically or economically rational objectives of the organization. Bateman and Zeithaml (1989:60), for instance, draw attention to the psychological context of strategic decision-making, to its incremental nature, the role of historical antecedents and individual biography, and the extent of convergence between personal and organizational goals.

As will be seen below, both the 'rational-outcome' and 'process' approaches to management strategy have important implications for the way in which HRM is approached.

Flexibility and quality

As much as anything, since the early 1980s the notions of flexibility and quality have been tied to industrial regeneration and, as such, provide important themes within HRM (see Chapter 2). Flexibility has been seen as a vital means of responding swiftly to changes in economic and technical environments and reducing costs by maximizing the utilization of employee skills.

Two forms of flexibility are usually identified. The first, numerical flexibility, refers to the ability of organizations to restructure their workforces so as to retain only workers with key skills as direct employees, less essential functions being placed with outside contractors, the self-employed or casual/part-time labour. In this way the organization reduces its direct administration and supervisory costs, and responds to changes in its markets/budget by terminating or extending contracts. The subcontract/casual 'periphery' thus acts as a buffer for the 'core' staff of the organization. This approach is epitomized in Atkinson's (1984) model of the 'flexible firm'. Functional flexibility, on the other hand, concerns the practice of 'multi-skilling' whereby workers are encouraged to acquire a range of different skills each of which, previously, would have been the preserve of a single occupational group. A mechanical engineer, for example, might also be trained as an electrical fitter and a plumber. In this way skilled labour can be deployed as and when needed.

Like flexibility, quality is also held to be a vital component in an organization's response to its environment. Quality management makes use of the notion of 'fitness of purpose', i.e. the idea that the quality of a product or service is defined not by some esoteric standard of technical excellence but by the demands of the customer or consumer. This necessitates constant monitoring of customer requirements and an ability to develop the product or service to meet, or preferably pre-empt, any changes. According to the principles of Total Quality Management, for instance, quality becomes a concern for every member of the organization (not merely a small group of 'controllers'): it is 'a business discipline and philosophy of management which institutionalises planned and continuous business improvement' (Hill 1991:554). From this perspective the management of both quality and flexibility is inextricably bound to the management of people, a fact which is being increasingly recognized in HRM thinking.

APPROACHES TO HRM

The three themes outlined above all appear to a greater or lesser extent in HRM. However, the interpretation of each theme and its relative emphasis does tend to vary, reflecting the fact that, like most other management disciplines, HRM is characterized by internal divisions. Indeed, it is possible to identify two extreme positions, distinguished primarily in terms of the way they conceive the strategic potential of HRM:

- **Instrumental approaches** draw upon the rational-outcome model of strategic management to view HRM as something which is driven by and derived directly from corporate, divisional or business level strategy, and geared almost exclusively to enhancing competitive advantage.
- **Humanistic approaches** utilize 'process' theory to emphasize the reciprocal nature of the relationship between strategic management and HRM and the latter's role in ensuring that competitive advantage is achieved *through* people, but not necessarily at their expense.

Instrumental approaches to HRM

Instrumental approaches place the emphasis firmly on human *resource management*. This is what Storey (1989:6) refers to as the 'hard' version of HRM, emphasizing the 'quantitative, calculative, and business strategic aspects of managing the head-count in as "rational" a way as for any other economic factor'. Dawson (1989), for example, points to the fact that the factors contributing to the emergence of HRM have also encouraged a renewed interest in human resource accounting (see Chapter 2 below) and that a closer relationship between the two is possible:

> what seems certain... is that there will be an escalation of the application of financial measurement techniques for planning, control and evaluation of HRM

activities.... With these 'harder' measures comes the notion that managers are able to make better, that is financially or economically rational, decisions.

(Dawson 1989:9)

Thus, taken from this perspective, HRM is concerned with the integration of human resource issues into business planning. All decisions about the acquisition, processing and management of human resources must, like any other organizational input, be tailored to increase or restore competitive advantage. The key question must be: 'What HRM strategy will maximise competitive advantage, optimise control, and minimise unit and labour replacement costs' (Keenoy 1990:5). From this standpoint, the notion of performance assumes central importance, this being taken as the primary objective of management strategy (Miller 1991). This has encouraged the development of measurable criteria for assessing the performance of people and their specific contribution to the organization in a manner comparable to other resources, e. g., in terms of business ratios such as profit per employee, added value per employee, costs per employee, etc. (Tyson 1985; Whitaker 1991). It has also led to an interest in the planning and forecasting of human resource needs in ways which match closely the organization's changing requirements and developing activities, making use of tools and techniques associated with, for example, portfolio planning (Purcell 1989) and social scientific research (Pearson 1991).

Indeed, the particular perspective on strategy adopted by Instrumental approaches tends to be very precise and makes a point of differentiating 'levels' of strategy. Thus, for Miller:

all issues associated with the management of human resources should be derived issues. In other words, we are probably dealing with a 'functional' or 'business' level strategy. HRM cannot be conceptualised as a stand alone corporate issue. Strategically speaking, it must flow from and be dependent upon the organization's (market oriented) corporate strategy.

(Miller 1991:24)

The assumption that HRM is 'derived' from corporate and business level strategy leads to what Boxall (1992) calls the 'matching model', according to which organizational effectiveness is achieved by ensuring a 'tight fit' between corporate/business strategy and HRM strategy.

A number of significant criticisms can, however, be made of the Instrumental approach. First, there is the charge that it tends to be overly rationalistic, that strategy is assumed to be formulated in advance of action and then unproblematically implemented. This, according to Boxall:

leads to a conceptualisation in which HRM is cast purely in a reactive, implementationalist role. It fails to perceive the potential for a reciprocal relationship between HR strategy and business strategy.... The theory seems to ask too little of HRM. Surely, any chief executive with long-term vision would want to use HRM not just to woodenly implement a preconceived business strategy, but to create a climate in which valuable strategising occurs...?

(Boxall 1992:68)

A related criticism is that this encourages a narrowness of focus. One of the early contributions to this approach, that of Fombrun *et al.* (1984), concentrated on four 'generic' functions: selection, reward, appraisal and development. While these undeniably have a central role, a strong case can also be made for the inclusion of other dimensions such as welfare, equal opportunities, employee involvement and industrial relations, on the grounds that these issues reflect both the practice of much organizational life and the realm of individual and societal interests which pervade all workplace activity (Boxall 1992:69; Hendry and Pettigrew 1990).

Finally there is the claim of excessive 'unitarism'. The so-called 'unitary frame of reference' describes an approach towards the management of people which regards the work organization as a harmonious unit characterized by a common purpose within which managerial authority is taken to be legitimate. Any challenge to this authority (such as trade unionism) is viewed as fundamentally pathological and destructive. From this perspective, interests and concerns of employees are frequently 'written-out' of the equation, it being taken for granted that what top management considers best for the organization will automatically (or ultimately) be best for the workforce. As Boxall (1992:68) has put it, from this viewpoint: 'HRM appears as something that is 'done to' passive human resources rather than something that is 'done with' active human beings'. This view has been echoed by Keenoy:

The irony is that the escape route from the ambiguity which is offered by the strategic pretensions of HRM may only be possible with the sacrifice of any claim to 'understand and articulate the views of the workforce'. While it is possible that the organizational legitimacy of personnel management may be reconstructed by its transformation into HRM... by embracing the very real power offered by involvement in strategic HRM, personnel managers may have to relinquish any claim to be the guardians of *humane* human resource management.

(Keenoy 1990:8–9).

In many respects, Humanistic variants of HRM can be seen as responses to these potential difficulties.

Humanistic approaches to HRM

These approaches are closely associated with what has become known as the 'Harvard School' of HRM. As the humanistic label implies, the emphasis is on the 'softer' aspects of HRM associated with organizational culture and employee commitment and, as such, its orientation is broader and less rigidly 'functional'. As Beer *et al.* the initiators of this movement, make clear:

Human resource management involves *all management decisions* and actions that affect the nature of the relationship between the organization and its employees – its human resources. General management make important decisions daily that affect this relationship.

(Beer *et al.* 1984:1; emphasis added)

This leads to a 'map of HRM territory', the core of which Beer *et al.* refer to as the 'four Cs' (p.16):

* Competence of employees.
* Commitment of employees.
* Congruence between the goals of *employees* and those of the organization.
* Cost effectiveness of HRM practices.

A summary of these factors gives a good flavour of what this approach entails.

* High **commitment** means that employees will be motivated to 'hear, understand, and respond' to management's communications relating to the organization of work. The resulting mutual trust enables 'management's message to be more believable to employees and to enable management to be responsive to employee's legitimate concerns as stakeholders' (Beer *et al.* 1984:36).
* High **competence** creates a positive attitude towards learning and development and, thereby, gives employees the 'versatility in skills and the perspective to take on new roles and jobs as needed' (p.36).
* **Cost effectiveness** 'means that the organization's human resource costs – wages, benefits, and indirect costs such as strikes, turnover, and grievances – have been kept equal to or less than competitors'... only a continual process of mutual influence about the realities of the business and the needs of employees can bring about this outcome' (p.36).
* Higher **congruence** is a reflection of policies and practices which bring about a 'higher coincidence of interests among management, shareholders and workers' (p.36), a situation encouraged by forms of employee influence which, in turn, reduce adversarial relations.

Humanistic approaches still exhibit a strong sense of unitarism (although here, rather than taking employee compliance for granted, as in the Instrumental version, the Humanistic variant assumes that it is only inappropriate HRM policies that 'obscure' legitimacy of the managerial prerogative). This emphasis, however, has been less apparent in UK developments of this perspective. Hendry and Pettigrew (1990), for example, draw explicitly on a process model of strategic decision-making which emphasizes the emergent, political and frequently non-rational nature of this process. This leads to a less prescriptive and more people-centred approach than that found in Instrumental orientations and a more realistically pluralist view of employment relations. The following account captures the main thrust of this position:

The impact of [contextual] factors on the HR system of the firm – on recruitment and selection, on appraisal, on career planning, on the training and development of people, on pay, on employee relations, on work organization – is mediated at times by the personnel/HR function, at times by line managers. The precise role of the personnel function in this is influenced by its record of successes and failures, its orientation, its vision and *capacity to enact* a 'strategic' HRM, and its organization. Similarly business strategy evolves in response to success and failure, and is the work of people acting in rational-analytical, *political, and emotional* ways through organizational structures. In so far as HRM is responsive to business strategy, it is perforce *'emergent'*. The criteria of coherence and appropriateness (fit) are therefore only very provisionally attained.

(Hendry and Pettigrew 1990:31; emphasis added)

What is important for this position is not simply whether HRM is, in itself, strategic, but the extent to which HRM programmes can be utilized to achieve policy and strategic objectives, as represented in Figure 1.1.

This utilization is based upon management choice (rather than environmental or situational determinism as with Instrumental theory) which, in turn, is conditioned by the power of other stakeholders to obstruct, modify or facilitate such action. This entails an awareness of alternative programme options and of their short-and long-term consequences at all organizational levels, thereby allowing an assessment of their congruence and an evaluation of their likely cost-effectiveness.

Thus there can be no standard or universal 'theory' or 'method' of HRM but, rather, a need for analytical knowledge of basic principles and how these can be adapted and developed innovatively to meet a range of individual, organizational and societal outcomes (Beer *et al.* 1984:19).

AN ANALYTICAL MODEL OF HRM

In a short introductory text such as this, it is not possible to provide an analysis of the ___ ___ic surrounding these differing approaches to HRM. At present it will be suﬃcient for the reader to appreciate in broad terms the nature of these differences and the general directions in which they point (see Storey 1989; Blyton and Turnbull 1992; Towers 1992 for more on these debates). For the purpose of exposition, however, it is necessary to develop a framework which allows the comprehension of the key components of HRM and their interconnection but which, simultaneously, is not committed irrevocably to any single 'variant'. The model which will now be advanced should be taken as a convenient analytical device, not as a statement of what 'genuine' HRM should be (see Figure 1.2). It is intended to capture the distinctiveness of HRM while being sufficiently flexible and 'open-ended' not to restrict discussion to a single school of theory.

The basis of this position is the view that, however defined, HRM must consist

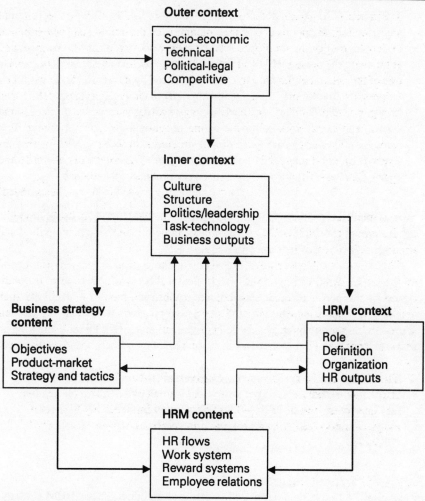

Figure 1.1 Strategic change and HRM
(*Source*: Hendry and Pettigrew 1990)

of a 'content': a set of techniques and practices that have been developed specifically for the management of people. These will fall into broad functional areas:
resourcing, assessment, reward, training, employee involvement, collective representation, welfare and equal opportunities being the most common. But in addition,
HRM must also exhibit a 'form': a conscious rationale according to which specific
techniques from within each functional area are selected and then integrated with
other organizational policies. It is this 'form' which constitutes HRM strategy and
distinguishes it from traditional 'fragmented' approaches to personnel management. As this is an expository approach, the existence of a formal rationale is
regarded as being more important than its precise nature (i.e. its theoretical

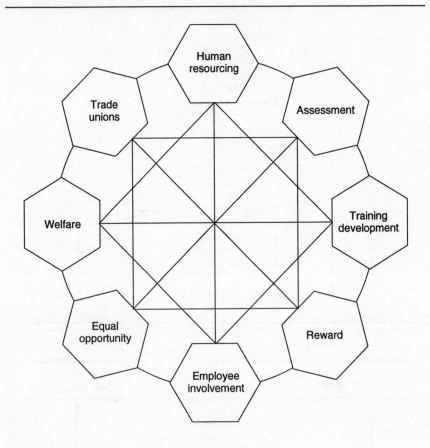

Figure 1.2　Elements of a HRM network

orientation). As such, no attempt will be made to outline a generic HRM strategy in its own right, although attention will be given to those features of specific policy levers which need to be taken into account in developing such a strategy. In this model each functional area is represented as a hexagon to emphasize (a) the multi-faceted nature of each field (the choice of a six-sided shape has no significance beyond aesthetic convenience) and (b) the variety of ways in which these 'units' may connect to give more or less 'clustered' network forms (Figures 1.3 and 1.4).

This form of clustering allows a great deal of flexibility and can be used to indicate a number of different properties of HRM networks, such as the centrality or isolation of particular functions, the 'tightness' or 'looseness' of the overall network, and, if additional hexagons are added, the connection with other non-HRM management functions (e.g. marketing, operations management, etc.). The crux of HRM thinking, therefore, is to understand the principles/choices at work

Figure 1.3   Tightly coupled HRM network

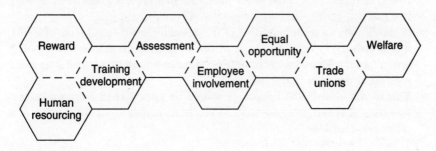

Figure 1.4   Loosely coupled 'string' network

in making these network connections and to be able to devise or adapt networks to meet particular organizational needs.

The objective of the following chapters is to equip readers with an understanding of HRM 'content' that encourages them to consider the possibilities and limitations of functional techniques in terms of their 'formal' implications. Thus, although attention is paid to the nature of specific techniques in each of the areas identified in the model above, their treatment is guided by an attempt to expose underlying assumptions and connections with wider organization theory. Thus, the emphasis is not on providing neatly packaged 'how to' recipes, but rather on the critical analysis of key themes and the exposure of their strengths, weaknesses and implications. This often involves drawing attention to diversity and contradiction between different sets of ideas and emphasizing uncertainty and contingency rather than certainty. Hopefully this approach will provide the reader with a basis from which the utilization and development of HRM strategies can be thought through within the context of their own organizations. The driving idea behind this book is that effective HRM cannot develop on the basis of *a priori* prescription, but only through the informed questioning of existing and future practice within specific organizational settings. It is such questioning that the following chapters seek to encourage.

KEY LEARNING POINTS

- **The development of HRM as a body of management thought in the 1980s can be linked to a conjunction of socio-economic factors, in particular, changes in international competition, domestic industrial and organizational restructuring, and the development of a 'new managerialism'.**
- **The key themes upon which HRM is based include Human Relations Psychology, Strategic Management Theory, and the doctrines of Quality and Flexibility.**
- **The relative emphasis which is accorded to each of these themes can give rise to different 'variants' of HRM. In particular, it is possible to identify two extreme positions: Instrumental and Humanistic.**
- **In developing an understanding of the possibilities and prospects of HRM, it is necessary to think in terms of the detailed content of specific policy levers and the formal ways in which these can be combined and integrated with other organizational policies.**
- **This means that HRM initiatives should be approached from an understanding of specific organizational realities, rather than from a set of *a priori* prescriptions.**

EXERCISES

1   Using the points listed in Table 1.1, consider the extent to which your organization has adopted the principles of HRM. To what do you attribute any movement in this direction, and what do you see as barriers to such movement?

2   Using the hexagon principle demonstrated in Figures 1.2, 1.3 and 1.4, analyse your organization's HRM structures (perhaps by cutting out hexagons and arranging them) and experiment by adding other (non-HRM) management functions to your model.

Chapter 2

Human resourcing

Planning and performance

HUMAN RESOURCING

The term 'human resourcing' is used here to describe a key set of principles through which the strategic possibilities of an organization's workforce and employment structure are evaluated. The methodologies of human resourcing derive from two concerns:

1 The auditing of current human resources in relation to possible future product/ service and labour market scenarios.
2 The promotion and maintenance of optimal human resource performance through the management of work patterns and organization structures.

While human resourcing encompasses what has traditionally been termed manpower planning, it also involves another dimension: that of managing motivation and activity in support of enhanced performance.

Manpower planning

The basic idea of manpower planning as developed in the 1960s was to manage the headcount of an organization in such a way as to achieve compatibility with predicted trends in performance over time. The emphasis primarily was on the relationship between numbers employed (in various capacities) and the rate of growth or contraction of the organization. This approach rested on three sequential steps (Bennison 1984: 4):

1 An estimation of the organization's future manpower needs in terms of numbers and skill composition.
2 An analysis of labour flows into, within and out of the organization, and the ability of relevant labour markets to supply existing or future demands.
3 The identification of gaps between supply and demand and the development of policies to 'close' these.

In theory, this approach had the advantage of combining sophisticated mathematical modelling with a range of potentially innovative policy options (i.e., step 3 above). In practice, however, this promise frequently seems to have been incompletely realized. From the outset, the mathematical dimension tended to dominate, giving manpower planning the appearance of an esoteric activity accessible only to those with a high level of quantitative knowledge. According to Pearson (1991:18) the prioritization of statistical analysis also encouraged 'an uncritical acceptance of existing categories of manpower and career structures, simply because they provided instant fodder for equations and computer data-bases', encouraging conservatism and myopia when innovation and clear-sightedness were necessary (see also Malloch 1988).

In addition, there was another more serious problem: the inability of this type of planning technique effectively to 'connect' with real organizational performance. As Bennison explains:

> The framework was logical, the techniques were well founded, and the idea of a manpower planning system seemed unassailable. Yet it failed to make the impact it should have done because it contained within it an immense practical difficulty. The notion that it is possible to estimate *future* manpower needs, with the precision necessary to match policies of supply, is quite fallacious. Demand is particularly susceptible to changes in the outside world; wars, commodity prices, and foreign exchange rates cause problems in managing economies which, in turn, affect the growth rates of organizations. These external events are essentially unpredictable and so the ability to estimate the demand for an organization's manpower is suspect.
>
> (Bennison 1984:5)

Such problems with traditional mathematical approaches to manpower planning led to moves away from forecasting and towards the auditing of organizational manpower. This 'practical' approach, following Bennison's cartographic metaphor, is concerned not with planning detailed routes between destinations but with producing a 'map' of the organizational manpower 'configuration' and the general direction in which it is heading, an exercise that can be undertaken with the assistance of techniques such as flow charts, histograms and pie charts, rather than complex mathematical functions.

Although these latter techniques have contributed significantly to contemporary human resourcing, there is another quantitatively orientated approach, human asset accounting, which has also exerted an influence.

Human asset accounting and human resource audits

The popularization of human asset accounting (or human resource accounting, as it is also known) is usually attributed to Likert (1967) although Flamholtz has been more influential in recent years. According to the latter:

> Human resource accounting may be defined as the measurement and reporting of the *cost* and *value* of people as organizational resources. It involves

accounting for investment in people and their replacement costs, as well as accounting for the economic values of people to an organization.

(Flamholtz and Lacey 1981:57; emphasis added)

This concern reflects a long-standing debate within accountancy about the precise nature of employees as assets: can something that is not owned by the company be regarded as an asset? (Hermanson 1964; for a useful overview see Gray and Maunders 1987: 161–7; also Giles and Robinson 1972). Historically, accounting conventions have treated employees as a (variable) cost of operation, with no value (Dawson 1989:6). Flamholtz's challenge to this 'accounting hegemony' suggested ways of measuring the value of an employee to the employing organization by means of the Stochastic Rewards Valuation Model (an accessible and brief account of which is provided by Dawson 1989). Although this relatively sophisticated tool failed to resolve satisfactorily either the practical problems of measurement or the dispute over accounting concepts, the general approach has attracted qualified support for its intentions. Tyson and Fell (1986:93), for example, suggest that it provides a major benefit by encouraging the perception of employees as assets: 'The notion of "investing" in employees encourages a view that one is looking for the profit to be gained from the investment and therefore the focus is on the development of people for a purpose.'

But, as with mathematical manpower planning, there has been a tendency for highly technical accounting principles to give rise to concepts with a lower level of technical specification and more general applicability. In this respect, although what is now termed 'human resource auditing' borrows its title and rationale from accountancy, it also makes heavy use of the methodologies of the social and information sciences. An example of this approach is provided by the West Midlands and North-Western Regional Health Authorities' Human Resource Management Audit, which develops measures of human resource outputs and effectiveness derived mostly from diagnostic questionnaires and financial and productivity ratios. The underpinning rationale of this approach, significantly, is analytical rather than prescriptive:

> it aims to encourage managers to develop their own ways of measuring performance against targets and objectives developed from the experience and needs of their own particular units. Managers are encouraged to revise, adapt and apply the various diagnostic instruments in ways which are best suited to their own circumstances.

(IRS 1992c:7)

A related but more sophisticated development has been the modelling of cost-based financial manpower decisions on computer spreadsheets. Dawson (1990), for instance, uses a computer simulation model based on principles of stylized stock control (Dawson 1988:33) to provide a form of scenario analysis whereby different inputs and outputs can be compared. A key part of this analysis is that it organizes the numerical and cost dimensions of human resourcing decisions in a way which emphasizes contingency and probability, rather than prescription and certainty. Importantly, this model also forces managers to engage in the prior processes of clarifying their own understanding of the ways in which employees are used and their value to the organization assessed. For example:

> The eight stages of the acquisition process [in Dawson's model] are broken down into 26 separate activities, for which the manager has to provide input data for both time and costs. Although some of these inputs may be given the value zero, it still requires the manager to go through the process of considering each. Moreover, if the manager feels that some time elapses whilst a particular activity takes place, there is a requirement to decide exactly how this is best expressed, by means of the choice of distribution and whether there are seasonal variations... it draws attention to the significance of the 'establishment level' and the convictions which lead to the setting of its particular size. The confrontation and subsequent thinking through of these issues, which are prompted by the use of the model, are potentially of considerable benefit.
>
> (Dawson 1988:36)

This use of computerized systems as a way of challenging managers to confront the basis of their human resource thinking raises a number of issues about the role of information technology (IT) in this area, a role which has increased significantly over recent years. However, whereas Dawson's approach is very much in the tradition of 'action research', aimed not only at modelling specific processes but also at the development of new ways of conceptualizing basic human resourcing assumptions, the widespread adoption of computerized human resource 'systems' has focused more on the collection and processing of large amounts of information in a manner which provides 'pre-packaged' results. Having already noted the potential danger of an over-reliance on data processing encouraging analytical conservatism (Pearson 1991), it does seem that the growing sophistication of IT systems is also supporting a more innovative and creative dimension.

IT and human resourcing

The role of computers in personnel has been the subject of increased interest and scrutiny over the past decade. Over this period, both the quantity and sophistication of applications has increased, the latter especially since the late 1980s.

The 1991 survey of computer use in personnel (IPM/IMS 1991) revealed that some 96 per cent of respondent companies were using computerized personnel information systems (CPIS), including 53 per cent of those with fewer than 1,000 people. These systems were utilized to provide electronic office facilities, recruitment administration, storing performance appraisal data, absence control and training administration. However, the full potential of CPIS is held to lie with the development of networked systems. Where, for example, a system can automatically drive the payroll, this may allow the remote input of overtime and absence data, abolishing the need for hard-copy time sheets and associated processes. Such a system also provides a basis for a manpower costing system that can be interrogated by line managers on a 'need to know' basis. Thus, instead of sending large quantities of manpower reports through the post to line managers, they can have remote access to the CPIS where they activate pre-written programs to generate the reports they need (Richards-Carpenter 1992:36).

This type of development has been projected into the future by Woodward and Winchurch (1991), who posit a 'molecular' human resourcing system as the next step in CPIS (see Figure 2.1).

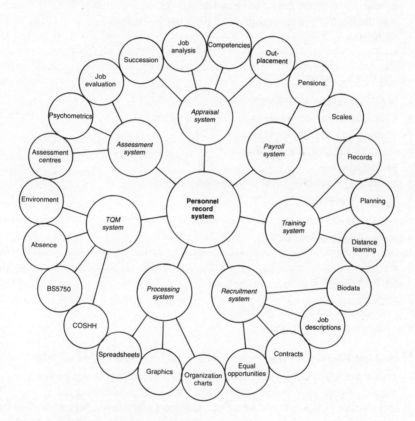

Figure 2.1 Molecular CPIS structure
(*Source*: IPM/IMS 1991)

Here, the nucleus of the system is composed of personnel records to which numerous other principal and subsidiary modules (in the form of specific software applications) are linked. Examples of the theoretical uses to which such a system, once operational, could be put are suggested by Woodward and Winchurch (1991:71) thus:

Recruitment

- production of detailed job/person profile
- biodata analysis
- psychometric testing
- using data on current employees for comparison and profile building
- job evaluation
- production of printed interview guides
- total analysis of all results to produce a shortlist
- producing rejection letters automatically
- cost analysis of the programme and costs per individual
- budgeting.

Succession planning

- appraisal results analysis
- matching of personal details to the job requirements
- training and development needs
- 'what if' organization charting
- projected costs
- matching of competencies to projected job profile
- team-role analysis.

Salary management

- payroll
- salary modelling
- absence
- pension and benefit calculations
- manpower planning costs.

The implications of this type of system architecture within an HRM framework are potentially significant, it being highly congruent with decentralized and/or flat organization structures, allowing the devolution of human resource information to line managers as well as its escalation to senior executives and strategists. The logic of this type of information configuration places the human resource manager in the role of a facilitator or internal consultant, assisting other managers with the accessing and use of information and (expert) systems relevant to particular operational personnel practices (Richards-Carpenter 1992:61).

However, although a study by Torrington *et al.* (1991:73) put forward claims to have found instances of this emergent role, the authors remained cautious about its rapid spread in the immediate future. Nevertheless, it is significant that many approaches to the use of CPIS give growing recognition to its applications in the socio-cultural dimensions of organization (see Legge 1989 for a comprehensive review) such as equal opportunities, appraisal and assessment, personal development, and planning organization structures. Securicor PLC, for example, has developed a computerized biodata/psychometric assessment package (see Chapter 3 below) which is used to screen candidates and quickly provide hard copy reports (in less than two hours) which can be used as the basis for personal interviews (Selby 1991:123ff.). Similarly, Spencer (1990:331) gives details of a job analysis and evaluation package which serves as an expert system, not only defining jobs, skills and person specifications, but also extending into organization design and career and succession planning, involving the identification and prioritization of options for moving or replacing the holders of specified jobs.

In these respects, therefore, there may be increasing opportunities for the integration of quantitative and qualitative human resource data, a prospect that appears especially propitious for the current concern to link human resourcing techniques to the management of performance at both individual and organizational levels.

PERFORMANCE MANAGEMENT SYSTEMS

Given the goal-directed nature of organizations, performance in terms of these goals is usually a central concern. To the extent that success in this respect can depend heavily on the effective deployment of human resources, one key aspect of human resourcing is to make the linkage between goals and performance explicit and manageable. A prime example of this type of endeavour is the strategy adopted by the computer company ICL and given voice in their company 'bible', *The ICL Way*:

> ICL is an achievement company. Recognition, rewards, promotion and opportunities for career and job development depend absolutely on results delivered. Performance is the way forward – for every individual and for the company as a whole. It is therefore vitally important that every individual has a clear understanding of his or her work objectives and responsibilities because performance will be measured against these. It is down to managers to make sure that these objectives and responsibilities provide maximum opportunities for the development of individual talent and to operate the company's recognition and reward systems on their achievement.

(Cited in Williams 1991)

The operational basis of this philosophy is a system of performance management involving 'a logical sequence of four steps linked with the company's business strategies'. The four steps in the cycle are defined as follows:

- **Step One**   The determination and setting of individual objectives which support the achievement of the overall business strategies.

- **Step Two**   A formal appraisal centred on what was achieved against these prearranged objectives. This results in the joint determination of a personal/job improvement plan, a career development plan and a training plan, plus the allocation of a performance rating by the manager.
- **Step Three**   A separate pay review in which the level of pay increase is based largely on the actual level of achievement made against the prearranged objectives.
- **Step Four**   An organization capability review which, as part of the normal business review process, focuses on the total organizational capability of each part of the organization to achieve the future business strategies.

(Neale 1991: 12)

What can be seen from this example is the emphasis which this type of approach to performance places upon the management process as this relates to human resources. In short, it takes a view which is broader and more encompassing than that which focuses merely upon the 'results' or 'ends' of a given task.

For this reason, models of performance management systems generally pay considerable attention both to the organizational 'climate' which the system presupposes, and to the motivation and development of the individual via the system. Thus, according to Armstrong and Murlis (1991:190), an effective performance management system (PMS) should include:

- A clear statement of mission and values.
- A procedure for establishing individual performance 'contracts' (based upon psychological contract principles).
- A clear process for establishing individual improvement programmes.
- Performance indicators and critical success factors.
- A performance appraisal mechanism.

The result, they suggest, is a system which works as a continuous cycle. A performance agreement is determined mutually between an individual and his/her manager which provides the reference point for the more formal performance plan. In many ways, the agreement can be likened to a psychological contract to which the individual is committed through mutual and open agreement (see Chapter 6 below for more on this form of commitment). Once committed in principle, the performance plan provides the concrete details of what performance will be sought and what will need to be done (e.g., training/support) to reach this level. Achievement of the planned objectives is the subject of continuous assessment and any changes/adaptations made in the light of this. The process is concluded by the performance review, which serves both to take stock of what has been achieved and to start a new cycle of the process again.

Initiatives such as PMS assume that the structure of employment within the organization is already effectively established and that appropriate performance measures have been identified. Such an assumption, however, needs careful consideration. We have already seen that one function of human resource auditing techniques is to cause managers to question the often taken-for-granted value which they put upon employees and their jobs. The same questioning needs to take place in the area of performance management as here, too, conventional measures may hinder as much as help when it comes to evaluating current practice and the need for change or innovation.

This problem has been highlighted by IDS (1990c), who point to the errors which arise from the 'obsession' which many business commentators and managers have with economic definitions of 'productivity'. In particular, they suggest that most organizations should be more concerned with questions of efficiency and that, even here, they should be cautious that numerical measures of efficiency are not treated as more real than the activities they represent.

All too often, it seems, productivity measurement has got the focus wrong – from the organizational point of view, what is important is the jobs that people do, rather than the balance of payments. This also means that measures of productivity based on worker effort are similarly ill-conceived.

It is not, IDS claim, a question of whether workers are working harder, but whether they are working better. As more organizations start to think about issues of quality and high value-added goods and services, the latter concern becomes absolutely crucial. An employee may work incredibly hard, but be involved in a process which is inefficient. In this respect, the key to measuring efficiency, and to cutting costs, is a qualitative one: namely, to identify what it is that managers and employees do that is necessary, to look at the effectiveness of organizations and their members from the standpoint of the customer. This is very different from merely cutting costs on a bottom-line basis. Instead it focuses upon the nature of the work that is done, the skills that are needed by employees, and the ways in which those skills are utilized. IDS give the following examples:

A comparative study of the hotel industry in Britain and Germany conducted by the National Institute for Economic and Social Research...revealed that German hotels were able to function with between 50 per cent and 70 per cent of the staff of their British counterparts. The key difference was the level and mix of skills in the German hotels, above all in the key craft functions. German hotels operated with many fewer unskilled workers and a larger number of qualified staff capable of a variety of roles.

A second case is the pioneering work on skill mix in the NHS done at the John Radcliffe Hospital in Oxford, since taken up at a number of other hospitals. The changes involved an increase in the number of registered nurses and a decrease in the number of less trained staff (enrolled nurses and auxiliaries). Routine tasks were delegated and skilled staff devoted more time to patient care.

Costs were held steady while all the measures of quality and effectiveness of care showed an improvement.

(IDS 1990c: 10)

One way in which organizations have attempted to rethink the organization of employment to enhance performance through greater efficiency is through a reassessment of working practice in terms of greater flexibility.

FLEXIBILITY AND WORKING PRACTICES

Flexibility, as discussed in Chapter 1, can be achieved at two levels: at the level of work practice (functional flexibility); and at the level of organization structure (numerical flexibility). To this can be added a third category, temporal flexibility, which involves the reorganization of working time (Blyton and Morris 1992).

Functional flexibility

An example of functional flexibility is provided by Storey (1992) in the case of Ford of Britain's 1985 agreement whereby discretionary productivity allowances were made available at plant level with the provision that they become payable only to 'employees who cooperate with local management in ensuring maximum capacity utilization and the efficient use of manpower' (ibid.:92). This involved accepting changed working practices, so as to encourage versatility and flexibility, the acquisition and use of new skills, and the elimination of inefficient demarcation lines. Wickens' (1987:52) account of flexibility at Nissan UK seems also to point in this direction (referring as it does to flexibility between production functions that can involve manual, non-manual and managerial employees), although the reality of this position has been questioned by Garrahan and Stewart (1992).

In practice it seems that most developments in terms of this form of flexibility have involved the relaxation of restrictive demarcation practices (Blyton and Morris 1992:306), rather than thoroughgoing multi-skilling of craft workers. This is confirmed by IDS (1990d), which compares surveys from 1986, 1988 and 1990 to conclude that although multi-skilling remains an aim, the 'real task across a range of industries is now to enhance and build on specific skills' (IDS 1990d:1), this position involving a greater recognition by managements of the importance of respecting craft attitudes and adapting working arrangements to deepen skills.

Temporal flexibility

Temporal flexibility, while not incompatible with functional flexibility, is primarily concerned with the fundamental restructuring of working time. This approach, (see, for example, Lynch (1991)), hinges around the notion of making optimum use of paid time – minimizing 'ineffective time' (i.e. where no productive work is undertaken) and maximizing 'productive time' (time spent in productive work). The most obvious method is the use of so-called 'bell-to-bell' working, whereby time spent preparing for work (e.g., changing into overalls, setting up machinery) or preparing to go home (e.g., washing, tidying work stations) is not considered paid time. Such savings, it is argued, can result in considerable productivity gains: if fifteen minutes of unproductive time can be transformed into productive time, there will be a 3 per cent improvement in productivity on an eight-hour shift. In addition, it is possible to make better use of 'plain-time' hours (basic working hours which do not attract premium payments) and to minimize premium hours (overtime and shift work which generally attract enhanced rates of pay).

A more radical move which relates directly to the quest to make better use of plain-time hours and to reduce overtime is the rearrangement of working time so that fewer hours are wasted in slack periods. This may mean the introduction of 'annual hours' contracts, which guarantee earnings over the year but allow for the working of longer hours during peak periods of demand and shorter hours during slack periods. This can both save on overtime and allow retention of more core staff. Other attempts might be to reduce overtime and maximize 'plain-time' working by the use of 'hours plus' contracts which provide a basic level of annual hours plus a quota allowed for additional hours (usually calculated by a formula for achieving existing pay levels, the base level hours being below this). This means that the worker has a positive incentive to get the work done in the minimum time and not to work the 'extra' hours, except in unforeseen circumstances (Lynch 1991:33).

According to a recent IDS investigation (IDS 1991e), annual hours arrangements have usually met with approval from managements. In the companies they studied they found that annual hours had allowed organizations to fit employee hours more closely to production requirements and, in addition, had frequently reduced both production and administration costs. The reporting of employee reactions, however, was a little more equivocal:

> Any lack of enthusiasm has tended to centre on the anticipated loss of earnings. Since a reduction in costs is often a major reason for introducing annual hours, this fear *may not always be without foundation*. And while rostered leave and five-crew shift working may afford workers more leisure at certain times of the year, the system may also require more intensive working at other times with no immediate financial reward.
>
> (IDS 1991e:6; emphasis added)

Another persistent question which has arisen with annual hours schemes has been the implications for equal opportunities, where there are two main concerns. The first centres upon the difficulties posed in relation to childcare arrangements, where 'long hour' periods in particular may cause problems. The second focuses upon the way in which annual hours totals are allocated to part-time workers, these often being higher than would normally be the case, thereby discriminating against part-time workers and, indirectly, women (IDS 1991c:6). Pickard (1991) provides the following contrasting examples:

ITN

The system...militates against job-sharing. Alixe Kingston, a mother of two small children, took voluntary redundancy after attempting a job-share under annual hours. She was contracted to work 900 hours a year and stated that she preferred to work Mondays, Tuesdays and Wednesdays, while her partner preferred Wednesdays, Thursdays and Fridays. But she says her managers argued that the system allowed them to call both job-share partners in at the same time, on any day they liked.

She says they could also extend the hours on a rostered day at almost no notice: 'One day I went in expecting to work until 6 pm, and at noon they told me I had to stay until 11 pm. I couldn't do it.'

She found the system of off-roster days frustrating, since it meant that, to guarantee time off on those days, staff had to deduct them from holidays. 'I said it was a nonsense to take holiday on days when I wasn't working anyway. If they had advertised this job on these terms, no one would apply....

'It's all changed now. People are going off sick like flies and women are leaving in droves, because they have made life impossible. It will all blow up in the end. Annual hours destroys incentives and doesn't work where the job is so unpredictable.'

Express Foods

Express Foods introduced annual hours in 1989 at its plant in Ruyton-XI-Towns [to cope with seasonal fluctuations in the supply of milk for cheese-making]. The idea was that, instead of relying on overtime and temporary workers in the busy season, the existing employees would simply work more hours then and fewer in the 'dry' period.

In complete contrast to the ITN experience, the workforce at Ruyton raves about the new regime.... The main attraction appears....to be the increased predictability of the work schedule.... Overtime was effectively bought out and the hourly paid workers went on to a salary, paid weekly.

Although some people's pay dropped slightly, the guaranteed pay went up.... The employees feel they know where they stand.

(Pickard 1991:47)

Numerical flexibility

In essence, the sorts of initiatives described above leave the basic structure of the organization relatively unaffected. Other writers, however, have attempted to locate changes in the structure of organization in terms of the performance requirements of organizations and to define these as strategic opportunities available to human resource planners.

The driving force of these approaches has been the assumption that changes in the environment of the 1980s and 1990s confront organizations with unprecedented demands for innovative responses in terms of human resource utilization. Of the early theories, the most influential was Atkinson's (1984) notion of the flexible firm. This approach was influenced primarily by the effects of increased economic competition and the supposition that to regain competitiveness organizations would need to restructure for rapid response. The 'flexible firm' (see Figure 2.2) was one way in which this might be achieved.

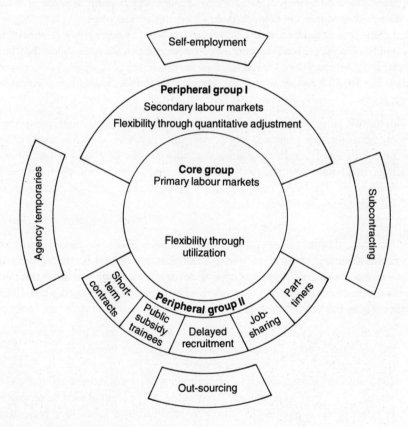

Figure 2.2   The flexible firm
(*Source*: Atkinson 1984)

This suggests the establishment of a 'core' group of key employees with flexible skills, around which are groups of peripheral workers whose tasks are either less central to the organization or who are needed on a less than permanent basis. These peripheral groups can be composed either of subcontracting self-employed or small businesses, or of temporary and part-time workers, or both. In theory, peripheral groups can be expanded or contracted in line with changes in economic demand or product structure without the problems of lengthy negotiation, costly redundancy payments, or industrial action, thereby acting as a buffer to the core workforce. This view of the flexible firm has frequently been subject to criticism on the grounds that, if treated prescriptively, it represents a crude form of employer exploitation whereby non-core workers can be subject to adverse terms and conditions of employment, often creating or perpetuating social division based on, in particular, gender or race (those belonging to groups traditionally regarded as 'socially inferior' finding themselves locked into employment in peripheral jobs). While such a view appears valid in some cases – there is, for example, evidence to suggest that many former public sector workers re-employed by private contractors under compulsory competitive tendering have suffered a considerable deterioration in their terms and conditions – it ignores serious theoretical and empirical deficiencies in the flexible firm model. Blyton and Morris summarizes some of these criticisms:

> The core–periphery distinction is over-simplistic and can be misleading in terms of the role and contribution of different work groups within the enterprise. Some organizations, for example, rely heavily on a part-time workforce, and others on contract workers. In these situations, such groups are often of central rather than peripheral importance to the organizations.... Similarly it is evident that in many cases, ostensibly 'core' groups of skilled workers do not necessarily enjoy the status suggested by the model.
>
> (Blyton and Morris 1992:300–1)

However, despite the attention given to debates about the flexible firm, the available data suggest that its widespread utilization as part of strategically in-formed human resourcing policy appears far from universal. Certainly there has been a substantial change in the nature of working patterns during the 1980s, especially in the UK. According to Hakim:

> In some respects the changes in Britain in the 1980s seem to have been more marked than in other European countries, suggesting that Atkinson's... model [of the flexible firm] might in a real sense reflect local developments. Between 1981 and 1987 the number of full-time employee jobs of indefinite duration fell sharply by 1.1 million jobs, from 70 per cent to 64 per cent of total employment. In effect these 'conventional' jobs were replaced by a 1.7 million increase in non-standard jobs which grew from 30 per cent to 36 per cent of total employment.... Temporary work, short-term contracts, agency temping, part-time work and self-employment all grew throughout the 1980s, with the largest share in the growth of the atypical workforce accounted for by an upsurge in the numbers of self-employed working entirely alone and who might be suspected of being labour-only subcontractors.
>
> (Hakim 1990:164)

Hakim questioned whether this apparent confirmation of the flexible firm thesis had been brought about by a 'sea change in employer strategies and choices' or merely as the result of a 'relatively minor intensification of existing practices which, multiplied hundreds of times over, produced a large aggregate change at the macro-level' (Hakim 1990:164). Her conclusion was that the latter was the more likely explanation, estimating about 5 per cent, but no more than 15 per cent, of workplaces in Britain to be pursuing a strategically informed core–periphery policy compatible with the flexible firm model.

Using the same data, McGregor and Sproull (1992) conclude that the main reasons for employers recruiting part-time and temporary workers were traditional ones associated with the nature of existing work, rather than being 'new' or informed by longer-term strategic thinking based on human resourcing issues. Indeed, Geary (1992) suggests that the flexible firm approach may generate serious contradictions for HRM. Referring to one of his case study firms, Astra, he reports:

> it is ironic that in striving to be flexible and in adopting a HRM strategy in response to business contingencies, management had unwittingly created a new status divide [between permanent and temporary workers] – a new *rigidity*. It is, perhaps, even more extraordinary in that traditional status divisions had been more or less obliterated in Astra. Where the original removal of status distinctions and the institution of harmonised conditions was to be the new basis of trust and commitment between employer and employee, the new divide between temporary and permanent staff was acting to undo the advantages that may have otherwise been gained.... The *peripheralisation* of a significant segment of the labour force would seem to have little in common with one of the main dictums of HRM – to value and develop employees as an organization's key resource.
>
> (Geary 1992:267–8)

Storey (1992), reporting case studies of two major UK companies, also points to developments in the strategic use of flexible working patterns, but cautions that such developments cannot be regarded as having been installed 'in perpetuity', or with total success. This observation seems especially pertinent in the light of the rapid changes in the UK economic environment between the 1980s and 1990s and the rapid shift from recession to boom and back to recession.

Partly to enable human resource planners to explore the possibilities of flexible structures in the context of changing environments, Leighton and Syrett (1989), for example, have developed planning models for assessing the strategic potential of flexibility. This approach rests on the identification of three categories of individual work pattern (in addition to subcontracting areas of an operation to another business organization), based on employment status and utilization. Thus:

- **Category A: directly employed**
  - full-time, open-ended contract
  - part-time work (supplementary and substitutional)
  - job-sharers

- – flexitime
- – sabbaticals
- – career breaks
- – homeworking
- – annual hours contracts
- – fixed-term contracts
- – fixed-job contracts
- – own pool temps

- **Category B: self-employed**
  - – casual
  - – freelance
  - – consultants

- **Category C: external**
  - – agency workers
  - – subcontract (labour only)
  - – government subsidy workers ('trainees')

Their contention is that traditional manpower planning approaches have considered only Category A workers and, of these, usually only full-and part-time workers. By broadening awareness of possible work patterns and of other forms of employment relationship, they point to the wider strategic opportunities that are opened up in the utilization of labour, in line with risk-assessment models of the type shown in Figure 2.3.

Among the examples they give is that of Rank Xerox which, in an attempt to reduce its labour costs – direct wage payments accounted for less than one-third of total labour costs in the Central London office, the remainder being taken up by outlay for office facilities – introduced its Networking scheme. This established many former direct employees as self-employed 'consultants' working from their own homes using computer equipment linked to the Xerox network. The company guaranteed an initial amount of work, but also left them free to find other clients independently. Stanworth and Stanworth (1991) have also explored the human resourcing implications of this and other types of 'teleworking' and point to a number of possible ways in which so-called 'remote' working can be organized, ranging from the home-based 'consultants', to combinations of home and office work, the latter either in a central location, satellite office or local centre. The advantages and disadvantages of teleworking are shown below:

Advantages

- gains in productivity (e.g. less time/effort spent travelling)
- reduction of overhead costs
- retention of rare skills (e.g. by keeping workers who might otherwise be lost as

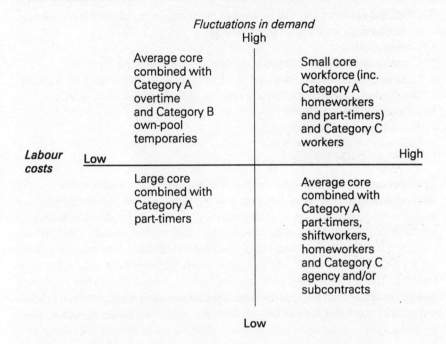

Figure 2.3   Risk assessment model of flexible working patterns
(*Source*: Leighton and Syrett 1989)

a result of a partner changing jobs geographically, or allowing more flexible use
of time to fit with domestic/caring responsibilities)
• penetration of unusual labour markets (e.g. workers with disabilities which
make physical transport difficult, or those in distant or overseas locations).

Disadvantages

• lack of commitment to organizational goals and culture (more likely to be a
problem with workers who are new to the organization or who have never been
part of its 'social' dimension)
• problems of communication and supervision (which can result from the limits
of the technology and the logistics of work organization in the case of the former,
and with the development of appropriate management styles not dependent on
the norm of face-to-face contact, in the latter).

As a guide to determining the type of employment structure an organization may
require, Leighton and Syrett (1989) suggest a systematic audit of the type of
employment opportunities available and their relationship to the economic and
social objectives of the organization. Important considerations include the following:

- Level and nature of demand for product or service (e.g., predictability, stability, which workers are affected by variation).
- Labour costs.
- Capacity to deal with changes in product/service provision.
- Centrality of each functional group of workers (e.g., importance to organizational goals, extent of supervision required, physical location of work).
- Labour market conditions.
- Equal opportunities requirements.
- Industrial relations constraints.
- Legal and policy considerations.

Leighton and Syrett's overall approach is to advocate caution and a careful thinking-through not only of the economic but also the legal and social impact of any new work patterns upon an organization: there will be direct and indirect implications for technical, cultural and individual processes in the short and the longer term. That this is sound advice has been evidenced by the recession of the early 1990s. Both for employers and for workers, the benefits of rushing into new working arrangements under conditions of rapid economic growth and increasing prosperity can be totally wiped out when the economic tide turns, especially if such a change in economic fortune had not been built-in to the change equation.

HUMAN RESOURCING: SYSTEMATIC INNOVATION

In theory, therefore, it seems that the approach to human resourcing which fits most closely with the general philosophy of HRM is one which is based on the planning principles of what Drucker (1989) has termed 'systematic innovation'. This is not the planning of the rigid five year plan nor of the deterministic forecast. Rather it is a dynamic and responsive discipline that looks at opportunities for innovation, for change, and for development that will improve organizational effectiveness.

In short, it is planning premised on uncertainty:

it is change that always provides the opportunity for the new and different. Systematic innovation therefore consists in the *purposeful and organized* search for changes, and in the *systematic analysis* of the opportunities such changes might offer for economic or social innovation.

(Drucker 1986:49; emphasis added)

However, the extent to which this theory has been put into practice is, as yet, difficult to ascertain. The evidence would seem to suggest that, not surprisingly, those techniques which do not involve fundamental organizational change are the most likely to be taken up. It may be some time, and under more settled economic conditions, therefore, before the full potential of human resourcing techniques is brought to bear on a more widespread scale.

KEY LEARNING POINTS

- **The term 'human resourcing' is used here to describe a key set of practices through which the strategic possibilities of an organization's workforce and employment structure are evaluated. The methodologies of human resourcing demand both quantitative and qualitative techniques that can be used to measure current human resource activity, and to plan for structural and/or cultural change.**
- **Manpower planning and human resource accounting techniques are an important part of this process, especially as there has been a shift away from mathematically-based forecasting and towards more accessible and flexible auditing processes.**
- **This process has been facilitated by developments in information technology, in particular the emergence of networked systems and specialist modules which allow not only the processing of quantitative data but also devolved access to qualitative data and 'expert' systems applications.**
- **One positive consequence of several new approaches to human resourcing has been to force managers to address the basic concepts and values that they routinely use in the evaluation of personnel processes, thereby encouraging a clearer understanding the overall human resource system.**
- **Such an understanding is closely linked to the success with which the performance of human resources can be evaluated. Such evaluation has tended to take two forms: a concern with systems of performance management; and the use of flexible working patterns and organizational structures.**

EXERCISES

1 Developments in computerized personnel information systems are now moving rapidly. Consider the following quotation and discuss the issues which these developments may raise for employers, managers and employees. In particular, how far should performance monitoring be taken, and what role should human resource managers take in promoting or regulating this?

Work can be monitored electronically in a number of ways. With telephone monitoring, supervisors can hook into a worker's telephone line while sitting next to the employee, or from a distance at his or her own desk. Another technique is to audiotape workers' telephone calls for later review. Video cameras can capture employee activities on tape. Certain computer systems can capture information about the number of keystrokes made per minute and the number of breaks taken. Other computer systems can even enable a manager to access an employee's computer screen and watch work from a distance.

(Laabs 1992:98)

2   Referring to the ICL performance management system outlined on pp. 25–6 of this chapter, consider the following points:
   (a) What *practical* problems would you anticipate with this type of PMS?
   (b) Would it work in your organization?
   (c) Could it be applied effectively to non-managerial staff?

Chapter 3

Assessment

Judging people and performance

ASSESSMENT AND HRM

Assessment refers to those processes used to make judgements about the attributes and abilities of individuals within a range of organizational settings and for a variety of purposes. Thus, although assessment techniques may be used for such diverse purposes as selection and recruitment, appraisal, training and development, and promotion, the underlying objectives are, from an HRM perspective, generally the same: namely, to ensure that the qualities of the individual are well matched to the human resourcing requirements of the organization. In some instances this match may be fairly loose (e.g., simple ability to do a specific job) but in others it may be extremely tight (e.g., where an individual has to demonstrate not only technical competence but also a specific personality profile and even a particular level of conduct in non-work life). Aspirations towards the latter position are certainly apparent in many approaches to HRM.

As clearly identifiable functions, assessment practices generally operate in three areas:

1 recruitment
2 selection
3 appraisal.

For the purposes of this chapter, appraisal will refer to those practices used to assess the actual or potential performance of existing employees, whereas recruitment and selection will be applied to processes associated with the entry of new members to the organization. It is, of course, important that none of these processes should be thought of in isolation, but as integral parts of a wider structure of human resource strategy. In particular, recruitment and selection will be closely tied to human resourcing considerations, and appraisal linked to reward provision, training and development; all three will have a bearing on levels of commitment and will be affected by equal opportunity issues. The level of integration will hinge on two dimensions: the extent to which specific techniques can deliver effective predictions of individual potential or performance in a given capacity; and that to which the social and psychological dynamics of the assessment process are congruent with individual expectations and organizational culture. Reliable and valid predictions allow proactive human resource strategies to be planned and structured with greater confidence, while the use of techniques which bolster rather than undermine the cultural expectations of the organization allow these strategies to have some chance of realization. Although not necessarily the case, failure to deliver on one dimension will often have the effect of weakening the other and, hence, the credibility of the assessment process in general, thereby marginalizing it from developments in other policy areas.

However, before their integrative potential can be grasped, it is necessary to understand the opportunities and constraints of each assessment function in more detail. The main characteristics of these functions are shown in Table 3.1.

RECRUITMENT

The principles of assessment which operate in the recruitment area can generally be regarded as 'gatekeeping' for the organization. They operate at the interface of the organization and the labour market and, as such, will be geared to the operating principles of these markets.

In this respect, assessment in the recruitment process deals with a series of choices, choices which are made both by organizations and (potential) employees: organizations need to choose people to perform particular jobs; job-seekers need to choose employers.

Table 3.1 Characteristics of assessment functions

Function	● Purpose	● Tool
Recruitment	● Generating a 'selection pool' ● Evaluating performance needs	● Labour market analysis ● Evaluation of employment structure and job categories
Selection	● Determining performance potential ● Succession planning	● Interview ● Biodata ● Psychometrics ● Assessment centre ● Graphology
Appraisal	● Performance review ● Reward determination ● Career planning ● Training needs analysis ● Development planning	● Interview/ self-assessment ● Assessment centre

Of course, the amount of freedom in these choices is highly variable and is shaped by economic and social factors: in a tight labour market, for example, employee choice is widened, but in times of recession employers have greater freedom of choice; alternatively, choice may be limited by institutionalized prejudice against certain social groups (young married women, for instance, may be thought to be 'unreliable' by some employers). The nature of these labour market processes and the role of organizations and workers in producing and reproducing them is complex and subject to much debate (see Fevre 1992 for a discussion). However, it is readily apparent that the definition of a labour market simply in terms of economic supply and demand is inadequate. Labour markets can also be conceived in terms of 'territories' in which job-seekers and organizations operate, these territories being related not only to geography but also to economic and social factors such as occupation (actual or potential), gender, ethnicity, age, education, physical health, etc. For example, senior executives may have a geographical labour market territory which is national and even international, whereas an unskilled labourer's territory may be local. In addition this geographical territory may be 'overlaid' by other territorial limits. For women, occupational territory is still unlikely to include, say, skilled work in heavy engineering or construction; for a married woman it is more likely to include part-time rather than full-time work; for a man it is very unlikely to include part-time work; for members of ethnic minorities it is unlikely to include senior professional roles in established professions (see Chapter 9 below).

From a broad HRM perspective, therefore, the task of recruitment is twofold:

1 It is obviously necessary to understand an organization's labour requirements in terms of its human resourcing plans.
2 It is equally necessary to assess how these needs can be met in the labour market, an exercise which, if it is to be undertaken seriously, must involve a careful questioning of the categories used to define both jobs and 'acceptable' workers.

However, although the ability to challenge and question established labour market definitions is likely to be crucial to strategically oriented recruitment, Fevre (1992:106) suggests that much practice is governed more by 'custom' than by strategy (see also Ashton, Maguire and Spilsburg 1990). Nevertheless, there is evidence that developments are taking place, not least among organizations which claim to have moved towards the adoption of HRM principles. A number of examples will make clear the sorts of recruitment initiatives that have been used:

• The NHS has set guidelines that shortlists for all top management jobs will be required to include women. This is accompanied by the setting of numerical targets for the proportion of women in such posts. To facilitate this, each health region will have to compile 'registers of talented women below general manager level. If insufficient numbers of women apply for vacancies, those on the registers will be approached'

(Brindle 1992; see Chapter 9).

- In an attempt to attack both the 'invisibility' or 'tokenism' of members of ethnic minorities in recruitment literature and materials, BP provides a brochure which presents a 'fair and not misleading' picture of BP people including a proportion from ethnic minorities. 'Inside the brochure are group and individual profiles and around one-in-ten of these feature a recent ethnic minority graduate. BP's equal opportunities policy statement has prominence inside the front cover'

(IRS 1990a:6).

- The emphasis on establishing links with schools as part of a (possibly long-term) recruitment strategy has also been taken up by (among others) companies in the chemical industry. Cecil Harrold of Glaxo Pharmaceuticals is reported as seeing 'the motivation for school links in terms of the needs of the community; of the recruitment needs of the pharmaceutical industry as a whole, and of the specific recruitment needs of his company: 'It's too early to say whether our links with schools help our recruitment, but I believe they are helping to dispose potential recruits in our favour'

(IRS 1990b:9).

Such initiatives, however, cannot be viewed as *ad hoc* or 'one-off' measures; they involve careful and critical scrutiny of existing practices and depend upon a willingness to implement changes which impact not only upon recruitment procedures but also upon working practices and organizational culture. Some indication of the extensiveness of such initiatives is illustrated by the case of Ealing Borough Council in London which, in an attempt to get 'the best people for jobs as quickly and inexpensively as possible' and to make equal opportunities more effective, established a joint working party with relevant unions, which formulated the following policy guidelines:

- Literacy was considered not to be a required skill for manual workers and therefore forms and procedures to recognize this should be introduced.
- The style of recruitment literature should be changed so as not to be written in local government jargon,
- All material sent to job applicants should be designed to be 'user-friendly'.
- Rethink employee specifications carefully.
- Establish a temporary register for people wanting temporary work with the council.

(IRS 1990a)

The results of this initiative are reported to have put staff in post with more appropriate skills, reduced the time taken to fill vacancies, decreased unfilled vacancies, reduced readvertising costs, and made cash savings through generally more effective recruitment processes.

SELECTION

The concerns considered above can be carried through into the wider area of selection techniques, where the issue of assessment for performance potential is likely to take a clearer focus. Wickens (1987:171) gives an example of the lengths to which Nissan (Sunderland) went to recruit supervisors who would be capable of meeting performance requirements in terms of flexibility, teamworking and quality consciousness. After initial screening and interviews which reduced 3,500 applications to seventy-five, these survivors were put through a specially developed assessment centre which involved the investment of over 100 manager-days to select twenty-two supervisors. It is significant to note that in this case a similar approach was also used to select production staff (see Exercise 1 at the end of this chapter). Storey (1992:99) also points to the use of psychometric tests designed to measure dimensions such as 'independence of thought', 'teamworking' and 'cooperativeness' by motor companies such as Jaguar for both supervisors and hourly-paid workers.

This concern to identify very specific forms of performance potential is responsible, at least in part, for the increased interest in systematic selection tools. However, some caution is necessary before assuming that 'new' techniques such as psychometric testing, biodata and graphology, etc. are at the top of the selection league in all companies. While their use is increasing steadily, it is also clear that the interview remains the dominant technique in most selection decisions. This is well illustrated in the results of an IRS (1991c; 1991d) study showing the selection method used by a sample of 178 UK employers (see Table 3.2).

Table 3.2 shows the selection methods considered first, second and third most important by employers. Although it seems that some organizations use only interviews, these figures show that many support these with other methods, notably psychometric tests. Additional information on interviewing approaches is given in Table 3.3 which, unsurprisingly, shows a direct relationship between the seniority of the vacancy, the number of interviews a candidate will have to attend, and the number of interviewers involved.

Table 3.2   Most important selection methods

	Interview	Assessment centre	Psychometric tests	Application form	References	N / %
Most important selection method (%)	85	7	3	5	0	178/100
Second most important method (%)	15	1	35	32	17	148/100
Third most important method (%)	0	0	35	20	45	96/100

Source: Adapted from IRS (1991c: 2-3)

Table 3.3   Numbers of interviews and interviewers

Interviews	Managerial (%) N = 72	Graduate (%) N = 78	Clerical (%) N = 102	Manual (%) N = 93
one	3	18	52	73
two	49	54	36	20
three +	32	22	0	1
varies	17	5	10	2
Interviewers				
one	11	24	38	41
two	46	40	41	43
three	8	17	5	2
four +	11	4	0	0
varies	22	12	14	13

Source: Adapted from IRS (1991d: 8)

Despite their widespread pattern of use, interviews have been subject to criticism as a selection tool. In particular, it is claimed that they have relatively poor validity and reliability, the former varying between 0.11 and 0.3 (1.0 being perfect validity), and the latter being suspect in terms of 'test-retest', 'internal consistency', and 'inter-rater reliability'. Moss (1992) elaborates on the reliability issues:

- **Test-retest reliability** (the ability to obtain the same results on different occasions)   Robert Half has shown that you will not be rated as highly if you were interviewed on a Monday as if you were interviewed on a Wednesday. If you are the first person to be interviewed, you are three times less likely to be hired than the last person on the list. [This presumably assumes only a single interview.]
- **Internal consistency**   This is likely to be low, since all the evidence shows that people are either very bad listeners, or do not believe what they hear... most interviewers make up their mind about the candidate in the first few seconds of the interview.
- **Inter-rater reliability**   In an early study by Hollingsworth, 57 candidates were interviewed by 12 sales managers. Every candidate received a wide range of rankings from the 12 managers.

(Moss 1992:110)

An attempt to explain the continued popularity of the interview in the light of these and similar doubts is provided by Anderson (1992:174) on the grounds of versatility, social communication and simplicity:

- The selection interview provides a sample of behaviour which illustrates sociability, interactions with others, and verbal fluency.
- Practical considerations make it a realistic choice, especially in situations where the number of applications is too small to justify more elaborate procedures.

- Interviewers maintain a high level of faith and confidence in their judgement and ability to make sound selection decisions.
- The selection interview provides an opportunity of both selling the job and explaining the job to applicants.

Despite the near universality of the interview, the wider recognition of its deficiencies as a *sole* method of selection has undoubtedly contributed to the expansion of alternative techniques.

In particular, and in line with the strong emphasis on individualism apparent in many HRM approaches, there has been a desire to 'get behind' the 'presentation of self' which the interview allows the candidate to project, and to 'uncover' the deeper psychological underpinnings upon which this 'social persona' is built. It is in this respect that techniques such as psychometric testing, biodata and graphology claim to be of service:

> more companies seem to be following the lead publicly made so evident by Nissan... and other Japanese companies.... While workforces are certainly much reduced there would now appear to be more care taken in the selection of that reduced employee stock. Behavioural and attitudinal characteristics are playing an increasing part in this. An inference that might be drawn from this increasing resort to systematic selection techniques is that there is some expectation that a workforce could gradually be constructed which would be more receptive to the broad span of HR philosophy than is the case with existing manpower stocks.
>
> (Storey 1992:100; see also Townley 1989)

To explore further the potential of this assertion, it is necessary to outline the principles involved in these 'systematic' selection techniques and how, specifically, they contribute to this more general HRM mission.

Psychometric testing

There was a marked growth in the use of psychometric testing as part of the selection process in the 1980s. A recent study (Bartram 1991) found that of a sample of 101 companies with over 2,000 employees, 74 per cent used ability and aptitude tests and 60 per cent personality questionnaires; of 189 with fewer than 2,000 employees, the figures were 62 per cent and 41 per cent respectively. Table 3.4 shows the types of test used by the IRS (1991d) sample and their application to different occupational groups.

Of particular note is the high proportion of managerial and graduate recruits subjected to personality tests, and the fact that between a half and two-thirds of clerical and manual recruits are required to undertake ability and aptitude tests. What is also interesting is that many of these more 'innovative' selection methods have been relatively recent introductions, over half of all personality test users, for instance, having introduced them since 1989.

Table 3.4   Use of selection tests by employee groups

Employee group	Cognitive tests (%)	Personality tests (%)	Literacy/ numeracy tests (%)
Manual	14	1	19
Clerical	31	15	43
Graduate	20	29	19
Professional/technical	6	5	5
Managerial/senior managerial	29	50	14
N	100 (115)	100 (136)	100 (174)

Source: Adapted from IRS (1991d: 11)

The growth of personality testing, however, has not been without controversy. While tests of aptitude (e.g. physical co-ordination, manual dexterity) and ability (intelligence quotients, reasoning) have generally been accepted on the grounds that what they measure can be related to the content of particular jobs, those which claim to identify and measure personality traits have had a more mixed reception. In part, this reflects a protracted debate about the technical merits of personality tests (i.e. about what exactly personality is and – assuming it can be measured – whether it correlates with performance in a job). Also it concerns a parallel debate about the ethics of personality testing – whether tests are biased in terms of either sex or race, and whether it is legitimate for organizations to seek to 'control' the personalities of their members.

There has been much recent debate about the utility of personality testing in relation to employment selection. The most trenchant criticisms of this technique have been mounted by Blinkhorn and Johnson (1990; 1991). Their argument can be summarized as follows:

When th[e] purpose [of personality tests] is to aid selection or promotion decisions, it should be possible to demonstrate that better decisions are made when using tests than when not.... The published research on the validity of personality tests for personnel decision-making is much thinner than many personnel professionals may imagine... there is not much of it, and what there is gives scant grounds for confidence in the method.... Even those studies which do exist concentrate on relating test scores to present performance rather than on prediction of future performance.... Our conclusion [based on computer simulation] was that there were no grounds for supposing that personality tests predict performance at work to any useful extent.... It is perhaps time we made up our minds: are personality tests serious measures of personal qualities which predict behaviour, or are they stage-managed bits of flummery, intended to lend an air of scientific rigour to personnel practice...? we fear the flummers are winning.

(Blinkhorn and Johnson 1991:38–9)

While some have found this view convincing (e.g. Gulliford 1991) others have been provoked to strong reaction. Robertson (1991) for instance, defends personality tests on the grounds that recent studies have revealed consistent, albeit rather small, correlations with aspects of job performance (of around 0.26) and that a 0.26 correlation can 'produce as much as a 26 per cent increase in hit rate' in the selection process, an improvement which he suggests would be useful to most personnel practitioners. Similarly, Lewis (1991) argues that Blinkhorn and Johnson's approach is to set personality tests up as a 'straw man', a view echoed by Mackenzie Davey (1991) who points out that relatively few organizations use personality tests alone to predict performance. Dulewicz (1991) also picks up this point and suggests that tests are a useful asset in personnel selection, serving as an aid to interviewing by 'flagging up' key points to be addressed in scarce interview time. However, most of Blinkhorn and Johnson's critics are cautious about the wisdom of relying solely on personality tests as the only factor in the selection decision (something which organizations would seem to be taking into account already, according to the IRS (1991d) data above). There is, though, a caution from Mackenzie Davey (1991), to the effect that while the administration and scoring of personality tests is relatively simple, the interpretation of the results is both difficult and complex, and should remain the preserve of qualified psychologists.

This concern has been reflected in a recent initiative by the IPM and British Psychological Society which seeks to redress what is noted to be an increasing abuse of psychological tests within employment, by providing independent accreditation for test users and a revised code of practice (Bartram 1991).

Apart from questions of technical effectiveness, there are also questions of a more ethical nature surrounding personality tests. It has been suggested that organizations have no right to seek to control access to jobs on the grounds of individual personality, an argument that can be viewed from both the individual's and the organization's perspective.

From the point of view of the latter, selecting only particular 'types' of personality may, eventually, lead to an 'incestuous' organizational profile where, weakened by 'inbreeding', the ability to think innovatively and challengingly is eroded in favour of a slavish conformity to established norms. On the part of the former, personality testing can represent an invasion of privacy, the organization seeking control over an aspect of individuality that should be outside employer 'interference'. At the heart of these concerns seems to be a fear about the totalitarian possibilities of work organizations and the role of personality profiling as a form of 'social engineering' for corporate conformity (for an early development of these ideas, see Whyte 1956). These views have been reinforced by accounts of personality testing being employed as a means of limiting potential employee resistance to the exercise of managerial prerogative. In the USA, for instance, this has been attributed to the work of so-called 'union-busting' consultants (Grenier 1988) who help employers select employees who are least susceptible to unionization: 'to stay non-union, hire dull, dumb, introverted, antisocial, unimaginative types' (quoted in Townley 1989:97).

In relation to other forms of testing there has been less controversy about the tests themselves, and more about their manner of application. In addition to questions of differential pre-and post-test treatment – who is selected to sit the test? Can it be shown that the (superior) performance of those who 'pass' a test is the result of innate ability or of raised expectations, the so-called 'halo effect'? – there are also concerns about social bias. In this respect, however, Wood and Baron (1992) point to the fact that while inappropriately chosen or administered tests can lead to unfair discrimination against members of ethnic minorities, this is not inevitable. In their view, the answer lies not in the total rejection of testing but, rather, in the careful evaluation of its appropriateness to the target job (via job analysis and evaluation), the informed choice of test design, professional interpretation of results, and the provision of 'positive action' where appropriate (see Chapter 9 below).

Nevertheless, the role of psychometric testing in selection remains controversial, a situation which shows little sign of change in the future.

The questions which need to be asked when considering testing depend upon a knowledge of the tests themselves and a clear understanding of the purpose for which testing is required. Thus, it needs to be recognized that even well designed and validated tests can still have implications for equal opportunities and that poorly designed or inadequately understood testing procedures can have serious repercussions, both for individuals (who may be wrongly selected or deselected) and for organizations; conscious and deliberate safeguards against such problems therefore need to be incorporated into the testing procedure from the outset. Overall, testing may have a useful role to play as one part of the selection process, but even where this can be demonstrated it seems undesirable that tests should ever be the sole method or principal basis for decision-making. The following case provides a salutary reminder of this.

Graduate recruiters may be using psychometric testing to too great an extent, and in an overly mechanistic way. Use of testing by graduate recruiters now appears to have become prevalent. Of the 737 undergraduates in a recent survey, 74 per cent had been asked to complete an aptitude test and 47 per cent had been requested to fill in personality questionnaires. Students in the course of their applications to prospective employers are thus now likely to be asked to sit tests several times. There is a three in four chance that a student lodging more than one application will be tested for aptitude more than once; and slightly less than a one in two chance of repeatedly completing personality questionnaires. Given the relatively small number of test instruments in use, the likelihood of being asked to complete the same test is correspondingly high. These results indicate that a 'practice effect' may be undermining the validity of testing for graduate recruiters.

(IRS 1992b:15)

Biodata

An alternative or adjunct to testing which is receiving increasing attention is biodata. This claims to find correlations between successful (or unsuccessful) job performers and aspects of individual biography on the basis of information provided on a specially designed application form. The most frequent use of biodata has been as a pre-selection screening method for sorting systematically through large numbers of job applicants and producing a more reliable shortlist (various examples of this type of use are detailed in IRS 1990a). In addition to 'screening out' potentially 'unsuitable' candidates, biodata selection has also been used by, for instance, the Civil Service, to 'sift-in' suitable candidates, who may have narrowly failed an admission test. The construction of a biodata system is described by IRS :

A group of people are chosen, usually employees, or they may be external job applicants. All should be connected with the same job. The group is split into two: good and bad performers (with middle-range 'triers' omitted) or, for applicants, into the successful and unsuccessful. All answer an identical list of broadly biographical or job-related questions and the responses of the two sub-groups are compared with each other to see which strongly distinguish between the good performers/successful applicants on the one hand and the poor performers/unsuccessful applicants on the other.... A smaller list of questions is produced after the trial, based on those that seem to be the most significant predictors. Usually, a weighting system gives a sliding scale of points to the answers, stating where there is most unanimity amongst good performers and greatest contrast with poor performers.

(IRS 1990a:16)

Although exponents of biodata claim that, used properly, it has an extremely high predictive validity, its critics point to the ease with which it could be misused so as to discriminate against individuals or groups by, for example, focusing on aspects of biography which are beyond their control, or which reflect social prejudice. Similarly, it has been claimed that the use of biodata lacks a developed theoretical base, one commentator referring to it as 'mindlessly and atheoretically empirical'. Although it appears that biodata will continue to develop as a selection technique there is, as yet, little research into its operation and effectiveness on a widespread scale.

Graphology

Despite widespread use in Continental Europe, graphology – the analysis of personality from handwriting – has met with a sceptical and often hostile reception in the UK and its use, although apparently increasing, remains low. Nevertheless, according to one report, Swiss companies use it in 75 per cent of general management appointments and it is, apparently, even more common in France (Rocco 1991). An account of one UK company's use of graphology to assist selection decisions is provided by Rocco:

> [The graphologist] holds the paper up to the light and speaks rapidly into the telephone. 'There is a tremor in the writing, a shakiness. I think there could be several explanations. Epilepsy. An incipient brain tumour. Alcohol perhaps. Or even drugs...'. The words hang in the air as the listener – a personnel manager at SG Warburg – digests the implications of this unexpected news.... The recent candidate interviewed for a junior job in Warburg's computer department provided an excellent CV, and seemed able and confident in the course of two interviews. His handwriting sample, however, was abnormally cramped. The lines were crooked and the letters spidery and badly squashed. At best it seemed like the writing of an ill-educated child. But [the graphologist] thought otherwise. For an employer like Warburg, the prospect of hiring a drug addict is too frightening to contemplate. The man was turned down for the job.
>
> (Rocco 1991:12)

Graphology involves the examination of handwriting characteristics such as slant, size, pressure and rhythm, in order to draw inferences about personality traits such as temperament, cognitive capabilities and sociability. The slant of the writing, for example, is claimed to indicate the emotional responsiveness of the writer, vertical writers being more 'object oriented', while forward slanting writers are 'more in touch with feelings'. Similarly, the space between letters and words is thought to be indicative of the distance that writers prefer between themselves and others, and the size of upper and lower loops to reflect traits such as emotional maturity and abstract reasoning (Taylor and Sackheim 1988:72).

According to its supporters, graphology can play a useful role in selection decisions, where it is claimed to be relatively cheap and easy to use in terms of candidate action, and free from sex and race bias. As with psychometric tests, it is usually suggested that graphology be used only as part of a selection process, and not as a stand-alone technique: 'it can give the interviewer new insights into a character, particularly its subconscious elements. It can help to focus discussions on areas of possible weakness or to give the interviewer a chance to draw out elements that perhaps did not come up [previously]' (*Personnel Today* 1988:18). Against this, however, must be set the various criticisms of graphology.

A traditional argument is that there is virtually no empirical evidence of a credible kind to support the validity of graphology as a selection technique. However, a recent paper by Gullan-Whur (1991) cites 212 studies, and Moss (1992) provides a summary of reliability and validity tests. Nevertheless, despite a sympathy towards graphology on the part of both writers, the overall results are less than conclusive: although some studies apparently demonstrate high levels of reliability and validity, others reveal correspondingly low scores on both counts (for an early and outspoken demolition of graphology's status as a means of personality assessment, see Eysenck 1968:223). On this score, then, it seems that the jury is still out.

In many respects, therefore, graphology raises similar issues to those associated with biodata, in terms of an intuitive appeal mixed with an all-too-easy potential for confirming social stereotypes and superficial judgements. In the case of graphology, however, the potential dangers are probably greater as the 'mysteries of interpretation' tend to be more esoteric and less directly derived from workplace experience.

APPRAISAL

According to a number of recent investigations it is apparent that the practice of appraisal is increasing, both in absolute terms and in relation to the groups of employees covered. From being almost exclusively the preserve of managerial employees, it now appears to be spreading down the line (Long 1986; Storey 1992; IDS 1989b). Between 1977 and 1985, for example, there were increases in the use of appraisal for first-line supervisors, clerical/secretarial staff and skill/semi-skilled staff of 18 per cent (from 60 per cent to 78 per cent), 21 per cent (from 45 per cent to 66 per cent) and 22 per cent (from 2 per cent to 24 per cent) respectively (Townley 1989: 98).

This extension of appraisal practices can be attributed to a variety of factors not dissimilar to those associated with the use of more systematic and individualistic selection techniques, performance management systems (see Chapter 2 above), performance-related pay, the redesign of reward systems (see Chapter 5 below), and the 'harmonization' of terms and conditions across manual and non-manual jobs.

The nature of appraisal, however, is by no means uniform, and tends to encompass two broad approaches:

- **Judgemental appraisal,** which relates to current performance in a particular job, often linked to pay.
- **Development appraisal,** which seeks to identify and develop potential for future performance, linked to succession and personal development planning.

Judgemental appraisal of current performance

Quite often, judgemental appraisal schemes combine the assessment of social/behavioural attributes and performance results data. On the basis of seven case studies, IDS (1989b) produced the following list of performance factors which are typically appraised:

- **Job knowledge/abilities**   (ability to perform in all aspects of the job)
- **Adaptability/flexibility**   (ability to cope with change; multi-skilling for craft workers)
- **Productivity**   (individual work output)
- **Quality of work**   (attention to detail; consistent quality)
- **Attitude to work**   (commitment; motivation; enthusiasm)
- **Interaction with others**   (communication skills; teamworking)
- **Originality/initiative**   (problem-solving)
- **Perception**   (ability to interpret job requirements)
- **Judgement/use of resources**   (setting of priorities; ability to plan and organize work)
- **Attendance/timekeeping**   (number of and reasons for absence; punctuality)
- **Safety awareness**   (awareness of health and safety standards)
- **Need for supervision**   (reliability; degree of independence)
- **Supervisory ability**   (leadership, ability to train and develop staff – where appropriate)
- **Performance against set targets**   (the extent to which previously set targets have been met).

(IDS 1989b: 3)

According to IDS, the assessment of these factors is achieved by a mixture of 'subjective' and 'objective' measures, almost invariably carried out by the employee's immediate superior, the most commonly used being job knowledge/abilities, attitude to work, quality of work, productivity, interaction with others, and attendance/timekeeping. This type of approach to appraisal falls into what Randell (1989) terms the 'performance control' category, an approach which he regards as underpinning most contemporary UK appraisal schemes. Within this approach, performance is typically appraised in one of three ways:

1   by the use of trait scales
2   by objective outcome measures
3   by behavioural observation scales.

Trait scales, writes Randell, are inherently ambiguous and are not recommended; 'outcome measures' can be extremely useful when they are available and relevant to the job; and 'behavioural observation scales' are always recommended, so that the means as well as the ends receive proper attention. Unfortunately, according to Randell, when performance appraisal is based on these principles there is always a probability that the measurement process will be inept and unfair because the technical problems in designing rating scales are overlooked (1989:161).

Nevertheless, it is this type of 'objectively' based appraisal that is most often seen as appropriate for determining the link between performance and pay. This link, however, has proved particularly controversial. Some commentators suggest that an explicit and direct link with pay, determined at a single appraisal session, is both fair and of greater motivational impact (because the reward is clearly related to assessed performance), whereas others regard the incorporation of pay determination into performance appraisal as an overburdening distraction such that the wider purpose of appraisal (i.e. to stimulate performance) becomes no more than a narrow pay review. Those holding the latter view generally argue for the separation in time of performance appraisal and pay review, to avoid conflation of purpose. The arguments for and against linking pay to appraisal are summarized below.

Positive arguments

- All parties, appraisers, appraisees and reviewers, take performance appraisal more seriously.
- Many individuals feel that, for reasons of fairness, there should be a close link between performance appraisal and pay.
- Organizations are more likely to develop performance-oriented cultures, in which high performers are seen to receive extra rewards, and vice versa.

Negative arguments

- When pay and performance appraisal are closely linked, the pay issue may overshadow all the other purposes of performance appraisal.
- There may be a tendency for employees to withhold negative information about performance, leading to a less than frank appraisal discussion.
- Employees may try to influence appraisers, in seeking to set lower, more conservative, goals.
- Employees may adapt their behaviour to target on receiving good ratings, rather than genuinely trying to improve their overall performance.
- Appraisers may be encouraged to over-rate employees if they think that adverse financial consequences may otherwise result.

(Derived from Anderson 1992:190–1)

In practice, the effectiveness with which pay review can be directly combined with performance appraisal is likely to be heavily conditioned by the organization culture. Carlton and Sloman (1991), for example, explain how the strongly individualistic and achievement-oriented culture of County NatWest bank mitigated against the separation of pay review and performance appraisal, to the extent that only by making pay dependent upon appraisal could (useful) employee participation in the latter be secured:

One of the features of an achievement culture is difficulty of control; the weak role culture is associated with a comparative lack of rules and procedures. At its simplest, this means that it is not an organization where people naturally look for guidance from above. They want to get on with the job and regard anything that deflects them from immediate client-orientated bottom-line activities as an unwelcome intrusion.... The appraisal cycle is deliberately timed to provide input to the remuneration review process so the results can be taken into consideration. Why is this a firm part of the programme when most of the commentators on the relationship between appraisal and salary review preach the opposite? The answer is a simple one. The culture would not accept two or more separate exercises.

(Carlton and Sloman 1991:80, 86).

The significance of appraisal in relation to organizational culture is reinforced by Townley (1989), who makes the point that even the most 'objective' assessment techniques also involve elements of behaviour control:

One of the functions of appraisal, rather than its being seen as the 'objective' measurement of individual performance, is to communicate organizational norms or 'culture' and reinforce this process.... Polaroid's job assessment or appraisal procedure, illustrates the operation of such a system... a lot of assessment is concerned with work behaviour – such as dependability and thoroughness, work habits and personal characteristics – rather than actual production achievement. What is learnt through the appraisal procedure are work habits, attendance, attitude and other personal characteristics. 'Exceptional' workers become defined in terms of those who set examples to others in methods and use of time, suggest ways of improving the job, increase the effectiveness of the group, display cooperation and enthusiasm etc. These criteria become the basis for promotion.

(Townley 1989: 103)

In recognizing this 'compliance element' in the appraisal process, Townley also points to its intensely personal and individual basis: ultimately, this form of performance appraisal is about the confirmation of a relationship of power between employee and immediate superior. Thus, it cannot be guaranteed that such initiatives, which essentially represent an individualization of the employment relationship, will meet with approval within workforces where collective bargaining is strongly established and where they are seen to challenge union power (see Chapter 8 below). Storey (1992:108) cites the case of Plessey Naval Systems, where a system of performance appraisal for manual grades which would have resulted in discretionary 'uplifts' within the existing pay grade structure was rejected by the EETPU. This view is echoed in a more extreme form by Grenier (1988), who details how ratings given by supervisors and team leaders were used to identify, coerce and eventually dismiss union sympathizers in an 'enlightened' US plant. However, whereas the analyses offered by Townley and Grenier suggest that the appraisal process may, under certain circumstances, operate as a mechanism of managerial control and manipulation to the detriment of employees, others have taken the view that appraisal contributes to building a 'performance culture' capable of 'liberating' and rewarding employee potential. From this latter perspective, the appraisal process is closely tied to the notion of individual development.

Development appraisal

It is in the area of appraisal for development potential that many have pointed to novel trends in terms of assessment centre technology. But despite the rapid growth of assessment centres, the bulk of work in this area is still largely dependent upon the interview as an appraisal technique. At its simplest, this stems from what Randell (1989) has termed 'qualitative assessment':

> All that a qualitative approach demands is the diagnosis of what an individual should be doing differently *next* in their job. This can be checked and discussed with the individual in an interview and this diagnosis turned into an 'action plan'.
>
> (Randell 1989:161)

Holdsworth (1991) provides a refinement of this position and points to four changes which he claims (albeit without citing any substantiating empirical evidence) characterize appraisal in the 1980s and 1990s:

1 **Purpose and content**   Here the change has been from pay and promotion to performance management and development. This has meant a shift away from mechanistic and depersonalized behavioural task assessment and towards a combination of task-and person-oriented assessment (the extent to which the latter assertion can be squared with the debate about management competencies will be returned to in Chapter 4 below) or towards a 'joint problem-solving' stance between appraiser and appraisee.
2 **Degree of openness**   Now, it is suggested, most appraisal schemes have moved from being secret and confidential (the data not being available to the appraisee) to a position where the appraisee sees 'most if not all' of the completed appraisal document, can comment on the result and, in some cases, upon the performance of the appraiser, both in general and in relation to the conduct of the appraisal exercise.
3 **Style of appraisal**   The shift here is towards greater dynamism, the process being less about the recording of information and more about changing and developing, again closely linked to the foregoing trends. This leads to an emphasis on the provision of open and constructive feedback designed to have a positive motivational effect.
4 **Ownership**   Apparently 'the ownership of appraisal has tended to shift from the centre to the periphery, from the personnel department to the manager and the appraiser [sic].' This, of course, ties in with the general thrust of HRM to decentralize key functions to line management level. This, of course, presupposes adequate training of such managers in appraisal techniques.

If correct, the last point is an important one, as the skills needed by appraisers within this context are not only those of assessing performance, but also of using

this information to diagnose development needs and provide coaching, encouragement and opportunities for these to be fulfilled. In this respect, therefore, appraisal
cannot be treated as a stand-alone practice but must be linked to other systems such
as career development and succession planning; top management has to be committed not only to assessing employees, but also to doing something with the results
of this assessment. One oft-cited case in this respect is that of IBM.

The IBM appraisal system is linked to a counselling programme which is geared
explicitly to the notion of employee development. In addition, however, it is also
used as part of the merit pay determination process. In most respects this system
reflects the trends described by Holdsworth (1991), in that it rests upon shared
information and aims at the establishment of consensus between appraiser and
appraisee over objectives and rewards (Sapsed 1991:8).

A somewhat different approach has been adopted by the Nuffield Hospitals
group to the extent that both assessment of performance for salary purposes and
the determination of work objectives are separated from appraisal for individual
development, each being tackled at different times in the year so as not to
'over-stress' the system (Wilson and Cole 1990:48). The basis for the personal
development appraisal centres on a short list of preparatory questions and a
nine-topic agenda for the interview, as shown below.

Preparatory questions

- What have I done particularly well at work in the past year?
- What have I done not so well?
- What obstacles have I met?
- What important abilities are not being used?
- In what aspects of my job do I need more experience and training?
- To help my personal development, what additional things might be done by:
  (a) my manager; (b) myself; (c) the company?
- Development actions agreed: (a) by me; (b) by my manager.
- What would I like to be doing in the future?

Interview topics

- Praise for special achievements
- Subordinate's assessment of their own performance
- Manager's response to subordinate's assessment
- Action to improve subordinate's performance
- Subordinate's assessment of manager
- Action to improve manager's performance
- Subordinate's career ambitions
- Action to achieve development target agreed above
- Summary of actions.

This approach to the assessment of development potential, especially the notion that it should not be conflated with other aspects of the appraisal process, finds a more sophisticated variant in the notion of the assessment centre. Here, although originally designed for selection purposes, increasingly the focus has shifted towards the assessment of the development potential of employees.

Assessment centres

The basic idea of an assessment centre (AC) is the assembly of a number of different but complementary assessment techniques that, specifically, can determine the ability of an individual to undertake a particular job. Proponents argue that in terms of thoroughness and effectiveness, ACs can be regarded as 'the Rolls-Royce of psychological assessment' (Fletcher 1982:42). Because ACs aim to match as closely as possible the competencies needed successfully to fulfil a particular job, it is claimed that the systematic and controlled nature of the data collected can show which competencies are present in an individual and which will need to be developed (and to what extent). Thus, according to Seegers (1992), whereas most assessment methods try to establish a person's suitability for a new position on the basis of successful performance in *previous* jobs (an approach which can only work if the new position is similar to the old one), an AC takes the new job as the *starting point* for assessment, thereby making it eminently suited for the assessment of promotability.

In 1989 over a third of UK companies employing over 1,000 people claimed to have used ACs in the past year (Woodruffe 1990: 5), and in the US the growth of AC usage has led to the establishment of standards aimed at eliminating 'non-valid' centres or their unprofessional use. To meet this standard an AC must comply with the following conditions:

- Multiple assessment techniques must be used, at least one of which must be a simulation closely related to the work situation.
- Multiple assessors, with prior AC training, must be used.
- Outcome judgements must be based on pooled information from assessors and techniques.
- An overall assessment of behaviour must be made by the assessors at a separate time from the observation of behaviour.
- Simulation exercises are used to tap a variety of predetermined behaviours and have been pre-tested prior to use.
- The dimensions, attributes, characteristics or qualities evaluated by the AC are determined by an analysis of relevant job behaviours.
- The techniques used in the AC are designed to provide information which is used in evaluating the dimensions, attributes or qualities previously determined.

(Source: (Blanksby and Iles 1990: 34)

The basic advantages and disadvantages of ACs have been summarized by Seegers (1992) thus:

Advantages

- **More accurate evaluation**   This assertion is based both on the experiences of users and on numerous technically controlled validation studies (such as those at AT&T) conducted on a longitudinal basis.
- **More specific training**   Criteria-based diagnosis allows the identification of very specific training needs which, in turn, allows the more effective targeting of training investment.
- **More effective use of human resources**   The method is claimed to allow greater insights into employee performance, both as a result of the assessment process itself and through the exercise of job competence necessary for the centre construction.
- **More effective communication**   A common language for assessment purposes is provided.
- **Cultural change**   Centres can help organizations change their work style because employees are taught to work in a different manner.

Problems

- **Acceptance by management**   Effective operation of centres demands the support and involvement of all managers; it cannot be driven only by personnel/training specialists.
- **Management time involved**   Because management time involvement (both in terms of assessee and assessor participation) is condensed into a determinate time period (e.g. one day), the cost becomes readily transparent.
- **Cost**   Costs of starting up a centre are often high, especially if consultants are necessary. Also there is the training of assessors, and the time factor alluded to above. Centres lasting more than one day may also require the provision of accommodation, etc.
- **Confusion with performance appraisal**   Centres focus primarily on future job behaviour, rather than job performance in the past.
- **Reactions to feedback**   As centres provide often detailed knowledge about a candidate's weaknesses, this information needs to be used both constructively and sensitively, if frustration and disillusionment is not to result.
- **Absence of policy**   Especially within a development context, centres need to be supported by integrated HRM policies in relation to career planning, etc.

In addition to the problems listed above, however, the issue of equal opportunities has been raised in relation to assessment centres. The main points have been summarized by Blanksby and Iles:

> It is important to remember that the whole centre *process* needs to be studied, not just the event itself. For example, if women have had to survive potentially discriminatory pre-screening hurdles, the proportionately fewer women who make it to the centre are likely to be highly skilled and highly able and will score

more highly on average than those men who were less stringently selected. Conversely a company which, as part of a positive action effort, sends all its women managers to a centre but pre-selects its male managers more stringently may find that its women managers on average score less highly.

(1990:35)

As AC usage has shifted towards appraisal and development, the level of congruence with HRM philosophy has increased, particularly in terms of emphasizing the integrated role of HRM within wider strategic objectives. Iles (1992), for instance, points to the use of ACs as part of a career development process and, more generally, as an aid to organizational development and cultural change. In the latter respect he cites the case of Cadbury Schweppes's use of ACs as a means of getting the company on the 'competence road' (see Chapter 4 below) and points to possible uses in the fields of leadership, decision-making, planning and communication, team-building, and as an input to human resource planning, by pointing to 'what skills should be hired, or developed so as to meet future and current needs, and to help construct talent inventories for succession planning or management development' (Iles 1992:81). This latter usage is illustrated by the case of Triplex Lloyd:

> Triplex Lloyd is a West Midlands industrial engineering group. The Centurion Programme is currently aimed at young people, between 18 and 30 years old, who may be qualified, part-qualified or have no qualifications at all and who have not had the opportunity to progress beyond shop-floor jobs. The programme is designed to identify people who are bright and creative. All employees within the age range were asked whether they thought they could take responsibility for managing 100 people. Interested applicants were invited to write to the group's chief executive. One hundred people wrote with reasons why they thought they should be given the chance to become managers. Two single day selection assessment centres were held. Senior management tested applicants' leadership skills, and ability to think logically. Applicants were divided into small groups and presented with problems to solve. A consensus solution had to be found by the group, which led to long debates. In addition to the group talks, participants took two individual tests: a personality questionnaire and a word association test. Out of the 100 applicants, 36 people were picked to go on the management development programme. In terms of immediate results of the programme, the company believes that it has recouped its costs of £60,000 by savings on recruitment fees and other training costs.

((IRS 1990c:2–3)

In summary, therefore, if human resourcing requirements are planned strategically, and if these include performance standards reflecting quality and quantity (see Chapter 2 above), it is to be expected that what will be required is 'right minds' as well as 'right actions'; just 'doing the job' may no longer be enough. As such it is perhaps not surprising that more attention is being given to assessment techniques which tap not only 'abilities' but also attitudes.

KEY LEARNING POINTS

- The assessment of employee attributes is nothing new: most employers, both large and small, have always recognized attitudes as a factor contributing to selection or promotion decisions.
- Where the HRM approach may differ is in the degree of formality with which this is approached and the sophistication of the assessment techniques used.
- Indeed, what may cause the adoption of systematic individual assessment techniques to spread is their interdependence with other human resource 'systems' such as human resourcing, training, development and reward.
- In this respect, even organizations which do not consciously aspire to the adoption of a total approach to HRM may find that initiatives in assessment practices push them towards development in other areas of human resource activity (and vice versa).
- Nevertheless, some caution is needed before embarking on the wholesale adoption of novel assessment approaches. It is important to be clear about what such approaches can and cannot deliver, why they are necessary (i.e., how they will be used, whether they will support other human resource strategies), what the cost (in time and outlay) will be if they are to be used effectively, and what their useful service life will be.

EXERCISES

1   Consider the following account of production worker selection at Toyota's new Derbyshire plant, which opened in 1992. To what extent would this be a desirable or practical approach for other organizations?

Employees have typically spent six or seven months in the extensive recruitment process, undergoing assessment for a total of 16 hours. Toyota's 'total production system' bases its management philosophy on mutual trust and respect which allows sharing of responsibility. This makes it a difficult club to join: out of more than 20,000 applicants, only about 400 have jobs on the production teams. 'We don't want the traditional 20-minute interview, and the 'you-go-to-the-same-football-match-as-me-so-you-must-be-okay' line,' Bryan Jackson, director of human resources, explained.... 'We want people who can work as a team and who have ideas for improvements and can demonstrate an ability to learn.' The detailed five-page application form – 'designed to test commitment' – includes detailed questions about personal values and achievements. Those whose forms were acceptable then entered a process of mental and physical testing.... First there was a three-hour 'testing and orientation' phase. A series of tests measured their numerical skills, attitude and ability to learn. A video-interactive test of learning asks candidates how they respond to a series of situations. Next comes the 'targeted behavioural interview', 75 minutes of questions.... Then came the crunch. The biggest test – six hours at a simulated production line. Candidates had to build fuel filters or wheel trims under real pressures. Those who reached the final interview – another hour – submitted two references and underwent a medical.

(Rowan and Milner 1992:18)

2   Discuss how the performance factors for worker appraisal, listed on page 52 above, could be measured and assessed.

Chapter 4

Training and development
Building bridges?

DEFINING TRAINING AND DEVELOPMENT

Although the terms 'training' and 'development' are frequently treated either as synonyms or as representing mutually exclusive activities, from an HRM perspective, they are better understood as being linked, such that training is seen as both a part of and a precondition for development. The traditional reason for regarding training and development as distinct personnel practices has much to do with hierarchical divisions within organizations. Training has evolved as something that is provided for non-managerial workers, whereas development has been treated as the preserve of management (hence the still common pairing, management-development). This type of binary divide has two difficulties within a HRM perspective. First, it undermines the assumption that all employees are a valuable resource to be 'developed' to their maximum potential; development therefore cannot be regarded as something to be restricted to a privileged section of the workforce. This is especially true where flexible, multi-skilled workers are employed, since such employees, like managers, are valuable organizational assets who cannot easily be replaced (retention and commitment being usual reasons for development). Second, it can obscure the fact that managers also need training: management work involves determinate skills and competencies for which training is necessary, besides more nebulous powers of reasoning, abstraction and personal growth associated with development.

From an HRM perspective, then, the connection between training and development must be regarded as highly interactive, each facilitating the other, in what may be thought of as a dialectical relationship.

Despite this close relationship in theory, however, the treatment of training and development in most of the literature is still largely one of separation. For this reason, therefore, it will be necessary for expository purposes to continue to use this convention.

TRAINING

Considered alone, training usually refers broadly to voc
training (VET) targeted at non-managerial employees. Eve.
neous category encompassing activities which may range fror.
college-based courses in scientific and technical skills (e.
through formal programmes of workplace training, to informal
of the 'sitting by Nellie' variety.

Serious concern about training in the UK surfaced during t   .ii of the
mid-1980s when, as a result of general expansion, employers in all sectors were
having to compete ever more vigorously for staff, a competition which exposed the
underlying weakness of the skills base in the UK labour market. This problem was
given added impetus by warnings about impending demographic change and the
opening of European frontiers, both of which were expected to make existing skill
shortages worse still. A series of reports and commentaries in the mid-1980s laid
the blame for this situation firmly in the hands of British employers who, it was
suggested, had failed, unlike their Continental counterparts, to invest in training:

> British management does not actually do very much [training].... For example,
> although expenditure on training is only a crude measure of activity, the
> comparative information that has recently become available suggests that the
> amount spent by British employers is considerably less than in other countries.
> Leading employers in Japan, West Germany and the USA, it has been suggested,
> spend of the order of three per cent of turnover on training.... In contrast [a 1985
> survey of 500 employers in Britain with more than 25 employees] found that on
> average the employers surveyed invested only £200 per employee per annum
> on training, which added up to only 0.15 per cent of turnover; that 24 per cent
> of establishments had provided no training of any kind in the last twelve months;
> and that 69 per cent of employees had received no training during this period.
>
> (Keep 1989:179)

Virtually all commentators, including both the CBI and TUC, have come to
regard increased training as a precondition for economic success in the 1990s, a
view captured by Lord Young, Secretary of State for Employment in 1986, thus:

> Training should be an integral part of the work and development of any company
> or organization, large or small. After all, a company's human resources are
> among its most important assets and the skills and motivation of its workers can
> be crucial to success. We all need to recognize that training is not a luxury, but
> a necessity.
>
> (Quoted in Kenney and Reid 1990: xi)

Although an unambiguous and direct causal link between better training and
improved organizational performance has yet to be conclusively demonstrated,
there is widespread agreement about the perceived benefits of high training activity
which it is argued:

ps employees learn jobs more quickly and effectively.
Improves work performance of existing employees and keeps them up to date in specialist skills.

- Leads to a greater volume of work resulting from fewer mistakes and greater rapidity.
- Frees management time, less of which is spent rectifying errors; also reduces wastage.
- Can help to reduce labour turnover among new and established staff.
- Can help to reduce redundancy and recruitment costs, through retraining.
- Incorporating safety training can help reduce accidents.
- Can help attract good workers.
- Is a precondition for flexible working.
- Creates an attitude more receptive to coping with change.

(Based on Kenney and Reid 1990:58)

These basic assumptions are endorsed by the CBI (1989) which, on the basis of a survey of 40 companies, identifies two extreme training positions: the 'road to failure' and the 'road to success'. The former reflects:

- a failure to recognize or implement management practices designed to meet, not only existing, but future skills needs;
- an unrealistic reliance by managers upon national and local labour markets to satisfy company skills needs at whatever level;
- a willingness to regard the practice of poaching the skilled labour of others as the chief response to skill pressures, regardless of the consequences at company level and in pay inflation terms.

(CBI 1989:8)

The 'road to success', on the other hand, involves:

- progress through the sharing of a common vision, from top management through to every level of the organization;
- high status being accorded to training and development practices based upon results and their relevance to the needs of the organization;
- company structures which allow for the development of individuals and encourage the acquisition of skills to meet business goals;
- business systems flexible enough to accommodate investment in people, with agreed budgets and clear targets subject to regular evaluation.

(CBI 1989:9)

The CBI's advocacy of this 'success model' as a guide to 'good practice' is supported by their strong intimation that this approach leads to economic benefits to the organization in the form of a lower vulnerability to skills shortages (see also Jones and Goss 1991; and Goss and Jones 1992 for more on this relationship).

Thus from this perspective, training is viewed as an integral part of core

organizational strategy rather than an *ad hoc* operational issue. Similarly the role of training is not seen exclusively in instrumental terms but also as an important employee motivator contributing to recruitment and retention opportunities.

The following cases of Rover Group and Lucas Industries illustrate this approach:

Rover Group

[The] commitment to giving people knowledge and skills, treating them as individuals and enabling them to adapt to change is reflected in the setting up of the Rover Learning Business, an independent unit with its own managing director and board of governors. Its sole business objective is the satisfaction of its customers – Rover's 40,000 employees.
    ... In May 1990 Rover started its REAL (Rover Employee Assisted Learning) programme, and by November 1,600 employees had applied for development. Rover aims at a 50 per cent participation rate after 18 months of the programme.
    The company is prepared to spend a maximum of £100 on every employee who attends an external further education course offered by an accredited institution. These are typically not work related and can range from a language course or a supervisory management course to computer literacy. Employees can also make use of extensive in-house programmes.
    ... During the '80s Rover's training expenditure per employee increased in line with inflation, and the 1991 budget of £33 million represents an average of £800 for each employee or six per cent of payroll. This puts Rover towards the upper end of British industry in terms of investment in education, training and employee development.

(Muller 1991:33)

Lucas Industries

In the period 1985–8, Lucas spent around £40m per annum on training which was equivalent to about 2.5–3 per cent of its total sales revenue. This expenditure was viewed as an 'investment' in that training and development was being called on to act as a major agent of change.... As Parnaby [Group Director Manufacturing Technology] observed: 'competitiveness to world standards requires a fundamental redesign of our manufacturing systems and far-reaching changes in traditional working practices, habits and culture. Our most potent engines of change are the multidisciplinary task forces which operate mainly at business unit and factory level. Once the members of each task force have been given basic training in systems engineering, they then redesign their factory or business units on the basis of 'Just-In-Time' control systems... they develop plans for marketing their products, improving quality, changing job structures, improving the performance of their suppliers and – not least – training all the people in the business unit.' This programme is so extensive that he estimated that by 1991 just about the whole of the workforce would undergo some form of training.... The delivery mechanisms included, in addition to the task-force methodology, an active central training function which has reoriented itself from training delivery to training development; open learning centres; modular courses in manufacturing systems; and external masters courses.

(Storey 1992:114–5)

In the case of Lucas Industries, however, Storey probes behind this initially encouraging picture of a 'training revolution', pointing not only to the relative novelty of this approach but also to the experience of this training initiative among shop-floor workers and middle managers. Here, it seems, both groups felt their recent training experiences to have been few; '[the] investment-in-people theme was countermanded by more visible messages of cost cutting and pressure' (Storey 1992:115). This is a salutary reminder that although a training culture may have to be 'driven from the top', it cannot be guaranteed that those further down the organization will necessarily be infected with the same level of commitment and enthusiasm.

Indeed, the enormity of this task is revealed by research into the link between training and corporate strategy. A major study conducted for the Training Agency (TA 1989a), for instance, found that two-thirds of all employers had no budget for training and three-quarters no training plan. Eighty-five per cent made no attempt to assess the benefits gained from training and only 4 per cent carried out any kind of effective cost-benefit analysis.

On a more qualitative note, a study of training needs and corporate strategy (Elliott 1989) suggested that training, compared to other business activities such as finance and accounting, was poorly represented in strategic discourse:

The language of training strategies, in the sense of a set of words commonly understood at the senior level of a company, is poorly developed when compared with other functions. Training appears weak in concepts and models as compared with functions like accounting and marketing, and thus weak in a language commonly understood by directors of businesses and those accountable for training strategies.

(Elliott 1989:1)

This view would seem to have some support from a sub-set of results contained in the *Training in Britain* report (TA 1989b). This analysis, closely linked to the Pettigrew and Hendry model of strategic change (see Chapter 1), suggested that developments in training generally were initiated by external competitive pressure, but that the nature of any such development was conditioned by factors internal to the organization (and not by, for instance, government infrastructural training pressures). Thus, firms that developed effectively tended to be those which had 'gathered together a critical mass of positive or supportive factors that drive [training] activities.' (A similar argument is made by Jones and Goss 1991.)

Although training may not always be among the top items on many corporate strategic agendas, its presence is being increasingly felt at this level, even if often only vicariously. One way, for instance, in which training seems to be gaining more attention, as *Training in Britain* (TA 1989b) suggests, is through general management initiatives aimed principally at resolving competitive challenges. One example of this, already alluded to in the Lucas case above and discussed further below, is total quality management (TQM); another is the attempt by some organizations to redress skills shortages through 'skill-based pay' whereby reward is linked to training acquisition in key skill-shortage areas.

Skill-based pay

The intention here is to reward the acquisition of skills by linking pay progression (totally or proportionately) to successful completion of approved training, thereby providing a proactive mechanism for giving breadth and depth to an organization's skills base. This linkage is also claimed to ensure that training is taken seriously at strategic level (since it has to be paid for on a continuous rather than an *ad hoc* basis), and that it becomes more attractive to potential trainees.

It is usual for such schemes to consist of both on-the-job and off-the-job training structured on a modular basis with employees being required to reach specified levels of proficiency in a number of competencies making up a particular skill module (see IDS 1992a). Although the principle of skills-based pay is relatively straightforward, the establishment of such systems generally requires significant amounts of management support and pre-training of those who will administer it and those who will take part (IRS 1992d). In addition, there is the problem of setting the limits of individual progress within a particular scheme (IDS 1992a): by establishing the principle that progression within the pay scale is dependent upon successful completion of training, such schemes require that access to training and ways of dealing with those who reach the ceiling of available skills training are both agreed and seen to be fair by all employees. Without such agreement, skills-based pay and related training programmes may rapidly become divisive, frustrating and demotivating. In practice, therefore, such schemes are likely to need to be connected to processes of appraisal and career development, an initiative which, in the case of non-managerial employees may involve significant changes in assessment practice (see Chapter 3). This necessity for skill-based pay to 'tie together' training, reward, appraisal and performance has close parallels with the philosophy of TQM.

Total quality management

A convenient characterization of the key principles of TQM is provided by Hill (1991):

Total quality management can be seen as a business discipline and philosophy of management which institutionalizes planned and continuous business improvement; indeed, many people prefer to talk of managing for continuous improvement rather than for quality, which has a 'product-centred' connotation. 'Quality' is much the same as 'excellence' in the recent management jargon, and the test of quality management is its ability to satisfy customers in the market-place. Total quality management assumes that quality is the outcome of all activities that take place within an organization; that all functions and all employees have to participate in the improvement process; that the organizations need both quality systems and a quality culture.

(Hill 1991:554)

Thus, a crucial contribution to successful TQM must be the provision of (often extensive) training, both in terms of specific techniques linked to quality monitoring and by providing a basis for continuous development of skills appropriate to rapid change. This is emphasized by an IRS (1992d) account of Michelin Tyres' quality initiative (which also makes use of skills-based pay):

The training programme had a number of elements but focused on three weeks off-the-job training followed by nine weeks of consolidation. Its aim was to strengthen existing skills and knowledge, and then teach the new skills and knowledge of inspection... at the end of each module there was a knowledge and/or skills validation. In addition, following the nine weeks of consolidation, a final validation of training took place. If everything was successful at this stage then the operator became a 'Post manager' with a rate of pay which 'reflected his or her total responsibility'.... The training resulted in an increase in delivered quality between departments from 75 per cent in 1986 to 98.5 per cent in 1991.

(IRS 1992d:6)

A further example of the centrality of training to TQM is provided by an IDS Study (IDS 1990e), which reports the introduction of TQM at Texas Instruments involving an increase in annual worker-hours of training from 10,000 to 39,000 hours across 1,100 staff between 1984 and 1989.

National Vocational Qualifications

The training initiatives associated with skill-based pay and TQM, essentially driven by organizational strategic concerns, can now be compared with a major state-sponsored scheme, the National Vocational Qualifications (NVQs). This approach has been developed not from the competitive demands of specific organizations but as a government initiative to provide a nationally consistent training framework linking training provision directly to work-based skills and to standardized accreditation.

NVQs aim to provide a national framework of competence-based qualifications appropriate to all industries and all levels of employment from shop-floor to the board level. These qualifications are intended to allow individuals to build continuously upon their skills and experience and to assist mobility between employers. The key method for attaining NVQs is through workplace activity monitored by an accredited tester (usually a supervisor or manager who has attended a designated training course). Underlying NVQs is the so-called 'competencies' approach to training which defines competency as: 'the ability to perform the activities within an occupational area to levels of performance expected in employment'. Thus, competence is understood to be largely about the visible signs of effectiveness in a job, demonstrable aspects of performance which can be assessed to determine whether someone is given an NVQ – there is only a pass or fail, and no other grading (IRS 1991f:15).

Although NVQs are concerned only with outcomes and do not specify the particular patterns or forms of training to bring employees to a given level of competence, there is a clear 'logic' of training implicit in the scheme as a whole. This has been well summarized by IRS:

> The NVQ approach offers a way of solving the conundrum that whilst training should not be an end in itself, it is often difficult to gain any precise understanding about what the 'end' is, or – more immediately – to evaluate whether the training itself has any effect. As NVQs are expressed in terms of performance required, then it becomes less difficult to link training with business need, and measure whether it has fulfilled its purpose. Assessment under NVQs largely involves on-the-job performance. It can show whether individuals meet the standard required and, if not, in what areas they have a training need. Training can then be driven by a full understanding of gaps in employees' skills. And the final assessment will show whether they have since attained them, thereby showing that training has succeeded.
>
> (IRS 1992a: 15)

In this respect, it is argued, NVQs can form a bridge between the individual training and performance of the employee and the whole organization's efforts such that individual profiles can be aggregated into an overall skills audit, a training audit, and a 'manpower plan'.

This approach, however, has been challenged on the grounds that it is both static and misguided in assuming that increasing individual competencies necessarily leads to enhanced organizational performance. In practice, it has been suggested, the competency approach leads not to a generalized 'ability' in relation to a whole job, but to discrete areas of activity *within* a job. Thus, as Holmes (1990) has pointed out, individuals 'have competencies' rather than become 'competent', such that, at root, the approach appears similar to Taylorian scientific management, i.e., extrinsic, mechanistic and alienating. Holmes's objection to this rationale is that it does not correspond to the real world and takes too little account of the complex and contingent factors which shape both the individual acquisition of skills and their transfer into organizational benefits. Missing, for example, is the consideration of corporate culture, environmental climate, organizational structure, managerial styles, career patterns, and individual learning abilities, etc. (These factors were precisely those identified by the *Training in Britain* study (TA 1989b) as being of considerable importance in shaping the organizational effectiveness of training strategy.)

Within the NVQ approach, therefore, there is a paradox. On the one hand, it seems to limit individual development by emphasizing a fragmented view of job skills and encouraging a narrow behavioural view of training which pays attention only to the physical attributes of a job, with little concern for psychological meaning. On the other hand, the 'progressive' structure of the NVQ scheme and its organization into five hierarchical levels can provide an accessible bridge between 'shop-floor', 'white-collar' and 'managerial' work, offering a framework for development which always points to a further step up the skills hierarchy (whether employers will be able or prepared to facilitate such progression for all who want it is, of course, another matter). In this respect the 'dual nature' of NVQs may mean that the scheme can be used either to facilitate or undermine individual development for trainees, depending upon the 'inner context' of the organization.

Another government training initiative, however, appears to address these particular concerns. The 'Investors in People' (IIP) scheme has been designed by the Employment Department but is administered and assessed through local Training and Enterprise Councils (TECS). This scheme focuses explicitly on the need to link training, development and business strategy. To achieve this strategic focus IIP provides a planning framework to allow organizations to develop systematically their own training provision to a standard that is nationally recognized. In this respect the emphasis is on encouraging organizations to assess the process, relevance and adequacy of training requirements in the light of their own business strategies, rather than upon detailed prescriptions of what any particular training course should involve, how it should be organized or to whom it should be delivered and although it may be appropriate for employers to link their training to the NVQ system, this is not mandatory.

In this respect the IIP 'national standard' involves a set of general principles, thus:

- '*An Investor in People makes a public commitment from the top to develop all employees to achieve its business objectives.*' (This involves providing a written but flexible plan of business goals and how employees will contribute to achieving these. The essence of this plan and the role of employees within it should also be communicated to all staff.)
- '*An Investor in People regularly reviews the training and development needs of all employees.*' (Here it is necessary to identify the resources that will be allocated to training, and the managerial responsibility for determining and providing training opportunities.)
- '*An Investor in People takes action to train and develop individuals on recruitment and throughout their employment.*' (This requires the ability to determine training needs on a regular and ongoing basis and to act upon these.)

- *'An Investor in People evaluates the investment in training and development to assess achievement and improve effectiveness.'* (Evaluation returns the training process to the initial objective: its continuing relevance to the business objectives of the organization.)

(Based on Employment Department 1991)

The process of becoming a recognized IIP involves careful planning and assessment of evidence of achievement. Thus, an organization will first have to audit its current training provision (with the assistance of survey instruments available through the scheme) and take appropriate action to meet the standards where necessary. When this is done, it can apply to its local TEC for recognition, at which point it will need to provide evidence of its achievements for assessment and be visited by an assessor nominated by the TEC. Following a report and recommendations, a TEC committee will make a decision on recognition.

It is clear that the intention of this scheme is to address a range of training issues in a manner highly compatible with HRM thinking. Thus:

- It challenges the binary division between 'training' and 'development' and attempts to establish the principle that all human resources have a potential worthy of development.
- It seeks to locate training as a strategic resource that has a direct relevance to all managers, not just those in the personnel section. This wider acceptance may be especially important if, as all too often happens, the tendency to cut a 'marginal' training budget when times are hard is to be avoided.
- It recognizes the fact that if training provision is to be accepted as a key strategic resource, then its contribution to organizational success must be capable of evaluation. Again, the overwhelming body of research suggests that proper training evaluation and monitoring is a rarity in most organizations (see below).
- It tackles the question of training needs systematically. It is all too easy to provide training for reasons which have no real relevance to organizational objectives. To be genuinely credible the relevance of training must be continuously established.

However, IIP has not been without its critics. A CBI survey claimed that some of the assessment costs were too high and the procedures overly bureaucratic (Hilton 1992:11). Such criticism is perhaps not surprising, given the lack of serious attention which many organizations give to the thorough thinking-through of their human resource management strategy at organizational level; the challenge for the TECs will be to convince potentially sceptical employers that the not inconsiderable level of commitment which IIP involves will be worthwhile.

DEVELOPMENT

The kind of scepticism referred to above has indeed confronted one of the key extensions of the NVQ scheme into the field of management development – the

Management Charter Initiative (MCI). The MCI was launched in response to a series of reports on the state of management education in the UK in the mid-1980s which painted an unequivocally damning picture when compared to competitor nations (Coopers and Lybrand 1985; Handy 1987; Constable and McCormick 1987).

In practical terms the intention of MCI is to build on the NVQ framework to develop four levels of management qualification – for supervisors, first-line managers, middle managers and senior managers – at supervisory, certificate, diploma and masters standard respectively. Like NVQs generally, however, the MCI approach has been challenged in relation to the practicality of devising a set of standard competencies that adequately capture the full complexity of managerial work across different types of organization and different industries. Indeed, this concern, together with a fear that the MCI scheme is overly bureaucratic, has led some companies to develop their own more flexible approaches (e.g., Brooke Bond's 'capabilities' model which combines 'skills and knowledge' with the even less tangible aspects of 'qualities and attitudes' (IRS 1991f:6)).

Such 'customized' approaches are, in fact, typical of the management development field and it remains to be seen to what extent attempts at standardization such as MCI can succeed (by voluntary means) in such a diverse and fragmented area. An indication of the task faced by MCI can be gained by examining some of the currently popular management development techniques. It is possible to divide various approaches to management development into two broad (and frequently overlapping) categories based on their key focus: those which centre on the development of the individual's personal career, and those which centre on the development of the employee within a social group.

1   Individual development focus

• Mentoring
• Continuous/self-development.

2   Social group focus

• Action learning
• Ourdoor training.

Mentoring

Rooted theoretically in behaviour modelling and vicarious learning, mentoring assumes that individuals learn and develop skills by observing, copying and adapting the behaviour of significant others (in particular those for whom they have respect). In an organizational context the mentor is usually a senior manager who is not in a line relationship to the 'protégé' and who may come from a different department/functional specialism; conventionally protégés are individuals who have been identified as 'high flyers' and potential senior managers. Thus:

Mentors' functional and managerial expertise enables them to provide on-the-job support and help with developmental projects and assignments. Using their superior knowledge of the organization, mentors can act as confidential sounding boards and confidants for protégés, helping them to understand the culture and politics of the organization, and to think about and develop their career. Their seniority and influence mean that they can be useful managerial allies, helping to secure attractive assignments, developmental job moves, visibility in other parts of the organization, and promotion for their protégés. A mentor can also open doors in other areas of the company; build confidence; encourage the protégé to develop other informal networks; provide informal assignments; help to involve protégés in the identification of their own training and development needs; and help the protégé to embark on a self-study programme or to attain professional qualifications.

(IRS 1990c:16)

Although mentoring systems are often instigated as a form of career development, Collin (1992) has suggested that they also serve an implicit function in relation to organizational culture, acting as a means through which core organizational values and meanings are transmitted and reinforced by being passed from senior managers nearing the end of their careers to those who will replace them.

On the down-side, however, mentoring can also lead to numerous problems. These include charges of elitism from those refused protégé status, reluctance and suspicion from line managers (as the mentoring partnership will often disrupt established reporting relationships), personal incompatibility between mentors and protégés, problems arising from cross-gender mentoring, over-dependence of protégés on mentors, and an inability of mentors to manage the relationship effectively.

Despite these problems, interest in mentoring seems to be increasing, although there is a case for approaching the technique with caution. In particular it is important to be clear that potential 'process problems' of the sort mentioned above have been addressed and that the advantages of mentoring have been evaluated relative not only to its potential difficulties but also in relation to other methods of development.

Self-development and continuous development

The philosophy of self-development is based on the twin assumptions that learning plays a crucial role in management activity, and that the process of learning can be controlled and directed by the individual. On the first point, it is suggested that managers, to be effective within any context other than the most rule-bound bureaucracy, must be capable of 'learning from experience' because only in this way can they respond quickly and innovatively to changing situations. Such learning, however, is neither natural nor easy and involves more than trial and error and avoidance of past mistakes, hence the need for a theory of learning.

Most approaches to the self-development of managers are influenced by the work of Kolb (e.g., Kolb 1984). A not untypical account of the so-called 'learning cycle' is provided by Honey (1986). This can be illustrated as in Figure 4.1.

Thus, self-development involves managers in diagnosing the situations in which they are involved, evaluating the options available, and planning a course of action to pursue the chosen goals. Through this conscious and reflective process, managers are more likely to make decisions that will enhance their job performance and, simultaneously, their personal levels of confidence: 'any effective system for management development must increase the managers' capacity and willingness to take control over and responsibility for events, and particularly for themselves and their own learning' (Pedler, Burgoyne and Boydell 1986:3). Methods of operationalizing self-development are various, ranging from individual programmes (available 'off the shelf' from bookshops, or customized for particular organizations) to group initiatives organized on a formal or an informal basis. In some instances, organizations and self-development consultants can co-operate to design in-house programmes which seek to link individual development and career plans closely with short- and long-term business planning. Here there may be a narrowing of the focus of self-development, away from the holistic notion of 'self' as object of development and towards a position where those aspects of self to be developed are contingent upon organizational requirements.

A variant of this approach has been promoted by the Institute of Personnel Management (IPM) in the UK through its 'ABCD' (A Boost for Continuous Development) initiative which focuses explicitly on the link between individual

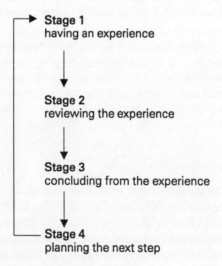

Stage 1
having an experience

Stage 2
reviewing the experience

Stage 3
concluding from the experience

Stage 4
planning the next step

Figure 4.1   A Kolb-type learning cycle

development and job demands. Continuous development (CD), according to Wood, Barrington and Johnson (1990:7), means: 'learning from real experiences at work; learning throughout working life, compared with useful but occasional injections of "training"'. There are, they suggest, five key facets of this approach:

1 **The integration of learning with work** All employees regularly need to learn 'something new', either in terms of task performance, organization, or interpersonal relations. CD enables employees to appreciate these needs and gives them the motivation to take responsibility for initiating relevant learning.

2 **Self-directed learning** The job-holder is uniquely placed to understand his or her learning needs, although support and training are likely to be necessary in helping employees to identify these needs and planning ways of fulfilling them.

3 **Process rather than technique** Following from the last point, CD is a function of the learner's commitment to the process rather than to specific techniques.

4 **CD as an attitude** CD is an approach to learning which encapsulates the following rationale: 'Let me think about what I'm doing. Can I do it better, quicker? What's changed since yesterday? Can I learn from that? Who can help me?' This involves making learning a habit and viewing problems as opportunities for learning.

5 **Simultaneous improvement in the performance of employees and organizations** The 'CD process helps individuals to develop, and thus helps the organization to achieve its objectives, through the intimate association of improved learning and improved performance'.

While CD has an undeniable intuitive appeal, it is not without its own difficulties. First, there is a presupposition of unitarism and commitment, whereby employees are assumed automatically to be willing to tie their personal development to that of their employing organization. In many respects this oversimplifies the difficulties involved in creating and sustaining a 'learning culture' and underestimates the constraints which face both learners and organizations undertaking such a course.

Second, the asserted link between individual learning and organizational performance is difficult to verify empirically. This is especially the case with self-development, where improvements may take considerable time and may be of a nebulous and indirect nature (this doubt is similar to the point about the aggregate benefit of competencies made by Holmes 1990 above).

Finally, where self-development is tightly coupled to job demands, the result can be a narrow utilitarian conception of learning and knowledge, perhaps ignoring issues such as ethical and environmental concerns. This is more likely to be the case where self-development follows a strongly individual pattern and where, for example, the learner does not have compatriots with whom to discuss progress or 'bounce' ideas. This point is made by Stuart in his discussion of Kolb:

The picture that emerges from Kolb's work is largely one of the manager making solo journeys around his learning cycle – experiencing, observing and reflecting, conceptualising, hypothesising and experimenting alone. However, the day-to-day activity of most managers is not a solo but a social one, being based in relationships with others in their work situation. Kolb's work does comparatively little to illuminate such relationships, not to inform the learning which arises directly from and through others.

(Stuart 1986:127)

Action learning

This recognition of the social dimension of management learning finds one realization in the action learning approach. This shares many of the assumptions of self-development in terms of learning from experience and locating this within a work context, but sees the process of learning as one which can progress most effectively through questioning and exploration of a sort which can only take place within a social group. The process is described by Lawrence:

The small basic [learning] structure is a 'set' – a group of five or six people who work to test and question each other until each is much clearer about what he [sic] wants to do and why. Each member knows that after he has taken his first step it will all be re-examined with him in order to learn from the particular event and to plan, with him, the next step – and the work of the set will proceed in this way until the set disbands.... The support of the other members of the set minimises the possibility of serious failure, and tests plans for 'trials' so thoroughly that even minor failure is unlikely. The support comes mainly from the set not from the 'teacher'.

(Lawrence 1986:221)

The essence of action learning, then, is a focus on real problems that enable learners to question the conditions which have led to these problems and to generate solutions which can be translated into action. The whole process is underpinned by a process of social dialogue which provides both for mutual criticism and mutual support. Thus, from the inception of the 'set' through to the operationalization and monitoring of solutions, the process is inherently active: learners must not only understand, but also be committed to their choices of action. As a result it has been argued that action learning is not appropriate to all aspects of management development. It is not, for instance, necessarily the most effective way of increasing technical competence nor of gaining new knowledge *about* management. It is, according to Lawrence (1986:227), 'useful only if the need is for more effective managerial *action*'. Even in this respect, however, action learning is by no means an easy or comfortable approach for organizations to come to terms with. It invariably involves criticism of and challenge to established orders and traditions; in short, a disruption of internal politics. Many organizations may be disinclined to stir up such potential 'hornets' nests'; others may embark upon action learning programmes and become disenchanted. On the other hand, there is good evidence to suggest that when there is commitment to this approach it can produce extremely useful results (Lawrence 1986; Revans 1980; Pedler 1983; Casey and Pearce 1977).

Development in the outdoors

Usually this form of training involves participants tackling a problem or conducting an exercise in an outdoor environment. Although these problems usually involve a physical dimension, most are not dependent to any significant degree upon high levels of physical fitness or athletic prowess; as with self-development, the underlying learning principles are frequently based on Kolb's learning cycle, with the emphasis on initiative, co-operation, and problem-solving skills. Often the outdoor component of the course is supplemented by theory sessions, and the analysis and evaluation of group and individual performance. The growth in the use of outdoor training in recent years is usually associated with the development of team-building and leadership skills. Although still at a relatively low level compared to more conventional forms of development, Lowe (1991) suggests that the provision of such programmes may be doubling every five years. An example of an exercise from one scheme is recounted by Lowe:

> [The] exercise... that combined 'ownership' of learning, high 'memorability' of the event and a 'personalised' learning experience was the so-called 'slippery slope'. This involved the whole group climbing a sheer rock face. Most of the exercise is carried out in the complete darkness of a mineshaft, the only light provided by a candle with three minutes of wick. The only solution is the formation of a human pyramid which everyone in the group has to build and climb systematically in order to reach the top of the shaft... great psychological closeness [was] generated by this event....it was striking how in the course of the subsequent interviews the sample continually referred back to this event, which reinforced the idea that they had gone through a highly distinctive shared experience.
>
> (Lowe 1991:49)

Accounts of the programmes adopted by two large organizations, Marks and Spencer and Exxon, are provided by IRS (1991b), from which are distilled the following key points for success:

- any course must fit in as part of an overall training programme;
- the programme should have very clear objectives;
- rigorous checks on providers' safety must be made;
- providers have to be familiar with the client organization;
- the programme has to be targeted to individual company needs and objectives;
- the course itself must have a high tutor-to-participant ratio;
- the programme and the tutors should relate each activity back to the workplace;

- the emphasis should be on reviewing the process, not the outdoor activity, from day one;
- the tutors must be capable of conducting ongoing reviews, both structured and unstructured;
- the course itself must be monitored by post-course follow-up sessions with managers in the workplace.

(IRS 1991b:9)

While Marks and Spencer and Exxon are claimed to be highly satisfied with their outdoor programmes, Lowe (1991) suggests that many organizations can find this type of exercise less than a complete success. First, problems can be caused by the non-attendance of senior managers, such that participants find themselves returning to a working environment in which their managers are unprepared to allow or share in experimentation and change inspired by the course. Second, there are difficulties in assessing the value of any changes such courses may produce against their not inconsiderable cost, especially since any 'direct' measurable effects are unlikely to be realized in the short-term. Third, there is always the possibility that the team spirit created by outdoor development may not automatically be channelled towards organizational objectives, but rather against them: group members may use their newly acquired unity to 'conspire against the bosses' more effectively. Fourth, where senior managers do take part, group dynamics may be disrupted by a tendency for the senior staff to impose their 'workplace authority' and for juniors to defer to this; alternatively, senior managers may feel unduly pressured by a fear of losing face or being seen to fail. Finally, there is the question of whether sufficient time can be devoted to feedback sessions in the work context. As Lowe reports, a lack of such time can mean that participants are not able clearly to identify the objectives of the course or to relate what they have learnt back to the workplace. Thus, 'when some of [Lowe's] sample were asked what use the outdoor training was back in the workplace, the typical response was, "We don't get much cause for abseiling in here"' (Lowe 1991:57).

EVALUATING TRAINING AND DEVELOPMENT

An issue which underlies all perspectives on management development and training is that of evaluation. This assumes greater importance within an HRM context as a means of demonstrating the link between training and other business objectives. Interest in training evaluation, of course, is not new and variants of cost-benefit analysis have been available for decades. Many of these, however, have been complex and cumbersome to administer and, for reasons similar to those discussed in Chapter 2, have usually fallen into disuse. Training evaluation, however, has not been abandoned; as with human resourcing, the impetus of HRM frameworks has provoked a rethinking of the methods and approaches used.

Of the more conventional approaches, the CBI's *Evaluating Your Training* provides a typical example. The underlying assumption is that training objectives must flow from a company's business objectives and that there are two key questions which lie at the centre of training evaluation: 'Is training achieving what it set out to do?'; and, 'Are there ways in which it could be done more effectively?'. To answer these questions it is necessary to examine four interlinked areas:

1 outlining strategic company objectives;
2 identification of major organizational activities;
3 setting standards for individual tasks;
4 setting training objectives.

This involves the application of a simple audit approach to each level, the techniques suggested including action planning, critical incident analysis, written and practical testing, and behavioural observation. These methods are intended to give a credible mix of quantitative and qualitative data to provide measures of return on training across a range of variables such as:

- **Manpower** Absenteeism, disputes, turnover, promotions, timekeeping.
- **Operations** Accidents, customer relations, decisions, downtime, errors, quality, productivity, etc.
- **Finance** Investment return, operating costs, profits, sales revenue, unit costs.

Although this method marks an improvement on traditional techniques, such as hierarchical task analysis which concentrates almost exclusively on a single job in relative isolation, it remains relatively abstract and formal, easier to plan than to implement.

A more 'active' approach has been adopted by Easterby-Smith and associates (Easterby-Smith and Tanton 1985; Easterby-Smith 1986; Easterby-Smith and Mackness 1992) by recognizing the role which organizational stakeholders and their differential interests may play in the evaluation process. This involves recognizing four main 'purposes' within evaluation:

1 **Proving** The attempt to show beyond reasonable doubt that a given training course has particular outcomes or consequences.
2 **Improving** Using the evaluation to remove problems and strengthen the quality of courses and development activities.
3 **Learning** Using the evaluation process to help people sharpen up on what they have got from a course.
4 **Controlling** the implementation of training initiatives.

On the basis of a study of the evaluation of a major computer training initiative at the Department of Health and Social Security, Easterby-Smith and Mackness (1992:44) use these categories to identify major stakeholders, their interests and the dominant purpose the evaluation process serves for them. Thus, the sponsors (the senior managers responsible for the overall success of the computerization project) had an interest in meeting project deadlines and comparing favourably with other units. Hence, their purpose was proving that the training was enabling effective implementation. The interests of the trainers (those who were delivering the programme), on the other hand, were to identify and correct weak areas of the course and, as such, the dominant purpose of the evaluation was improving the quality of the training and their own performance. Finally, for the trainees (the managers using the system) theirs was an interest in learning what was needed, the evaluation purpose being that of learning what is required to implement the strategy effectively. Such recognition of the potential 'political' dimension of evaluation hammers home the important message that the ultimate success of an evaluation exercise depends upon the ability to clarify purposes; in particular, what is the purpose of evaluation and whose purposes are being served.

To accept this point should lead to the basics of any evaluation exercise being scrutinized very carefully. McEvoy and Butler (1990), for example, suggest that all too often the purpose of training evaluation is not sufficiently thought through. Their argument is that before an organization embarks upon a training assessment exercise, it should carefully determine exactly what objectives it is trying to achieve through its training policy. Although this may seem a rather obvious statement, they point to the fact that there are, in practice, a variety of possible training objectives and that, very often, these may not be explicitly articulated or even realized by managers. As an aid to this assessment process, they suggest four sets of dualisms representing different training objectives:

1 **Substantive vs. symbolic**   Is training intended to meet an objective skills gap or does it constitute a cultural symbol? For example, training can signifying the organization's commitment to developing its employee and contribute to its public image as a 'good' employer.
2 **External vs. internal**   Is the training intended to address external behaviour (e.g., physical motor skills, or mastery of a standard practice) or is it focused on internal psychological processes such as attitudes and values?
3 **Change vs. results**   Is the product of the training to be measured in terms of behaviour/attitude change (which may or may not lead to concrete measurable outputs), or will it relate only to observable results?
4 **Work vs. perk**   Is the training given to those who need it to improve their performance in a given area, or is it given as a reward to those who have already demonstrated good performance?

To properly evaluate their training needs organizations need to understand where they see themselves in terms of these four dimensions because evaluation techniques and methods will differ radically depending on the nature of the objectives. For example, if management training such as 'outdoor activities' is regarded primarily as a 'perk', or if access to training has a largely symbolic function within the organization, then attempting to evaluate such training solely in financial cost-benefit terms will be a fruitless and costly exercise. Similarly, the use of complex behavioural observation procedures and attitude scales will be unnecessary (not to mention expensive) if the real concern is simply a change in employee output results.

KEY LEARNING POINTS

- **To understand the role of training and development within an HRM framework it is essential to think through exactly what these activities are supposed to achieve in relation to other organizational objectives and to plan and assess them accordingly.**
- **In particular, this will involve thinking in terms of a more flexible definition of development, one which transcends the traditional distinction between training for operatives and development for managers.**
- **A wider conception of development must involve an awareness of how**

Table 4.1 Evaluation table

Examples of priorities for evaluation	*Data sources*	*Methodology*	*Concepts*	*Timescale*
1 Awareness of corporate training strategy at line manager level	line managers all divisions	telephone survey	awareness measures	within four weeks of activating strategy
2 Evidence of behaviour change as a result of management training course	trainees and their line managers	self-administered rating scale	BAR dimensions and items	one week /six months after course completion
3 Effect of equal opportunities sensitivity training on representation of target groups at senior level	personnel records	statistical analysis	category measures	to follow each promotion round
4 Cost-benefit analysis for organization of customer care training programme for front-office staff	cost data, benefit data	secondary analysis, performance observation	cost and benefit measures (e.g. customer satisfaction surveys, increased bookings, repeat bookings, staff turnover)	to cover one-year period after course

Note: BAR = behaviourally anchored rating scale

individual potential and growth is realized by making experience meaningful. This is premised upon understanding and upon action, but action which
is not restricted to a mechanistic and unreflected set of behaviours. Rather,
'development denotes those processes which engender enhancement of
capabilities whilst leaving scope for discretion, creativity and indetermi-
nacy' (Storey 1989:5).

- The key challenge in this area for HRM is to marry training and development in such a way as to benefit *all* organization members while
simultaneously serving the performance needs of the organization itself.

EXERCISE

One way of approaching training needs analysis is through the use of an evaluation
table. These tables demand that the purpose of the evaluation is first determined
and then the methodology for achieving this purpose is considered. This will
involve not only the choice of appropriate research methods (e.g., questionnaires,
interviews, etc.) but in many cases the development of appropriate concepts. These
may be available 'off the shelf' (e.g. attitude scales culled from psychological
textbooks; questionnaires borrowed from research reports) or they may have to be
developed specifically for the organization in question. Some examples are shown
in the table.

Chapter 5

Reward

Motivation and control

THE NATURE OF REWARD

A central and recurrent debate about the role of reward policy within HRM centres upon the extent to which reward should be treated as an individual or collective phenomenon. There has been a strong rhetorical commitment to the view that reward should directly reflect an individual's contribution to the organization, a commitment which has resulted in considerable interest in performance-related pay (PRP) and other forms of individually oriented benefit packages and reward policies. As Smith (1992) has pointed out, however, to conceive of reward merely as 'payment for performance' is an unnecessary (and uniquely British) limitation:

> American organizations, and indeed the American literature, have moved the debate about reward to the level of 'reward systems' integrated with human resource management. The emphasis here is not on some crude link between pay and performance outputs but rather on a much wider set of motivational issues including attraction, retention, expectancy, skill development, culture, and the reinforcement of organization structure.... In America rewards have been linked to business strategy and to other related features of the organization, with the ultimate goal being: 'an integrated human resource management strategy that is consistent in the way that it encourages people to behave, attracts the kind of people that can support the business strategy'.
>
> (Smith 1992: 172–3)

While one might question the rather sweeping generality of this view, it does indicate the issues that are at stake in this area and points towards the need for a broader and more complex understanding of the reward process. One way to move in this direction is to deal with reward dynamics in terms of two interrelated levels:

1 Individual meaning and behaviour.
2 The systemic character and function of particular policies.

Meaning and behaviour

The most basic form of reward for employment is pay. But even here, the question of meaning is far from simple. Thierry (1992), for instance, suggests that pay is meaningful to the employee precisely because it conveys information about important aspects of employment other than pay.

In this respect pay can 'send messages' to an employee, not only about access to material welfare, but also about the level of recognition for work contributions made, about behaviour which is valued by the employer, and about the organization's attitude to individual performance and achievement.

However, Thierry also points out that these meanings are neither universal nor static, but may be affected by individual background, life-style and personality, by job level, and by situational conditions. There are, thus, four 'domains' to which pay can refer:

1 **Salient motives** Pay is meaningful because the employee expects that it will allow him or her to satisfy important motives and to reach relevant goals. Because of this instrumental nature, pay may stand, for example, for avoidance of insecurity, for feelings of competence or for opportunities for self-realization. This domain relates to... the motivational properties of pay.
2 **Relative position** First, pay provides feedback on how the employee's task performance is progressing (or has progressed) with respect to the goals or targets set. In giving information about the effectiveness of the contributions made to his/her work (such as care for quality; setting adequate priorities) as well as about the impact of external events (e.g., machine breakdown; loss of a customer), pay may call for the redirection of the employee's efforts during (or after) task performance. Second, pay provides feedback about the employee's effectiveness in comparison with others, such as co-workers, other employees up or down the hierarchy, or professional colleagues.
3 **Control Pay** is meaningful because it signifies to the employee the extent to which she or he has been successful in influencing others, such as the supervisor, workmates, people in other departments, or customers, during task performance, in order to reach his/her goals. Also, characteristics of the particular payment systems in use reflect the degree of control exerted by and upon the employee. This relates to the employee's impact upon the total amount of pay, the variation in pay from time to time, the composition of the pay package, the principles upon which payment systems are based, etc.
4 **Spending Pay** is meaningful because it reflects the products and services that the employee can afford to purchase. In this, it also mirrors the ease with which this is done. Consequently pay is perceived in terms of individual welfare.

(Thierry 1992: 146–7)

Thierry's proposition is that the extent to which an employee's behaviour at work will be affected incisively by pay will reflect the extent to which the reward system provides meaning in terms of the four domains outlined above. For example, for a young person working in a part-time job, the meaning of pay may be only in terms of 'spending', whereas for someone with pressing domestic responsibilities, the salient motive to provide security may overshadow all other meanings. In a more complex example, a sales person early in his/her career may find that an individual performance-related pay (PRP) scheme is meaningful in all four domains: it affords a level of income sufficient for security; it indicates relative success in the job; it provides an opportunity to exercise control over the 'effort bargain'; and it gives spending power commensurate with status expectations. However, at a later stage in his or her career, the same person may find that these meanings have changed. Once domestic stability is secured the salient motive may be less clear. Similarly, with increased experience in the job, the level of income may be a less meaningful indicator of relative position than promotion to managerial grade. Also the attraction of control over one's own effort may have levelled out, whereas promotion depends on exercising control over others, a task which may not be rewarded by the PRP scheme. Spending power is likely to remain important, but less so over time. In these respects, therefore, the meanings which a PRP scheme creates may be experienced as increasingly 'inappropriate' as an individual develops in his or her job.

It is, of course, no easy matter to establish a consistent match between these potentially unstable domains of individual meaning and a payment system in a manner which is wholly consistent with organizational objectives although, as will be seen below, developments in the area of 'flexible benefits' have attempted to address this question directly. More often, however, the design of payment systems can evoke behaviours which, although meaningful to the recipient, are quite different from those expected or desired by those designing or implementing the system.

This type of 'mismatch' has been described by Kerr (1991:485) who suggests that many reward systems are 'fouled up in that the behaviours which are rewarded are those which the rewarder is trying to *discourage*, while the behaviour he [sic] desires is not being rewarded at all'. He gives the following examples:

- **US universities** Society *hopes* that teachers will not neglect their teaching responsibilities but *rewards* them almost entirely for research and publications.... Rewards for good teaching usually are limited to outstanding teacher awards, which are given only to a small percentage of good teachers and which usually bestow little money and fleeting prestige. Punishments for poor teaching also are rare. Rewards for research and publications, on the other hand, and punishments for failure to accomplish these, are commonly administered at universities at which teachers are employed.... Consequently it is rational for university teachers to concentrate on research, even if to the detriment of teaching and at the expense of their students.
- **Business ethics** Assume that the president of XYZ Corporation is confronted with the following alternatives: 1. Spend $11 million for antipollution equipment to keep from poisoning fish in the river adjacent to the plant; or 2. Do

nothing, in violation of the law, and assume a one in ten chance of being caught, with a resultant $1 million fine plus the necessity of buying the equipment. Under this not unrealistic set of choices it requires no linear programme to determine that XYZ Corporation can maximize its probabilities by flouting the law. Add the fact that XYZ's president is probably being rewarded (by creditors, stockholders, and other salient parts of his task environment) according to criteria totally unrelated to the number of fish poisoned, and his probable course of action becomes clear.

(Kerr 1991:488–9)

In both cases the behaviour of those being rewarded is meaningful in relation to the practice of the reward system, but these meanings are not those which the organization would necessarily want or intend.

A related point is made by Pearce (1991) in relation to individual merit pay which, she suggests, can work against desirable behaviour such as team-building and co-operation by rewarding, instead, self-centred individualism. In particular, she attacks the assumption that overall organizational performance is the simple additive combination of individual employees' separate contributions (often the justification for individual merit pay) and suggests that where uncertainty, interdependence and complexity are characteristic of organizational work, successful performance depends more on co-operation among employees. Individual merit pay, however, can provide powerful disincentives for such co-operation, not because money is not a powerful motivator but, on the contrary, because it so effectively individualizes motivation at the expense of co-operative action that may be more functional for the organization:

Paying people on the basis of their recent measured individual performance simply does not build on the relative advantages of the organizational form. Most kinds of organizations succeed because of cooperation among their members, not because of members' discrete, independent performances. Such cooperation is particularly critical among employees with either valuable expertise... or the discretion to commit the organization's resources.... It is simply not in the organization's interest to encourage short-term single transaction expectations among such important employees.

(Pearce 1991:505).

This is an issue that will be returned to in the discussion of performance-related pay below.

System and function

The foregoing discussion should be seen, not as suggesting the absolute unworkability of policies such as individual merit pay but, rather, the need for clarity about (1) the ways in which meaning and behaviour are related to the systemic character of a reward policy, and (2) how this can be used functionally to support wider organizational objectives.

The systemic character of a reward policy can be clarified by reference to the following typology based on Steers and Porter (1991), set out in Figure 5.1. This uses two axes: one representing the distinction between intrinsic and extrinsic rewards (respectively, psychological rewards which arise from an individual's own sense of 'fit' or satisfaction with a particular work role, and tangible benefits, e.g., money, provided by an organization in return for the performance of a particular work role) and the other that between individual and system-wide (or collectively offered) rewards.

When considering this model it is useful to think of the quadrants not as mutually exclusive categories but as aspects of a particular reward policy that may be present

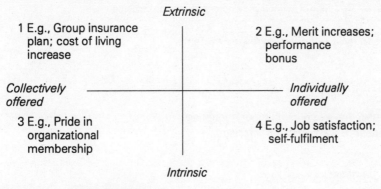

Figure 5.1   Types of reward
(*Source*: Based on Steers and Porter 1991)

(in combination) to a greater or lesser extent. In this way the model allows the scope of a given reward policy to be mapped out clearly and simply. For example, a system of performance-related pay based principally upon individual merit increases is likely to fall mainly in quadrant 2, with some coverage of quadrant 4 but little of 1 or 3 (see Figure 5.2). On the other hand, an approach linked to the harmonization of conditions and single status is likely to have a large coverage of quadrants 1, 3, and 4 and perhaps less of quadrant 2 (see Figure 5.2).

In terms of the design of reward policies, therefore, it is possible to determine what motivational effect is required and then to evaluate the potential of different policy initiatives in terms of their relative abilities to 'hit' the motivational targets identified.

However, in addition to analysing the motivational impact of a given policy, it is also necessary to relate this to the function which it is intended to serve within the organization. Such functions have generally been grouped under two headings:

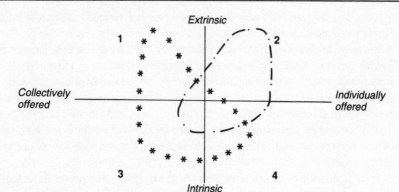

—·—   Coverage of individual PRP scheme
＊ ＊ ＊   Coverage of harmonized single-status reward scheme

Figure 5.2   Maps of different reward systems

1.   Participation

- Membership – either joining or remaining
- Attendance – avoiding absenteeism.

2.   Performance

- Normal job performance
- Extra-role performance (e.g., innovation, high commitment).

The point to be made is that managers need not only to be clear about what they want to achieve through a payment system but also to understand what sort of system is most likely to achieve that result, given that, as the foregoing discussion has shown, different pay policies have highly variable coverage and create different messages and meanings about expected or desired behaviour.

To be functionally effective, therefore, some amount of 'alignment' or matching is required between the objectives, scope and meaning of the policy. Ultimately this must be an empirical question that requires careful analytical consideration within the context of particular organizational situations.

REWARD SYSTEMS AND HRM

Certainly during the 1980s there was a greater willingness to experiment with different forms of reward policy, and there does seem to have been a more self-conscious attempt by many managements to use reward policy to achieve determinate organizational objectives, at least in terms of the broad categories of recruitment, retention and performance. Lockyer (1992), for example, points to a tendency for the 'logic of HRM' to encourage a shift away from 'fixed' or 'bargained' payment systems and towards 'variable' reward policies in order to emphasize the contribution which employees, individually and collectively, make to organizational performance.

It will be useful, therefore, to examine some of those policies which have attracted most attention within the HRM context. In the consideration of these different approaches the complexity of the underlying motivational processes should be kept in mind, especially the possibility of contradiction in terms of functional objectives and internal policy dynamics.

Job evaluation

Job evaluation is a well-established and basic principle of most payment systems. However, its exact form and purpose has varied over time. The underlying principle of job evaluation is the assumption that all jobs within an organization can be ranked hierarchically relative to one another, based on their value to the organiza-tion. This ranking is then tied to pay bands, the level of which can be determined by a combination of market conditions and collective bargaining. One common approach is the so-called 'point-rating' method, whereby several bench-mark jobs are selected and their 'contents' presented in a job description. Then these jobs are analysed in terms of key characteristics, such as required knowledge, responsi-bility, and social skills. Points are allocated (weighted according to their relative importance) to each characteristic, and the total job value is set by adding all the points together. The value of all other jobs is derived by comparing these with the nearest bench-mark job, and the salary rate allocated/negotiated accordingly (Thierry 1992: 150).

Such systems can and do lead to extremely complex grading schemes, which are capable of reflecting fine distinctions and giving the appearance of objectivity, rationality and equity. Nevertheless, despite this sophistication, job evaluation approaches increasingly have had both their validity and operational effectiveness called into question. Such questioning has been directed at the frequent arbitrari-ness of the initial choice and weighting of bench-mark jobs (an arbitrariness often masked by the ensuing statistical manipulations) and at the 'bureaucratizing' effect of elaborate schemes. Wickens (1987:112), for example, points to the rigidities of practice and attitude which such schemes can engender, such that 'the preservation of the system becomes more important than reacting rapidly to change – in short the tail begins to wag the dog'. Attempts to overcome this tendency towards bureaucratization (which sits uneasily with the encouragement of flexibility and adaptability found in most HRM thinking) have often led to a reconsideration of the very fundamental principles of job evaluation and, as a corollary, of other key dimensions of organization. Indeed, Wickens contends that, for job evaluation to be made sufficiently simple and clear to allow true flexibility, there must be a parallel commitment to the 'delayering' and flattening of organization structure. As an illustration he cites the case of Nissan UK:

> To maximise flexibility it is necessary to minimise the number of job titles and to make them as general as possible. It is helpful to reduce to the lowest possible level the number of layers between the top and the bottom of the hierarchy.... In Nissan all tasks are covered by 15 job titles... and within the production department, it takes but six steps to go from Managing Director to Manufacturing Staff... Nissan has no job descriptions and no numbered grades.
>
> (Wickens 1987:117)

Within this simplified structure, allowance can then be made for the adoption of performance appraisal and associated variable salary ranges or bands, a development which would otherwise cut across the boundaries a of highly categorized job evaluation system.

This move towards a simplified grading structure is usually a precondition for the adoption of a unified pay scheme whereby a majority if not all employees are covered by a single salary structure, thereby representing a further erosion of detailed job grade differentials and, in particular, of the status divide between manual, white-collar and in some cases managerial employees. Indeed, according to IDS (1988b), two of the main reasons for introducing integrated pay systems are flexibility and simplicity:

* **Flexibility** The major reasons cited by the [nine] organizations in our Study for introducing integrated pay was as part of moves towards greater flexibility.... Changing technology has often led to the blurring of demarcations between skilled, semi-skilled and craft workers and between manual and non-manual tasks. The introduction of the multiskilled craftsman and the rise of the 'operator technician' are examples of this development.
* **Simplicity** A single pay structure, which incorporates overtime, shift and bonus payments within an annual salary, can lead to much simpler administration. This can result from the [removal of the] plethora of payments created by 'productivity bargaining' in the past.... One of the aims, therefore, [is] a much simpler structure. Shell Chemicals was able to reduce three different agreements, in three separate volumes, down to a single four-page agreement.

(IDS 1988b: 1)

There is, however, some debate over the extent to which integrated pay systems should allow for differential reward based on performance. The Nissan case described by Wickens, for instance, makes use of salary bands, progression within which is determined by performance appraisal. Others have argued that the use of banding and performance-related pay detracts from objectives of integrated pay schemes and can erode group co-operation. Of those schemes that do not involve performance-related elements and salary bands, most make use of a 'spot' system whereby salary level is determined by fixed 'rates for the job'. Arguments advanced for this latter approach include the view that this is a 'cleaner' and simpler structure than banding (with the inevitable complexities of performance measurement and appraisal). Thus, although integrated systems using spot salaries may represent an advance upon mechanistic and bureaucratic job evaluation approaches, in terms of motivational potential they still face some challenges. According to Thierry (1992), for example, where wages or salaries are set strictly in line with job evaluation categories alone (as in the case of 'rate for the job' spot systems) the motivational effect upon employees can often appear paradoxical. On the one hand, the perceived fairness and security which such a system provides is often appreciated but, on the other, the very predictability of pay and the lack of scope to reward performance is often resented.

Performance-related pay

Although there are various systems which claim to reward employees according to their performance (e.g., piecework, bonus and tariff systems) most of the recent debate has concerned performance-related pay (sometimes known as 'merit pay'), the general principles of which are usually defined as the explicit link of financial reward to individual, group or company performance (or any combination of the three). This rather simple definition, however, begs a number of important questions regarding both the construction of a PRP system and its operation. According to Kessler and Purcell (1992), PRP schemes can be categorized according to three dimensions:

1   The nature of the performance criteria (usually either the inputs or outputs of the employee).
2   How performance against such criteria is assessed (which may vary according to how, when and by whom the assessment is made).
3   How this assessment is linked to pay (e.g., in terms of a percentage increase, a lump sum or incremental progression on a pay scale).

Using these dimensions it is possible to identify the two groups of PRP system which have received the most attention within HRM perspectives: individual schemes and group/company approaches. (Table 5.1).

Individual PRP

One aspect of the attractiveness of PRP has been its promise to fulfil a number of functions relevant to organizational effectiveness. Its supporters point to the following features in its favour. First, there is the prospect of financial gain to the organization if a system can be used to reduce the fixed paybill, i.e., by making as much as possible of the total benefit an individual receives contingent upon revenue-earning performance, as, for example, in the case of sales persons payed mainly on commission. (This, of course, is not without difficulty: it assumes that an individual's contribution can be measured and that the level of contingent reward

Table 5.1   Types of PRP scheme

	Nature of performance criteria	How performance is assessed	How performance is linked to pay
Individual PRP schemes	Individual results, either in terms of inputs or outputs	By individual appraisal with a superior, often against mutually agreed targets	Either by a predetermined bonus or by movement within an incremental salary band
Group/company profit or share schemes	Group or company performance, either in terms of profit or project targets	According to a pre-determined formula based on company results for a specified period	In terms of a regular bonus or various forms of share options applicable to all those involved in the scheme

available is sufficient to motivate performance. The real gains in this area may be made where PRP is tied to employment relationships based on subcontract, self-employment or consultancy contracts.)

Second, PRP is seen to be effective in terms of aiding recruitment and retention because of the assumption that it will be attractive to 'quality' employees (who can be rewarded in direct proportion to their effort) and, conversely, unattractive to 'poor' workers whom the organization is not sorry to lose. Such an argument, of course, is likely to carry more weight at a time of economic buoyancy than in times of recession.

Third, PRP can be claimed to be 'fairer' than across-the-board cost of living increases which reward high and low performers equally. Certainly, there is consistent evidence to support the view that most employees agree with the *principle* that people should be rewarded roughly in proportion to their contribution to the organization. The perennial problem, of course, is that of convincing people that such contributions can be defined and assessed to ensure fairness *in practice*.

Fourth, PRP is held to focus effort where the organization wants it, strengthening the performance planning process and generally encouraging a performance-oriented culture, emphasizing results rather than effort.

Kessler and Purcell (1992:21), however, approach the analysis of PRP with greater sophistication by suggesting that PRP can be seen as more than simply sending messages to individual employees about organizational values.

They argue that the very mechanics of these schemes involve a fundamental restructuring of the employment relationship which can result in greater managerial control over staff by isolating the individual

from the work group and forcing the personalized design and evaluation of work.

Thus, although performance criteria may be discussed and agreed with employees at the appraisal stage (see Chapter 3), assessment and final evaluation remain firmly in the hands of management.

This is not dissimilar to the view expressed by Pearce (1991) referred to earlier; indeed, the complaints voiced against individualized PRP usually concern its tendency to fragment team behaviour and the perception that the appraisal of performance is not conducted fairly (either because of the incompetence of the appraiser or the measurement deficiencies of the system). Perceived fairness is an especial problem where performance in a job cannot effectively be measured by 'output' and where inputs are measured instead (i.e., effort rather than results). Both difficulties are illustrated in an account of a PRP system applied to British Telecom managers:

> Based on a survey of members of the Society of Telecom Executives (membership 36,000, response rate 60 per cent) conducted in January 1991 the following results were obtained.
>
> Only six per cent thought that PRP had improved their performance; 70 per cent thought it had not. Although nearly 40 per cent felt that PRP rewarded individual effort, over 50 per cent thought that it was applied unfairly in practice. 60 per cent disagreed that bonuses were paid for the achievement of objective, measurable targets, and 70 per cent thought bonuses were arbitrary. Nearly 90 per cent thought bonuses did not encourage team work.
>
> One respondent commented: 'Our percentage PRP was paid as standard irrespective of an individual's performance. Furthermore we were not counselled on the figure at all. We only discovered what figure we had been paid after receiving the pay slip.' The survey even threw up a number of instances where one or two members of a team had been paid bonuses which they then shared out amongst the rest of the team.
>
> (IRS 1991e:2)

A summary of the critical success and failure factors associated with individualized PRP is represented below.

Success factors

- Individual differences in job performance are great enough to be worth the time and effort it takes management to measure and relate pay to them.
- The pay ranges are wide enough (35 per cent or greater) to allow for significant base-pay differences among employees on the same job.
- Management is able validly and reliably to measure individual differences in job performance.

- The appraisers are skilful in employee performance planning (setting and communicating expectations) and appraisal.
- The organization's culture supports performance-based pay.
- The level of compensation technology in the organization is reasonably high – the pay structures are equitable and competitive, and management knows how to relate pay to performance.
- The levels of trust between managers and those who work for them are high.
- The managers have the 'will to manage' – that is, the willingness to establish and communicate performance criteria and standards and the willingness to make tough human-resource decisions.

Failure factors

- The factors which encourage success can also result in a preoccupation with the task at hand and do not relate individual performance to the larger company objectives.
- PRP works against creating a climate of openness, trust, joint problem solving and commitment to organizational objectives.
- PRP can divide the workforce into those supporting the plan and those against it, which can create adversarial relationships.

(Applebaum and Shappiro 1991:32)

Group, profit and share schemes

An attempt to avoid the problem of divisiveness associated with individual PRP is to be found in team/group or company-based schemes. These are generally linked to some measure of organizational profitability (or budget targets) or share ownership and can range from full-blown profit-sharing to the payment of a regular bonus proportionate to profit targets (or in the case of some group schemes, project completion) related either to the work group or the whole company.

Both profit-sharing and share ownership schemes are claimed to have benefits to the organization in terms of enhanced performance and, especially, commitment. These advantages normally include:

- A closer identity of interest between the employee and the organization, either because the employee is a part-owner or has a direct benefit from higher profits.
- Following from this, a reduction in 'them and us' attitudes between workers and management.
- A greater awareness among employees of how individual performance can affect profitability, and a greater cost-awareness and more profit-consciousness in relation to wage claims.
- A flexible and tax-efficient way of rewarding loyalty and service and, concomitantly, a reduction in labour turnover.

• The possibility of cushioning the effect of an economic downturn by allowing the profit element of pay to be reduced, rather than making immediate lay-offs.

In many respects the resurgence of interest in profit sharing has been stimulated by government action, in particular the favourable tax treatment given to profit-sharing bonuses by Chancellors since 1978. In the latter part of the 1980s, particular attention was given to the notion of profit-related pay whereby the Inland Revenue specified recognized schemes that would be more tax-effective than unrecognized profit sharing. Generally, payments are made from a pool related to a specified proportion of profits, with possible tax savings of between £500 and £800 for participants.

In terms of performance, recent UK data from 470 companies (113 with profit sharing) shows that:

the companies with all-employee profit-sharing schemes outperform similar non-profit-sharing companies to a statistically significant extent. The before-and-after analysis provides some evidence of an improvement of performance, particularly in respect of growth of sales, soon after the introduction of the schemes. The results also indicate that the stock market appeared to recognize this improvement.

(Hanson and Watson 1990:180)

The authors of this survey, however, offer the caution that other factors may account for these results, especially 'a reflection of good corporate management and industrial relations', i.e., profit sharing may be introduced by better-managed and performing companies, rather than creating them.

This point is reinforced by Hammer's (1991) analysis of US 'gainsharing' schemes. These schemes, developed in the 1930s and associated especially with the American trade union leader Joseph Scanlon, and Allen Rucker, are characterized by a 'management philosophy of worker participation in decision-making and two structural characteristics: a bonus payment formula and a committee system established to facilitate worker participation and adopt productivity improvement suggestions' (1991:532). In the case of the Scanlon Plan the reward bonus is calculated according to a formula based on the ratio of labour costs to the sales value of production which is averaged over a given time period and then split (usually 25–75) between the company and all employees. In this respect gainsharing represents a form of profit-sharing, but what is important is that its exponents regard it as much more than a reward strategy. As Hammer (1991) makes clear, the gainshare itself is only one part of a complex motivational system that is intimately connected to notions of worker commitment and involvement.

The extension of employee shareholding is another area where change in the reward structure is intended to bring about a change in attitudes and performance. There are two main forms of share-based scheme in the UK: Approved Deferred Share Trusts (ADST) and Save As You Earn (SAYE). The former involves the establishment of a trust which holds shares on a firm's employees' behalf, whereas the latter uses a savings contract for five years which, with accumulated bonus, can be used to buy shares at a (discounted) option price established when the contract is entered. Financial benefits in both cases are tax free. Although having grown from a very small base, there were only 890 ADSTs and 891 SAYE schemes operating in the UK in 1990 (covering about 8 per cent of the workforce) (IDS 1990b). Research results, although at present thin on the ground, present a somewhat ambivalent picture. According to one study of participation in SAYE schemes:

> attitudinal differences between participants and non-participants across a range of criteria have been marginal, and in some instances barely discernable, notwithstanding the different profiles presented by the two groups. Participants tend to be male, white-collar, non-union employees, often with medium to long periods of service with their companies. Pay seems to be a crucial factor, influencing not just participation/non-participation, but also directly relating to savings levels and... to retentions or disposals of shares... the most frequently expressed reason for non-participation was given as inability to pay.
>
> (Ramsay *et al.* 1990:200)

The conclusion of these researchers is that participation in share-ownership schemes by employees is, contrary to management objectives, more closely allied to financial opportunism than organizational identification. Thus, 'it is doubtful whether share schemes make other than a marginal contribution to the development of unitarist values within the organization' (Ramsey *et al.* 1990)

Thus, although they met with considerable enthusiasm in the 1980s (with high rates of growth and inflation), both individual and collective forms of performance-based pay have faced increasing scepticism in the wake of the recessional conditions of the 1990s. In part this has arisen directly as a result of the disillusion of employees: PRP appears less attractive when economic conditions prevent improvements in performance being made. As such, the motivational gains provided by such schemes, which may in any case be relatively small, can easily be outweighed by the administrative and management costs. An IDS report (IDS 1991d), for example, lists two issues that should be examined when considering performance pay 'in a new climate':

1 For many organizations growth will not be easily realized.... The team effort and contribution to corporate success may well be more important than the individual. Should the criteria and weighting of performance pay systems change to reflect this?
2 The budget available for merit payments will be tighter, the room for manoeuvre more constrained.... It may be more sensible to squeeze the merit budget completely, or look for different forms of rewarding performance.

(IDS 1991d:6)

Cafeteria or flexible benefit systems

The disenchantment with PRP as a core reward system has contributed to interest in more subtle approaches to remuneration. One such approach currently attracting attention in the USA is the so-called 'cafeteria' model or flexible compensation package. This is aimed primarily at the organization and distribution of so-called 'fringe benefits' which organizations may offer in addition to basic money salary, although as Woodley (1990) points out, some systems can have direct effects upon salary level also:

> Cafeteria benefits can sometimes mean a limited choice between a few benefits, but it is more commonly used to describe the choice from a full 'menu' of different benefits at different levels, each with attached price tags. The term focuses attention on benefits, but in practice the concept usually covers the compensation package as a whole, allowing individuals to alter the balance of benefits and cash pay as they wish.
>
> (Woodley 1990:42)

Simple versions of such schemes might, for instance, offer, say, five benefits (e.g., pension, life cover, car, medical insurance, holidays) at three different levels, the middle level corresponding to the current fixed package. Individuals can then opt up or down from the standard position to suit their preferences, with a corresponding increase or decrease in basic pay.

A recent study by IDS (1991a) examines those factors associated with the adoption of flexible benefit schemes in the UK in the following terms.

Changes in the workforce

As a result of demographic changes, the increased participation of women and older workers may push towards the provision of flexible benefits to reflect different needs and changes over time. Similarly, in professional grades the growth of 'dual career' families may make such flexibility attractive as a means of minimizing over-provision of a particular type of benefit (e.g., medical insurance).

Cost management

Here it seems that possible gains in the longer term by having a more selective and better value-for-money benefit portfolio, may have to be offset against short-term increases in cost arising from additional administration, possible loss of economies of scale and extra take-up as employees swop under-utilized benefits (e.g., full holiday entitlement) for ones that they will take up.

Perceived value

Gains may be made to the extent that employees may place a higher value on their benefit package, with associated improvements in commitment. The process of communicating the scheme can improve the visibility of the total benefit provision, reminding employees of the full value of the benefits they receive.

Total compensation

Because of the breakdowns and costings necessary to operate a flexible system, it is likely to be possible to derive more precise data on the costs of employing each member of staff.

Administration

Although often cited as a major worry with the introduction of flexible packages, companies with these systems seem to take the view that the administrative headaches are overplayed, or that the benefits achieved are worth the additional effort required. Computerization is generally regarded as having made the process considerably more manageable.

Tax implications

Here there may be problems with year-on-year changes in the tax on various benefits and in the provision of cash alternatives to benefits where there is some kind of favourable tax treatment. Although some commentators suggest that the Inland Revenue is becoming more accommodating in this respect, this problem is unlikely to be resolved completely except by governmental action.

Employee and union reaction

Most UK experience of flexible benefit schemes has been with non-unionized companies or with employees at a level where unions are not recognized for bargaining purposes. There is some evidence to suggest that trade unions can view such schemes as potentially undermining standard packages of terms and conditions. This does not mean, however, that unions could not have a role to play in the determination of flexible benefit provision.

Conflict of principles

As with individual PRP, this type of package, with its strong emphasis upon individual choice, may lead to tension where teamwork ideologies are strong. On the other hand, it can be seen as a recognition of the maturity and responsibility of employees.

Supporters of such schemes, which appear to be relatively rare in the UK (IMS 1992) claim that they can be cost effective by reducing the provision of unappreciated benefits and, most importantly, by generating commitment as a result of the implicit message of trust, maturity and openness which a choice of reward gives. Against this, however, must be set the disadvantages of complexity (particularly in the field of taxation of benefits, administration) and a general resistance to change and innovation with associated problems of communication and initial commitment.

Although the reasons for the growth of cafeteria systems in the US are largely associated with that country's tax system and with a desire by employers to find ways of controlling escalating medical insurance costs, in the UK (where these issues are less relevant) their modest but noticeable expansion seems to be more associated with the notion of flexibility and individuality, and in this respect they may also offer greater scope for motivational 'coverage' than other schemes.

KEY LEARNING POINTS

- Given the complex nature of the relationship between performance and reward, a key challenge for HRM is the design of reward systems that align individual expectations with organizational objectives and to integrate these with other human resource policies.
- From a purely motivational perspective, reward systems need to be flexible and dynamic over time, responsive to unique individual needs, and able to reflect changes in performance requirements. In practice such flexibility and dynamism is likely to be difficult to achieve, being crucially affected by factors such as organization size, the range and diversity of jobs, the nature and role of collective representation, the attitudes and values held by employees (both workers and managers), and the stability of the organization's economic base.
- While it is clear that during and since the 1980s many organizations have attempted to establish more 'individualized' and variable reward systems, it is also clear that this is neither an easy nor an effective solution for all organizations or all sections of a workforce.
- Given this less than perfect record, it is unwise to expect a reward policy, no matter how thoughtfully and meticulously constructed, to affect individual performance on its own. 'The design of a compensation system should rarely be the place to start in solving business and human resource problems, though it will always be an area that will have to be managed to complement other HRM changes' (Beer *et al.* 1984:115).

EXERCISES

1   Consider the ways in which reward is (or is not) linked to performance in your own organization, and the effects of this for both employees and the organization.

2 Evaluate the views of writers such as Pearce and Kerr (this chapter, above) on the problems associated with individual performance pay in the light of your own and your organization's experiences.
3 To what extent do flexible benefit systems represent a viable option for organizations in the UK?

Chapter 6

Commitment and employee involvement

HRM's Holy Grail?

COMMITMENT, EMPLOYEE INVOLVEMENT AND HRM

The previous chapters have revealed a strongly held view that to be successful, an integrated and consistent HRM initiative must rest upon an organizational climate in which employees feel a sense of positive identification with and commitment to the goals of the organization. In this respect particular attention has been given to various forms of employee involvement (EI) as a means of generating commitment on the basis that, once obtained, this provides the bedrock upon which flexible and quality-conscious attitudes and behaviours can be built (Guest and Peccei 1992; Ramsay 1991). Thus, according to Marchington *et al.* :

> the last decade has seen a renaissance of business interest in improving com-
> munications with and the involvement of employees at work. These 'new'
> employee involvement initiatives have been much more management sponsored
> than in the past, and as a result they have been more concerned with employee
> motivation and commitment to organizational objectives and performance than
> with issues of joint regulation and power-sharing at enterprise level.
> (Marchington *et al.* 1992:1)

While there undoubtedly is a link between EI, commitment and various aspects of human resource performance, there is also a good deal of social scientific evidence to suggest that it is neither as strong nor as inevitable as is often supposed. That this is so is evidenced by the many EI initiatives which either fail altogether or simply do not live up to the high expectations many managers have of them. Much of the misunderstanding which stimulates unrealistically high expectations of EI can be traced to overly simplistic conceptions of 'commitment'.

The evidence suggests that commitment is a complex phenomenon that operates in different directions and at different levels. It is not something which can easily be generated or sustained, neither does it necessarily lead to improved performance.

Thus, although EI techniques can play an important part in generating commitment, are by no means the only factor in this equation (others being reward, training d development, selection and assessment, and job design). Nevertheless, and bearing these qualifications in mind, the centrality of the 'involvement-commitment-performance' connection within HRM thinking demands detailed investigation if an adequate assessment of its potential is to be realized. This chapter begins, therefore, with an evaluation of the notion of commitment and, on the basis of this, considers the nature and scope of a variety of EI policy levers.

THE NATURE OF COMMITMENT

The link between commitment and HRM has been made in a fundamental sense by Walton (1991). This is perhaps best typified in his influential article which appeared in the *Harvard Business Review*, asserting that, 'At the centre of this philosophy is a belief that eliciting employee commitment will lead to enhanced performance. This belief is well founded.' For Walton, 'commitment' represents the latest stage in the evolution of managerial practice, a successor to the supposedly moribund regime of 'control/compliance' characteristic of Taylorist management during the early and mid-twentieth century. Walton points to changes in organizational structure and practice associated with the putative shift from control to commitment models. These have been conveniently summarized by Oliver and Low (1991) such that the Commitment Model involves:

Job design

- Multiskilling and flexible job definitions
- Work teams as the unit of accountability
- Emphasis on complete tasks.

Structures/systems/culture

- Flat organizational structures
- Co-ordination via shared goals and values
- Horizontal communication flows
- Task culture.

Employee–organization relationships

- High employment security
- Extensive company-based system of employee involvement
- Emphasis on mutual benefit
- Individual pay linked to skills/performance
- High trust.

The epochal nature of this change is made clear by Walton's claim that the rate of transition from control to commitment strategies 'continues to accelerate', fuelled not only by economic necessity but also by 'individual leadership in management and labour, philosophical choices, organizational competence in managing change, and cumulative learning from change itself' (Walton 1991: 455). Walton, however, provides little hard evidence to support this claim, other than a handful of sketchy allusions and an unsubstantiated 'estimate that at least a thousand plants are in the process of making a comprehensive change'.

Nevertheless, this approach attracted considerable attention during the 1980s, and many writers have reconceptualized Walton's approach in terms of organizational culture and the role which this plays in generating commitment. The notion of organizational culture has had a relatively long currency in organization theory (e.g., Handy 1985, Deal and Kennedy 1988, Graves 1986, Schein 1989), and its explicit link to HRM is now being more fully explored. Quinn Mills and Balbaky (1985:256), for example, distinguish the 'cultural approach' as a step beyond traditional 'morale-building' activities associated with personnel management, representing 'a more substantial framework of employee commitment':

> To be successful a company needs competence – the right people – and it needs commitment – people who really perform. Today, it needs flexible and innovative people who can respond to and initiate change. This has led to a new element of people planning – planning for the quality of the organization as a way of creating a more committed and involved workforce. Companies are moving from simple workforce planning to planning for organizational and cultural development. For an increasing number of companies, the human resource planning process includes plans for organizational revitalisation, the creation and maintenance of a specific culture, and morale building and productivity programmes.
>
> (Quinn Mills and Balbaky 1985:269)

The nature of this 'committed culture' remains rather vague in Quinn Mills and Balbaky's paper, although it eventually emerges as something akin to the notion of 'mutuality' espoused by the Harvard School (see Chapter 1) and emphasizing the 'greater identity of interest between company and employee'. In particular they associate these cultures with 'new entrepreneurial companies'. Such companies 'recognize and make use of the importance of symbols, celebrations, and the frequent articulation and communication of the company's values. The culture of the organization is said to be both a means of commercial success and an end in itself – a *community* for those who are its members' (Quinn Mills and Balbaky:281–2, emphasis in original). However, against this somewhat rosy picture Quinn Mills and Balbaky raise the issue of the possible conflict between a committed culture and the instrumental search for profitability. Whether or not management can preserve a culture of mutuality in the face of declining profitability, or rapid expansion is, they claim, a test of its sincerity. How or if management can pass this test, however, is left an open matter.

An attempt to answer this type of question is provided by Oliver and Lowe

(1991), who report case-studies of two UK companies, similar to Quinn Mills and Balbaky's 'new entrepreneurial' type, with strong commitment cultures. These findings throw an interesting light onto the question of commitment and culture and, in particular, raise questions relating to the commonly accepted notion that a key element in the mutuality/commitment nexus is stability and security of employment. This connection has been particularly emphasized by those who draw lessons from what they perceive to be the Japanese approach (to manufacturing industry). According to Saunders (1984:25), for example, 'The Japanese employee has security. He is employed for life. Labour turnover is very low; employees rarely leave of their own accord and dismissal is virtually unheard of'.

One of Oliver and Lowe's high commitment firms, however, demonstrated a marked departure from this stability pattern:

> At Company A, the picture was... one of higher *in*security, a situation which appeared to be accepted as a fact of life and compensated for by generous benefits.... Around the time of our [Lowe and Oliver's] visit two senior people were being made redundant due to reorganization.... The Human Resource Director described it thus: 'We've agreed that it's a no-fault divorce.... If you are going to try and reach a truly flat organization there are stages in both the organization and the person's life where you are not appropriate for each other. That doesn't mean that there is a fault on either side'. A further justification for the insecurity was expressed in a phrase that is in common currency within the company: 'You accept that [Company A] is an experience, not a career'.
>
> (Oliver and Lowe 1991: 442)

These writers suggest that commitment may continue to be high under conditions of insecurity if workers have been hired on the understanding that the situation is 'an experience' for which they will be well rewarded. Such antecedent awareness and matching of expectations may well contribute to subsequent commitment. At the same time, these individual expectations may need to be bolstered and reinforced by cultural expectations within the organization.

Views of commitment and culture based on Walton's notion of commitment as a 'paradigm shift' in managerial thinking captured the imagination of many commentators and provided a general sense of legitimacy and appropriateness for the idea of commitment as a natural corollary of HRM (see, for example Michael Armstrong's (1989) eulogy in *Personnel and the Bottom Line*: 188). However, this approach tends to treat commitment as a *strategy*, involving a collection of policy levers (usually centring on EI initiatives) and ideological techniques. This easily leads to the assumption that, if applied properly, such techniques automatically elicit commitment from those subject to them, but it is this all-too-easy slippage that has often given rise to expectations of performance that the techniques cannot realistically be expected to deliver.

Such an approach, which effectively ignores a detailed examination of the antecedents and consequences of commitment has, however, been challenged by writers approaching the issue of commitment from the perspective of social psychology rather than sociology. This perspective starts from a more tightly defined concept of commitment (generally as an individual psychological state) in relation to which causes and consequences can be identified and tested empirically (usually via measures of statistical association).

In terms of a theory of commitment, the most frequently cited is the work of Salancik (1977). This approach (which emphasizes employee *behaviour* rather than *attitude*, see chapter 1) suggests that commitment is 'the binding of the individual to behavioural acts' and that there are four major elements which determine commitment:

1 **Explicitness** relates to the 'deniability' of an act: put simply, with what level of certainty can we say that a specific act has taken place (i.e., did we actually observe it or did we have to assume it?) and with what level of conscious determination (equivocality) was the act undertaken?

2 **Revocability** concerns the 'reversibility' of an act: many actions are reversible to the extent that if we do not like them we can change our minds and do something else ('jobs can be quit. Marriages can be dissolved; engagements broken. Contracts can be torn up'); others, however, are irrevocable, once committed they cannot be taken back ('Consumption of food or drink may be regretted but not reversed. Pulling the trigger of a loaded gun pointed at a friend commits all to its gross reality').

3 **Volition** refers to the complex relationship between freedom and constraint in the making of choices: very crudely, to what extent an individual 'causes' a given action to happen. This will depend upon a variety of factors (both psychological and social) including the choices available, the nature and intensity of external demands, and the presence or absence of co-actors (e.g., 'A person who works hard because his superior stands over him constantly is not perceived as having as much volition as one who does as much on his own').

4 **Publicity** is the factor which links action to its social context. Thus, publicity refers to the extent to which others know of an action and their importance to the actor: 'One of the simplest ways to commit yourself to a course of action is to go around telling all your friends that you are definitely going to do something. You will find yourself bound by your own statements. The same commitment will not develop from proclamations to strangers you meet on trains'.

(Salancik 1977:6–7)

Thus, the extent to which these four factors are present in a given situation will determine the level of commitment which an individual experiences. Within an organizational context, the extent to which those in control can expose others to, and control the intensity of, such factors will have important behavioural implications. The notion that commitment is a quality which managers can, and should, utilize in the control and manipulation of employees is made more explicitly by O'Reilly (1991:247): 'We need to understand what commitment is and how it is developed. By understanding the underlying psychology of commitment, we can then think about how to design systems to develop such an attachment among employees.' Here, however, O'Reilly regards organizational commitment as part of a system of control within the organization with a stronger emphasis on attitude than behaviour. Thus:

> Commitment is typically conceived of as an individual's psychological bond to the organization, including a sense of job-involvement, loyalty, and a belief in the values of the organization.
>
> (O'Reilly 1991:247).

This leads him to identify a number of mechanisms through which commitment can be fostered.

1 **Participatory systems** encourage people to be involved and send signals to individuals that they are valued. Such systems may range from the formal (e.g., quality circles and advisory boards) to the less formal (such as opportunities to meet with top managers at informal social gatherings). These processes encourage people to make incremental choices and develop a sense of responsibility for their actions. When we choose of our own volition to do something, we often feel responsible.

2 **Symbolic action** refers not only to the dissemination by top management of a clear message which affirms the organizational culture, but also to the accompaniment of this by supporting symbolic action:

> When top management not only says that something is important but also consistently behaves in ways which support this message, we begin to believe what is said.... An important function of management is to provide interpretations of events for the organization's members. Without a shared meaning confusion and conflict can result.
>
> (O'Reilly 1991:250).

3 **Information from others** emphasizes the conformity-effect of interaction with others, in this context co-workers, based on the proposition that 'we often take our cue from others when we are uncertain what to do'. From a management perspective the goal is

> to create a strong social construction of reality by minimizing contradictory interpretations. In cults, this is often done by isolating the members from family and friends.... In corporations, 60 hour work weeks can also isolate people from competing interpretations.... With the commitment of time, workers may be as isolated as if they had joined a cult.
>
> (O'Reilly 1991:251)

4 **A comprehensive reward system** is taken to include both intrinsic and extrinsic satisfactions, much along the lines of Herzberg's motivation theory:

> Recognition by your boss or co-workers for doing the right thing can be more potent in shaping behaviour than an annual bonus.... the trick is to

catch someone doing the right thing and to reward it on the spot. While tokens such as scrolls and badges can be meaningless, under the right circumstances they can also be highly valued.

(O'Reilly 1991:251)

Against this 'manipulative' approach to commitment, however, there is now a well-developed body of literature which points to the fact that under certain circumstances, commitment can be as dangerous as it is beneficial. Randall (1987), for instance, points to the complexity of commitment levels and outcomes for both individuals and organizations. Randall distinguishes between high, medium and low levels of commitment, where commitment is defined as (1) a strong belief in the organization's goals and values; (2) a willingness to exert considerable effort on behalf of the organization; and (3) a strong desire to continue as an organization member. This allows him to identify positive and negative outcomes for both organization and individual at high and low levels. At low levels of commitment, for example, there can, apparently, be positive consequences for both the individual and the organization:

By engendering an environment of conflict and uncertainty, a minimally committed workforce can promote originality and innovation.... Also, minimally committed individuals may seek alternative employment... this may be a more effective use of human resources, and it may improve the mental health of those who leave the firm.

(Randall 1987:461)

Randall suggests that low commitment may be functional for the organization if the higher turnover and absenteeism associated with uncommitted individuals reduces the disruption which they might otherwise cause while at work. Alternatively, uncommitted employees may be more prepared to be 'whistle blowers' on the firm, reporting bad practice or illegal activity to internal authorities, an activity which, according to Randall, may have long-term positive consequences by prompting pre-emptive remedial action on the part of management to rectify potential misdemeanours.

The negative effects of low commitment are more commonly rehearsed. For the individual these can range from being passed over for promotion or excluded from development opportunities to being dismissed or harassed for whistle-blowing. At the organizational level the negative effects are those usually cited by 'commitment enthusiasts', i.e., high labour turnover, high absenteeism, poor performance, and sabotage (Randall 1987:463).

Of particular concern to Randall are the under-researched negative effects of high levels of commitment. For the individual such consequences may include the stifling of creativity and innovation, resistance to change, and personal danger and damage, e.g, stress and even suicide:

For the overcommitted, the organization is dominant in life. A victim of role-overload, these corporate employees may be unable to compartmentalise their lives and may have little energy left for their personal lives.... There may be no life/work balance.

(Randall 1987:465)

In terms of organizational consequences, over-commitment may lead to a loss of operating flexibility, as employees cling to the traditional practices to which they are committed and become organizational zealots whose behaviour alienates outsiders and less committed insiders alike. But more importantly, for Randall, is the possibility that highly committed employees 'may be more willing to commit illegal or unethical behaviour on behalf of the organization. Often if there is a conflict, highly committed individuals put corporate dictates above their own personal ethics or societal dictates' (1987:466). Randall's solution to the dilemmas posed by over-and under-commitment is to opt for the middle path:

the commonly assumed linear relationship between commitment and desirable consequences should be questioned. An inverted U-shaped curve between these variables with an apex at a moderate level of commitment may be a more accurate description of the relationship. Individual and organizational needs appear to be in balance with moderate levels of commitment.

(Randall 1987:467)

It is certainly useful for the concept of commitment to be broadened in this way, and Randall's analysis does challenge the simplistic assumption that commitment is an unequivocal benefit for any individual and all organizations. Others, however, have taken the critique of commitment further by giving greater attention to the notions of power and control.

A pluralist view of commitment, for instance, recognizes the multi-faceted nature of the concept (Iles, Mabey and Robertson 1990), and suggests that it is necessary to abandon 'global' notions and to speak instead of organizational commitments with 'multiple foci'. Thus, according to Reichers:

commitment is a process of identification with the goals of an organization's multiple constituencies. These constituencies may include top management, customers, unions, and/or the public at large. This approach may represent a natural evolution of the commitment construct, from a general construct concerned with *organizational* goals and values, to a more specific formulation that specifies *whose* goals and values serve as the foci for multiple commitments.

(Reichers 1985:465; emphasis in original)

The scope of such multiple commitments is depicted by Reichers in Figure 6.1 where the broken line indicates the (permeable) boundaries of the organization and the area of white space within this boundary is the scope for global commitment to the organization. Thus, the more 'constituencies' the individual is committed to, the potentially more fragmented the possibility of global commitment.

This approach has been extended more thoroughly by Iles, Mabey and Robertson (1990) who suggest that in addition to 'affective commitment' (i.e., based on

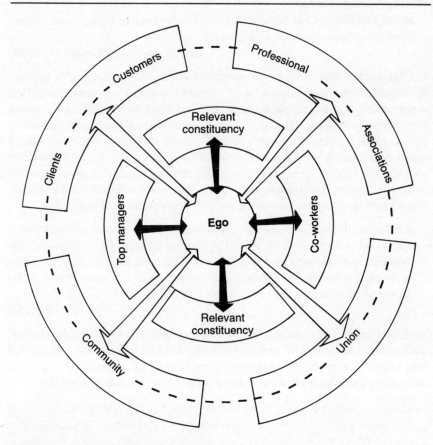

Figure 6.1   Organizational commitments
(*Source*: Reichers *et al.* 1985)

value-attachment), organizational commitment may also be seen in 'compliance' terms, as when people are committed to their organization 'because they perceive few existing alternatives and some sacrifice and disruption if they leave' (1990: 150). Compliance commitment, according to Iles, Mabey and Robertson, can take two possible forms: 'instrumental-calculative', or 'alienative'. The former, as the name implies, involves 'an instrumental exchange of involvement in return for rewards. Continuing commitment is seen as a function of an individual's evaluation of the costs and benefits of maintaining organizational membership' (1990:150). Alienative commitment, on the other hand, is a condition where

individuals perceive themselves unable to change or control their organizational experiences and also perceive a lack of alternatives. A negative attachment then exists, combining weak intentions to meet organizational demands with intentions to maintain organizational membership.

(Iles, Mabey and Robertson 1990:150)

For Iles and his co-authors, the acceptance of a multi-faceted concept of commitment rather than the global notion of a single organizational commitment, has important implications for HRM practices. In particular it can assist in explaining some of the paradoxical effects that can occur when commitment-boosting policies are introduced. They point, for example, to the case of a stress counselling programme introduced by the British Post Office (Sadri, Cooper and Allison 1989) which, while resulting in employees reporting less anxiety, depression and somatic anxiety and higher self-esteem, also reported lower organizational commitment. Iles, Mabey and Robertson suggest a possible explanation for this paradox:

counselling enables employees to identify more clearly the causes of their stress. Conceivably, these might be related to poor supervision, poor job design, role ambiguity or frustrating company policies. Achieving such clarity might result in employees being less attached to their organization because they become more critical of it.

(1990:154)

An a similar note they cite the case of the introduction of 'development centres' (Rodger and Mabey 1987) into organizations with the intention of assisting individuals to plan their career development, and the expectation of thereby committing them more firmly to a career within the organization or industry.

However, participants in a development centre run in a major British financial services organization were more likely to report less clear career goals, plans and strategies and stronger thoughts and intentions about leaving their career field after participation in such a centre.... Perhaps employees' ideas about their skills, strengths and weaknesses, and their existing career plans, had been shaken up and challenged by the centre experience; perhaps they had come to realise that their expectations and abilities did not match up to organizational requirements, stimulating thoughts of withdrawal.

(Iles, Mabey and Robertson 1990:154)

Thus they conclude that commitment should not be viewed as a 'linear, rational process... imply[ing] that high levels of commitment lead to certain behaviours in a prospective logical fashion' but rather as a complex, multi-faceted and paradoxical process.

The pluralist critique suggests that in terms of HRM practices, commitment is not something which can be easily or unproblematically harnessed to achieve predictable and determinate outcomes, a view supported by Coopey and Hartley (1991:25), who point to the

free-standing, context-free assumptions of many global, single-commitment models.

Against what they perceive to be a tendency to borrow uncritically from perceptions of Japanese practice, they suggest that for western organizations there is a need to ground the study of commitment in the western cultural context. This might involve accepting the greater levels of individualism and pluralism characteristic of western societies and, especially in Europe, the commitment to collective pluralism through membership of independent trade unions and (with the partial exception of the UK) a willingness to give legislative support to forms of worker participation.

EMPLOYEE INVOLVEMENT

Despite a lack of statistical data establishing a significant positive correlation between levels of commitment and EI practices, the latter have continued to enjoy a reputation as important contributors to this process. Marchington *et al.* (1992:14) divide EI practices into four broad categories:

1 Those concerned with downward communication (e.g. team briefing)
2 Those concerned with upward problem solving (e.g. suggestion schemes, attitude surveys, quality circles)
3 Financial measures
4 Representative mechanisms.

Of these, the present chapter will be concerned only with communication and problem-solving practices (financial participation having been dealt with in the previous chapter, and representation featuring in Chapter 8).

Team briefing

There is little doubt that in the UK, team briefing is now a widely used strategy of downward communication. Storey (1992) cites figures from a survey of 222 large organizations, showing that 86 per cent had installed team briefing systems; the Industrial Society helped to introduce 400 to 500 such systems between 1984 and 1986 (Storey 1992:106; see also IDS 1992c). Indeed, the Industrial Society has been instrumental in promoting this practice and it seems likely that a majority of UK systems are based, more or less closely, on their model:

Team Briefing is a system of communication operated by line management. Its objective is to make sure that *all* employees know and understand what they and others in the company are doing and why. It is a management information system. It is based on leaders and their teams getting together in groups for half an hour on a regular basis to talk about things that are relevant to their work.

(Grummitt 1983:1)

Particular emphasis is given to the need to make the information imparted relevant to the recipients, a rule of thumb being that only 30 per cent of information should relate to wider corporate matters. Recommended group size is usually between five and fifteen members. The same guide to team briefing lists the following benefits of the system:

- **It reinforces management** by allowing the manager to be seen as a leader. For first-line managers and supervisors in particular, it 'makes them manage... because it clearly differentiates them from their people and reminds them and their team that they are accountable for the group's performance'.
- **It increases commitment** because it informs them about what their team is doing and whether they are meeting targets. 'It is extremely difficult to be committed to something when you do not know what it is. Talking to people regularly about how we are doing and whether we are overcoming the problems gives people an objective to work for'.
- **It prevents misunderstandings** by reducing the impact of the inevitable 'grape vine' and also by allowing important information to be passed quickly and 'cleanly' to all those who need to know.
- **It helps to accept change** as it gives people an accurate understanding of why change is necessary and the time to adjust to it.
- **It improves upward communication** by filling what is frequently an 'information gap' at the level of people's jobs. By relating problems to people's jobs they are more likely to see it as a direct concern of theirs and to want to voice ideas, views and suggestions for solving them (see also IDS 1992c). Such upward communication, however, should be regarded as a useful 'side effect' rather than a principal function of team briefing (it is not the same as quality circles or consultation).

(Grummitt 1983:3)

Despite a long-standing enthusiasm for the technique, there is now a growing body of case-study material indicating a number of difficulties with the team briefing approach. Storey (1992) for example, points to an apparent gap between a company having team briefing, how it was used in practice, and which departments it covered:

it was rare to find a case where the system was being uniformly applied in practice. There were usually whole departments where briefings had not successfully taken root. The initiative in the unionized settings was also complicating collective relations. The shop stewards were in some cases rather better informed than the first line supervisors who were supposed to be giving the briefings. These supervisors said they felt exposed in transmitting a brief about topics where they might be challenged and be made to look foolish.... In about half a dozen of the cases the trade unions had sought to oppose the introduction of team briefings on the grounds that it was, they said, designed to bypass union channels. And of course it was. Though this was not usually it sole or main purpose.

(Storey 1992: 106)

It could be suggested that these sorts of problem reflect ineffective or poor implementation of the team briefing system by the management responsible. However, the difficulty in obtaining local 'consistency' is also highlighted by Marchington and Parker (1990:146ff.) and Marchington et al. (1992), the latter study drawing attention to the forms of local responses to team briefing systems, ranging from completely ignoring them to subjecting the system to piecemeal, informal and largely pragmatic adaptation.

The same study also contains the results of a survey of workers in a range of industrial sectors which further confirms the diverse picture of team briefing (see Table 6.1)

As these figures show, the response of employees to team briefing is not easy to interpret. On the one hand, it seems to be a system they value as a means of providing information (89 per cent of the above sample wanted the system to continue) but, on the other hand, the substantive outcomes appear more limited. Of particular note is the fact that over three-quarters of the sample felt that team briefing made no difference to their level of commitment to the organization; similarly the relatively small increase in the understanding of management decisions suggests limited potential as a means of significant employee involvement. Clearly, team briefing is not intended primarily to offer a mechanism for upward communication, although this may be one (not insubstantial) consequence. Other methods, however, do take this as their principal focus.

Suggestion schemes

Suggestion schemes, where employees are invited to submit ideas to improve aspects of organization performance, have a history going back to the nineteenth

Table 6.1 The impact of team briefing on employees (%)

Impact on:	Increase	Decrease	No change
Amount of information received	59	4	37
Understanding of management decisions	29	5	66
Commitment to the organization	19	4	77
Upward communications	31	6	61
Management openness	27	8	65

Note: N = 623
Source Adapted from Marchington et al. (1992:35)

century (Slee Smith 1983), although their use seems to have received a boost in the 1980s, inspired by the Industrial Society and culminating in 1986 in the formation of a co-ordinating body, the United Kingdom Association of Suggestion Schemes (UKASS). It is claimed that, in addition to cost savings and process innovations, suggestion schemes can also have other beneficial effects. These have by listed by IDS (1991c) as follows:

- By rewarding good ideas they involve employees in the search for improvements
- Schemes can encourage a climate of change in the organization
- They help to identify employees who may have creative/lateral thinking skills
- A scheme may allow employees with good ideas to bypass their immediate (and possibly obstructive) managers in a non-confrontational manner, without undermining the latter's authority
- Schemes can assist in management development by giving managers the opportunity to practise skills of evaluating and implementing ideas which the scheme throws up
- The quality and quantity of responses to the scheme can give an indication of the state of organizational morale.

On the basis of nine case studies, IDS (1991c) report that all have seen significant savings arising from employee suggestions, and four organizations saved over £1 million each. UKASS claim that if all UK companies operated suggestion schemes, the total savings could be more than £1 bn.

However, against these benefits there are also a number of potential difficulties which may arise with suggestion schemes. These are commonly associated with poor administration, such as lengthy delays in evaluating and rewarding ideas, thereby leading to demotivation and a disinclination to use the scheme. But problems may also arise from a conflict of ideologies where, for instance, the adoption of a TQM regime dictates that constant improvement is a normal part of the job, not something for which employees should receive an additional reward (Marchington et al. 1992:16). Other complications in the practical running of suggestion schemes include eligibility (i.e., who can take part, and what ideas are acceptable) and the type of award that is made.

Participation practices are variable and may extend for blanket coverage of all employees to specified grades. Under the latter practice, schemes are usually restricted to non-managerial employees, the rationale for this resting with the eligibility of ideas: to be rewarded, ideas should fall outside an individual's own area of responsibility, in that he or she could not make the change without higher authority, nor should he or she be open to criticism from management for not having made the change. Thus, as one ascends the management hierarchy it becomes progressively more difficult to argue that suggestions lie outside the sphere of one's responsibility. In addition, specific topics may be deliberately excluded from suggestion schemes, these usually relating to ideas which might affect collective agreements with unions or the legal obligations or corporate objectives of the organization.

Types of award made for successful suggestions are also variable, but usually fall into three categories: 'encouragement awards' which are given for effort, even though the idea is not implemented (in the IDS cases, these ranged from £5 to £50); 'valued awards' given for suggestions leading to clearly quantified savings (usually based on a percentage of savings made, frequently between 20 per cent and 50 per cent over the first year); and 'special awards' for savings which cannot be easily quantified, such as health and safety improvements (usually decided on a points system, with maximum payments of around £2,000 to £3,000).

In terms of their contribution to the generation of commitment, suggestion schemes are likely to be heavily influenced by the organizational climate in which they operate. The volition which such schemes make available to employees is heavily conditioned by the ability and willingness of management to reciprocate this involvement which will mean ensuring that top management are aware of and actively support the scheme and recognize its importance by being prepared to put into practice ideas which have not emanated from formal managerial channels. In many respects, however, it seems that the commitment-generating potential of suggestion schemes is also limited by the fact that many schemes are primarily concerned with the 'technical' as opposed to the 'social' dimensions of work organization, a fact reflected not only in the way they are presented in the workplace but by the frequent domination of assessment panels by 'technical' specialists. It is to tap responses to the social dimension of organization that attitude surveys have developed.

Attitude surveys

The use of attitude surveys to tap employee opinion developed in the 1980s and appears to be continuing. NOP and MORI between them claimed to have organized such polls for over 350 organizations in the past decade (IRS 1991g), with many more organizations likely to have conducted their own in-house surveys. On the face of it, attitude surveys seem to have more to do with gauging and measuring employee commitment than with serving as a form of EI. While the measurement function is certainly crucial, a good deal of case study data also indicates that many employees do value the opportunity to express their views through such surveys and see it as a means of having their voice heard. The benefits of this technique are reported by IDS (1990a):

> Whether surveys are conducted on a one-off basis or regularly, many companies find that they increase the involvement of their workforce, and check that management's perception of the organization's strengths and weaknesses corresponds to staff's. They also allow management to assess the extent to which their policies are having the desired effect. Most of all though, the companies we spoke to were surprised at how much thought employees put into answering

the questionnaires they were sent. Simply being asked for their views often raised employees' morale.

(IDS 1990a:1)

The success of attitude surveys as a means of generating commitment, therefore, is dependent upon not only providing the opportunity for employees to express their opinion, but also on management feeding back the results of the surveys and being prepared to act on them. However, unlike suggestion schemes, the information elicited from attitude surveys is likely to be critical, less specific and to require responses at the level of policy and organization rather than purely technical systems. Such questioning of existing organization practice can pose management with difficult challenges for change. The following illustrates the sorts of response to which attitude surveys can give rise:

> In 1990 results from a BP survey revealed that 'BP is secure and healthy – but over-complex and bureaucratic. Staff are loyal and proud to work for the company but feel that it cares too little for them'. Fifty-nine per cent felt that staff in their areas were proud to work for BP, and 66 per cent said they themselves were proud. But management came in for criticism. Under 40 per cent felt that senior managers had the qualities needed by the company, and in the UK this figure was barely over 20 per cent. Particular worries were expressed about communications, efficiency and planning.... On BP's record on equal opportunities staff were less convinced.... Particularly worrying for the company was the view, expressed by more than half of the respondents, that too little attention was paid to the interests of employees. Only a minority agrees that the company's actions demonstrated that it believed its people to be its most valuable asset.

(IDS 1990a:19)

Thus, attitude surveys are also likely to stand or fall on the ability of management to act upon the views expressed. Again, the implication is that such measures, if they are to succeed as a means of employee involvement, must be part of an approach to management which is prepared to take seriously the contribution of employees. Such an approach, however, is not necessarily integral to the attitude survey technique – it is the precondition for its success, but it also needs to exist independently and, probably, prior to it. In many respects this is not so true of quality circles, and even less so of TQM, where the wider culture of the organization is inherently and explicitly tied to the EI techniques themselves.

Quality circles and TQM

Quality circles normally involve a group of employees meeting voluntarily and regularly to solve work-related problems of their own identification and, where possible, implementing solutions (with management approval). Normally circles number between six and twelve members and are led by the supervisor or team leader in the area concerned. Although managers are not usually circle members, they are frequently invited to put their views as 'experts' in various fields. If operated successfully circles should:

• Improve the quality and reliability of the product or service
• Make suggestions leading to cost savings
• Increase employees' interest and commitment in jobs
• Encourage an aware and flexible response to problems
• Enhance supervisory authority and leadership skills.

(Ramsay 1991)

However, although quality circles still have their supporters, there is good evidence to suggest that the boom in adoption which characterized the early 1980s has now halted and is probably in decline. Accounting for the rise and fall of quality circles involves the consideration of numerous factors, not the least of which are the difficulty in sustaining the early impetus, the problem of integrating them into existing organization structures, and the emergence of TQM as an alternative means of addressing the quality issue.

One of the best recent reviews of the effectiveness of quality circles is provided by Hill (1991), and the following account draws heavily on this work. Hill suggests that the rapid growth of quality circles can best be understood as a response to two challenges while faced British companies in the late 1970s and early 1980s. First, employee relations, perceived by many to be more conflictual, antagonistic and lower in trust than in other industrial societies, were seen (rightly or wrongly) as a major contribution to lower levels of productivity and efficiency. Second was the growing awareness, especially in the face of Japanese competition, of the inability of manufacturing industry to compete in terms of high (and improving) quality standards at low cost. In this climate the hopes which managers held out for quality circles were, apparently, high:

> Quality circles were intended to do more than just improve communications: the aim was for rank-and-file shop-floor and office employees to participate actively in the improvement process. It was hoped this would in turn increase job satisfaction, stimulate personal growth, lead people to identify more with the quality of their own work and the managerial objectives of higher quality and efficiency throughout the company, and so increase employees' sense of involvement in their firms.... A senior manager with responsibility for quality put it thus: 'Quality circles promote personal development and job satisfaction by harnessing ideas and opening up communications, which in turn leads to improved quality, a more effective company and a new attitude among *everyone* who works here.'

(Hill 1991:546)

However, Hill's research into companies that had run quality circles for several years indicates that seldom, if ever, were these hopes realized in full. Managers pointed to relatively low levels of participation in circles (at most, 25 per cent of those eligible to join, and at least 2 per cent), to widespread indifference on the part of most employees, and to the active opposition by some groups. Indeed, a survey of those employees who chose to participate in circles revealed no differences in attitude from non-participants in relation to job satisfaction, long-term commitment to working for the company, perception of the company as a 'fair' employer, and the amount of trust and 'us and them' feeling between managers and employees. Only in one area were there significant differences: namely in terms of the desirability of greater participation in managerial decision-making, with quality circle members endorsing this more strongly (Hill 1991:547–8). Although the companies studied all reported that some business improvements had resulted from the circles, little attempt had been made to measure these rigorously, and most felt that the returns were disappointing and showed a tendency to decline over time. Those companies that retained circles 'chose to do so for "social" rather than economic reasons, believing that they were good for their members and the overall climate of human relations even if they no longer delivered significant financial or technical improvements' (Hill 1991:548). In terms of the attitudes of middle managers towards the circles (frequently identified as a 'problem' area), the main concern was not primarily of attitude or culture, but of the general 'cost' of circles (in terms of disruption and time commitments) in relation to their benefits, both to the organization and the majority of employees. To this was added the difficulties caused by the 'dual structure' to which quality circles give rise: because circles require a facilitator to oversee and co-ordinate their activities and, usually, a committee to assess the ideas generated, this establishes a distinct quality circle hierarchy, separate from the normal structure of the organization but also leaving the existing authority relations untouched, resulting in a confusion in normal lines of command and authority.

Thus, Hill's assessment of the effectiveness of quality circles, based on his own research and that available from other sources, is less than encouraging:

The dominant impression, conveyed by companies with and without circles alike, was of fragility. Every programme needed constant stimulus to keep it alive. [One] company... had been forced to relaunch its programme once before, after it collapsed in the mid-1980s. Facilitators in two other firms gave identical accounts of how, after they had been on sick leave for several months, they returned to find that more than three-quarters of the circles had not met in their absence. Every company experienced a continued ebb and flow as circles went into suspension or collapsed and others started. The continued flux meant that companies were never certain how many circles were in operation at any moment.... Thus, all the evidence points to the widespread failure of circles to become institutionalized. The rhetoric of the early days of the boom, that circles would become a normal way of doing business, was hollow. Circles never really took hold in the great majority of these firms, remaining both experimental and marginal throughout their lives.

(Hill 1991:551)

While recognizing the limitations of quality circles, Hill also accepts that they can represent part of an evolutionary process, a first step on the road to a more sophisticated and sustainable pattern of employee involvement through quality management, in particular TQM.

TQM, it is claimed, has the advantage over quality circles in that it represents a total system, as opposed to just part of such a system: early enthusiasts of Japanese management often failed to realize this and regarded quality circles as a 'free-standing' institution. As a result, quality circles in the UK and other western countries tended to be structurally and strategically fragmented, unsustained by a core organizational commitment to quality. By locating quality issues within a strategic perspective driven by top management and by making use of existing management hierarchies (albeit delayered and horizontally integrated via the identification of internal customers) rather than 'dual structures', TQM makes employee involvement more 'directed' and purposeful than semi-autonomous quality circles. Thus, problem-solving groups and team working are likely to be retained – and developed – but they become more a part of 'normal' working practice for all employees (frequently with membership of teams being mandatory) rather than voluntary 'extras'. This approach is characterized by Wickens' (1987) account of kaizen or 'continuous improvement' teams incorporating a quality circle element at Nissan UK:

> The key to success... is in ensuring that Quality Circle activity is fully integrated into the job and is not seen as a separate activity. We therefore regarded QC activity as just one aspect of a programme aimed at achieving employee commitment to continuous improvement in all areas.... Because we regard it as part of everyone's job to strive to improve continuously, the question of whether the activity is voluntary or compulsory does not really arise.

> (1987:71–2)

In practice this form of involvement, however, is likely to be more constrained than that associated with quality circles. Problem-solving teams under TQM are normally restricted to working on issues identified by management rather than of their own choosing, and the resulting action is more firmly under the prerogative of managers. The result of this more limited form of involvement, however, may be more effective in engendering employee commitment, simply because it is more likely to achieve the results intended, relatively quickly and easily. In short, because the initiative lies with management, albeit shared with employees, there are likely to be fewer 'political' and organizational barriers to be overcome, with the result that quick and effective success breeds a greater sense of achievement than the familiar quality circle experience of limited results achieved only after long and protracted struggle.

Such an 'optimistic' assessment, however, must be balanced against the views of writers such as Sewell and Wilkinson (1992) and Grenier (1988) who point to the possibility that the rhetoric of employee 'empowerment' often associated with TQM and quality circles may, in practice, conceal practices which, on the contrary, 'emasculate' employee influence. Both point to the ways in which sophisticated quality-monitoring technology can be used as a means of employee surveillance which, when coupled to carefully designed team-working practices, limit the scope of employees to question managerial decisions ('genuine' empowerment) other than on management's own terms. Sewell and Wilkinson's case-study of a consumer product manufacturer documents a system which they equate with 'electronic tagging':

> During the period of our research at Kay a significant extension of the issue of quality information was made.... [This involved] a system of highly visible displays based on 'traffic light' cards suspended above their heads from the production-line superstructure. Depending on their quality performance on the previous shift... the cards are at either green (no [errors]), amber (between one and four [errors]) or red (four or more [errors]). Thus, in addition to providing the individual member with a reminder that they must improve their performance, it also relays that information to the wider audience constituted by the team.... The combination of the cards and the selective display of both individual and team performance indicators... enables the team to identify those members who 'aren't up to it'. This creates a climate where a horizontal disciplinary force, based on peer scrutiny, operates throughout the team as members seek to identify and sanction those who may jeopardise its overall performance.
>
> (Sewell and Wilkinson 1992:107–10)

This critical analysis of forms of employee involvement raises an issue which has ethical implications in the whole field of 'commitment management': namely, the tension between a management philosophy of HRM which claims to value and respect the involvement of employees, on the one hand, and the adoption of policies which manipulatively seek to limit such involvement to only those issues and outcomes acceptable to management, on the other hand. As will be seen in Chapter 8, this dilemma is reflected in the field of trade union recognition and collective organization.

KEY LEARNING POINTS

- **The practical contribution of 'commitment' to organizational performance is ambiguous. First, the extent to which it can be defined and 'targeted' as a dimension of managerial strategy is open to debate. In practice, commitment is a complex and multi-faceted phenomenon that does not operate in a single direction or lend itself to easy manipulation.**
- **In terms of individual psychology the causal link between EI, commitment, and performance is both partial and relatively weak.**
- **The sociological concept of commitment emphasizes the link with organizational culture. In this respect commitment is not the result of a single policy but the outcome of a wider set of initiatives covering not only employee**

involvement but also reward, training, selection, and organizational design factors.

• Thus, employee involvement, while an important factor in building a 'committed culture', cannot alone deliver these results.

• Because of the heavy reliance on socio-psychological techniques involving behavioural and attitudinal change, the search for commitment may give rise to ethical issues concerning manipulation and surveillance.

EXERCISES

1   Using the models of commitment developed by Salancik and O'Reilly, consider the extent to which these techniques are employed, deliberately or unconsciously, in your own organization, and the consequences.

2   Explore the nature of multiple/overlapping commitments within your own organization using the model proposed by Reichers and expressed in Figure 6.1.

Chapter 7

Welfare

Health and efficiency?

WELFARE, PERSONNEL MANAGEMENT AND HRM

Welfare provision generally refers to those policies which are directed at some aspect of employee well-being. Clearly this is a diverse field and many provisions which bear upon well-being will be part of reward and development packages (e.g., holiday entitlement, sick-pay, access to education, job satisfaction). Usually, however, it is aspects of the physical and emotional health of employees which form the core of secular welfare policy, and it is with this area that the present chapter is concerned.

Within HRM thinking the role of welfare has not received as much attention as other areas. This seems to be due to a concern on the part of some commentators to distance HRM from traditional personnel management, which has often been caricatured as having a 'welfarist' orientation and, in consequence, lacking a 'real' business focus.

This dismissive view of welfare is usually a response to the historical circumstances in which many company welfare provisions have developed. It is, in fact, possible to identify three common 'welfare rationales', each of which appears to limit the potential of welfare policy to 'connect' with wider organizational issues:

1 **Legalistic–reactive** In the UK there has been a close association between welfare and health and safety legislation. Where welfare policy has been driven primarily by these legislative requirements imposed from outside the organization, it has invariably been cast as something 'separate from', rather than genuinely 'of', the organization's core objectives: a prescription to be complied with, rather than genuinely embraced.
2 **Corporate conscience** This reflects the influence of nineteenth and early twentieth-century social reform movements (the Institute of Personnel Management, for example, was originally founded as the Industrial Welfare Society in 1913), and later ideas from the Human Relations tradition emphasizing the need for social cohesion in a potentially alienating work environment. These influences often cast personnel departments in the role of a 'loyal opposition',

representing the interests of workers to management (Sisson 1989:18). In the 1980s in particular, however, this approach was often perceived as 'soft' and 'indulgent' in its treatment of employees, and subversive to the extent that it questioned the legitimacy of managerial prerogative as the principal axiom of work organization (see Chapter 1).

3   **Company paternalism**   As a form of welfare provision, paternalism is 'encompassing' and tied closely to a company identity (as opposed to a secular personnel policy). This approach, often associated with the large Quaker manufacturers of the nineteenth century, sought through the provision of benefits such as housing or other 'rewards' to regulate and control the attitudes and behaviours of employees, often along religious or 'moral' lines. Henry Ford's 'Sociological Department', for example, formed in 1916, set out to administer a generous reward system (based on the, then, high rate of $5 per day) but linked this to a programme of 'social monitoring' of employees in their homes by inspectors charged to ensure that no one strayed from the path of 'rectitude and right living' (Beynon 1975:22–3). However, many commentators on company paternalism have pointed to the fact that its survival is continually threatened by an erosion of the dependence of employees upon the jobs (and values) of their employers. As such it is a deeply conservative form of authority which is simultaneously resistant and highly vulnerable to change. The decay of many forms of industrial paternalism has, in fact, been associated with the removal of local restrictions on movement (better transport provision), the growth in the availability of alternative employment, and the diffusion of 'outside' ideas made accessible by the growth of a mass media (Newby 1977; Norris 1979).

Now, given that HRM typically emphasizes individual initiative, flexibility, and adaptability to change, there are clear incompatibilities with the legal–reactive, corporate conscience and company paternalist approaches to welfare. There is often an open aversion in much HRM thinking to the notions of dependence and reactivity implicit in these approaches, expressed forcefully by the distinction between 'soft care' and 'tough love':

The needs of our business will be most effectively attained if the needs of people for fulfilment, success, and meaning, are met. If people are in poor shape, the company's objectives are unlikely to be achieved. Yet the needs of the business still come first. People need to be developed, but this will not be achieved by treating them with 'soft care', by allowing issues to be smoothed over without being properly addressed. To treat people without care will cause them and, therefore the business, to diminish. Experience suggests that the needs of people and the business will be best met if we treat ourselves with 'tough love'.... This is very different from 'macho-management', which basically does not involve care. Tough love requires courage. Respect for the individual does not mean pandering to the individual's weaknesses or even wishes. Involving people through tough love to secure both their development and good performance requires managers to take initiatives.... People, of course, are far and away the most important resource in any company. But they are not more than that. It is very easy to forget when endeavouring to develop people and to care for them, and even to love them, that the needs of the business must come first. Without that, there can be no lasting security. A fool's paradise in which effort is concentrated only on the present well-being of staff, without regard for the future, will eventually disintegrate and it may well be the staff that suffer most.

(Barnham cited in Legge 1989:33)

Here, it seems, the notion of welfare is very differently perceived. It involves 'care' for employees, but it is a care which is driven by organizational needs and not by a wider, more embracing, social or religious philosophy.

From the perspective of 'tough love', welfare is about the provision of benefits and services which employees want and value and which simultaneously link strategically with the needs of the organization by enhancing performance.

To this end there has been a tendency to rethink certain areas of welfare along HRM lines. In particular, there has been a growth of interest in areas of 'health and efficiency', an issue that fits well with a good deal of HRM thinking because it focuses attention first on performance and, second, on individual responsibility.

Poor (psychological or physical) health, it is suggested, leads to deteriorating performance, hence the need for an organizational response emphasizing prevention and treatment. In theory the emphasis of such responses should be on rehabilitating the 'problem' employee in line with organizational requirements, commitment to rehabilitation therefore becoming synonymous with commitment to the organization. Thus, from such a perspective, a concern with health can be both practical and symbolic. Symbolically there is often the suggestion that the virtues of a healthy lifestyle are also those of a healthy organization. In some cases this has been reflected in a renewed interest in the values engendered by team sport:

Japanese and American companies are much better at this than the British... but gradually five-a-side football, badminton, athletics, table tennis and even parachute jumping have emerged. At the five-a-side competition half the company was involved and this has led to spontaneous matches between numerous departments. Badminton courts have been marked out between the production lines in the plant, people asked to wear Nissan tee shirts in the Great North Run. Once such activity develops – because people want to socialise with others within the company – then the company can, unobtrusively, help.

(Wickens 1987: 92)

Other more individually oriented initiatives can be found in the areas of:

- Health promotion
- Alcohol and drug abuse

- Stress
- Counselling.

Proponents claim that initiatives in all these areas can have direct benefits to the organization in terms of cost savings and performance enhancement.

HEALTH PROMOTION POLICY

The 1980s witnessed a growth in workplace health promotion, often involving programmes geared to the provision of advice and services linked to preventive medicine, e.g., screening services, information and education provision covering matters such as cervical cancer, heart disease, diet and smoking. According to one UK study, companies that had implemented such programmes were concerned mainly with 'a felt need to improve employee relations by displaying a sense of caring and concern, and staff morale' rather than the intention of deriving a quantitative improvement in performance' (cited in Sigman 1992:25–6). However, according to IDS (1991b) there is now evidence from the US to suggest that health promotion programmes can result in quantifiable benefits to organizations both in terms of cost savings and individual performance improvement. It reports the results of the Du Pont company programme which is claimed to have paid for itself in the first year and to have provided a return of between two and four dollars for every dollar invested in the programme by the end of the second year.

Although such *general* health promotion policies are increasing, there remains a strongly held view that some health-related issues are best treated by means of specific policies. This has sometimes been argued in relation to HIV/AIDS and, more strongly, for policies on substance abuse.

HIV/AIDS

Acquired Immune Deficiency Syndrome (AIDS) emerged as an important concern for human resource strategy and welfare provision in the 1980s and is likely to remain a concern for the 1990s. The spread of HIV and AIDS has always been accompanied by an element of moral panic. The disease was widely perceived as the result of morally questionable behaviour – either homosexual promiscuity or intravenous drug abuse – and its very potency marked it out in the public imagination as one of the most serious threats of the late twentieth century. Although the intensity of this panic has now diminished, it has not disappeared. Indeed, HIV/AIDS continues to pose a substantively different set of problems from other life-threatening or terminal diseases, involving as it does complex layers of meaning, intimately connected with sexuality and morality, with which many people who think of themselves as 'normal' feel distinctly uncomfortable. This situation has been exacerbated by the very novelty of the disease, its sudden 'discovery' and apparently incurable effects: new hazards, especially those for which there is no immediate remedy, generate significant levels of fear and anxiety which, in turn, fuel perceptions of risk. In these respects, therefore, HIV/AIDS is dissimilar to other serious diseases and its occurrence in workplace situations (as in other areas of social life) gives rise to questions which go well beyond those posed by other illnesses.

The implications for welfare policy arise from the effects which fear and/or experience of the virus/disease can have on organizational behaviour. The latter can include prejudice against people with AIDS (manifested in recruitment and promotion discrimination), dismissals (lawful or otherwise), anxiety and fear among employees about contracting the disease, and confronting the expression of attitudes about sexuality. Certainly these difficult questions have often been handled badly, quite frequently as a result of lack of understanding or ill-informed perceptions of risk. Past UK cases, for example, have involved a woman sacked from her shop assistant job because her son had AIDS, a man dismissed because co-workers suspected him of having AIDS and did not want to share toilet facilities, a homosexual chef dismissed because it was thought that he might 'get AIDS' and transmit it to diners (see Adam-Smith *et al.* 1992 for a fuller discussion). The most recent examples are provided by a National AIDS Trust report; for example:

> Steve, a wages clerk, was a haemophiliac. Because bleeding tended to occur in his knees and ankles he had always delivered wages to company outlets by car. However, when he was diagnosed HIV positive he experienced a change in attitude from his employers. The company took away his car and told him he would have to deliver the wages on foot. After one such journey he had severe bleeds and had to have a long time off work. Eventually he was dismissed from his job on grounds of ill-health.

> (Wilson 1992:11)

Similarly, a study of 181 people with HIV/AIDS by Tolley *et al.* (1991) noted that among those who were employed, several had changed jobs or working positions to relieve stress or better accommodate HIV/AIDS-related health problems. Of those who had worked since being diagnosed HIV positive, 63 per cent reported that their working conditions had adversely affected their health. Most frequently cited were fatigue and the strain of working in a situation where their HIV status was unknown to colleagues. Forty per cent of those employed since diagnosis gave instances of hostility or discrimination at work because of their known HIV status. On the other hand, almost as many respondents spoke of their colleagues being supportive in terms of rearranging work schedules, allowing time off and being understanding. In particular, over half of the sample spoke of the need for increased education for the public, employers and employment agencies, as well as expressing a wish to see the establishment of further HIV policies in the workplace.

Since the mid-1980s the formulation of corporate AIDS policies has been a key plank in organizational responses to the disease. In both the US and the UK, AIDS policies appear restricted to a relatively small number of large firms, although in the US that number is claimed to be growing rapidly (Kohl, Miller and Barton 1990). In the UK, one of the few studies of AIDS and the workplace (IRS 1991h) surveyed 118 organizations from a population of the 1,000 largest employers. This revealed that 70 per cent of respondents had developed AIDS policies, that private sector companies were less likely to have a policy than public sector employers, that most policies were developed between 1985 and 1987, and that private companies were less likely to provide information or education about AIDS for employees. All but six of the respondent organizations had at least one known HIV+ employee. But as IRS point out, this high figure should not be used as a basis for generalization, given the low response rate and the expected tendency for non-respondents to be organizations without policies.

The policy approach taken by the UK government has been one of general education about the nature and spread of AIDS. In the context of employment, the Employment Department/Health and Safety Executive's updated booklet *AIDS and the Workplace* (1990) explains the limited chances of contracting the virus through work and recommends that employers provide information about AIDS and HIV to their employees as part of a policy to prevent future difficulties. It suggests a need

> to think through in advance how to deal with any AIDS cases among... staff and how to handle any fears and prejudices that may arise. The most effective way to do this is to have an AIDS policy.
>
> (DOE 1990:6)

Such policies are intended to deal specifically with HIV/AIDS and most contain all, or some, of the features suggested by the Department of Employment (DOE 1990), such as:

- A general statement of the company's commitment to non-discrimination
- Commitment to an employee-education policy
- Affirmation of usual hiring procedures
- Assurance of continued employment
- Equitable benefits
- Guarantee of medical confidentiality
- Access to employee assistance plan.

In practice, however, even policies which appear to share this framework can exhibit significant differences. Analysis of UK company policies by the University of Portsmouth 'Centre for AIDS and Employment Research' (see Adam-Smith *et al.* 1992; Goss *et al.* 1993; Goss 1993; Adam-Smith and Goss 1993) suggests two broad policy approaches: defensive and humanitarian. These different approaches have implications for the nature of welfare responses.

Defensive policy

Although defensive policy has a stated concern to deal fairly with employees who have contracted AIDS, it also embodies an assumption that HIV/AIDS poses a threat to workplace operations. In line with much popular reporting of the disease, this type of policy is couched in terms of a defensive response to the threat of attack, with the emphasis upon protecting the (presently) 'healthy' organization from risk. This is often evidenced in references to the damage which could befall the organization should its managers inadvertently contravene employment laws or generate 'bad publicity'; the implicit emphasis usually being on the consequences of being 'caught out', rather than the ethical nature of the action itself. The following extracts from different policies illustrate this approach:

> To dismiss an individual who is infected or thought to be infected, because of pressure from work colleagues or the client, *may expose us to an unfair dismissal claim, and furthermore to potentially adverse publicity.*
>
> Suspension or dismissal solely on the grounds that an employee has become infected is not considered a *practicable* course of action.
>
> In order to protect our trading position against the risks which can stem from public ignorance and alarm, the PR aspects of individual cases will require careful handling. The prime aim will be to eliminate or at worst minimize publicity in each case. If publicity is unavoidable, the PR department should be asked to advise. (Emphases added.)

This approach to the issue of HIV/AIDS is reflected in the detailed content of much defensive policy. Where statements relating to the treatment of employees with AIDS are made, these are framed in highly conditional terms requiring any action to be assessed against organizational interests, with an implied preference for exclusion where HIV/AIDS is suspected.

For example:

> *in general* the company will not dismiss an employee purely on the basis he/she has become infected.... At this stage medical tests for AIDS are not considered appropriate, unless required by legislation or exceptional commercial contract arrangements.... [Managers] are advised to contact their Personnel department for advice *before contemplating* making a job offer to an AIDS carrier.

> Should an applicant identified at recruitment as being an AIDS victim or virus carrier, discretion will need to be used as to whether the person should be engaged – depending upon the position being sought, general site circumstances or *other sensitivities believed to be likely to have a bearing on the decision.*

> An employee carrying the HIV virus will be considered for any appointment... subject to the same conditions as would apply to any other applicant. The employment prospects of an employee suffering from AIDS are so limited that such a person would not be considered a suitable candidate for promotion... applications from people suffering from AIDS will not be considered since their

work performance and attendance would be adversely affected by their condition as to make them unsuitable for employment.

Following this, defensive policy usually provides for mechanisms of surveillance (ranging from testing to reporting procedures of employee's own or others' health states) designed to identify those with, or suspected of having, HIV/AIDS. As a corollary, considerations of confidentiality and its consequences are given relatively scant regard. Thus:

> In circumstances where it comes to the attention of the unit manager that it is suspected/confirmed that we are employing a potential AIDS suspect, he/she should immediately notify the Operations Manager. The OM should notify his General Manager Operations, who in turn should notify Personnel and the Regional Director. The RG is responsible for notifying the Divisional Operations Director.

> Should it become known to management that an employee is carrying the HIV virus or suffering from AIDS this information will be held in the strictest confidence and will be made known only to such others as need to know... and only with the employee's permission, except where, permission being withheld, Management concludes, after proper consideration of all the circumstances... that disclosure is necessary in the best interests of the employee, other employees, or the Company.

> Should you have any fears arising from the behaviour or state of health of any of your fellow employees, you must immediately discuss the matter with your immediate superior.

In summary, then, defensive policy presents HIV/AIDS as a potentially 'dangerous' problem for the organization, the interests of which are prioritized as the standard against which 'acceptable risk' must be assessed.

Humanitarian policy

The impetus behind the development of humanitarian policy is attributable in no small part to the efforts of AIDS agencies and pressure groups, which have fought to safeguard the rights of people with AIDS. One of the best known policies, frequently held up as a model of good practice, is that of Levi Strauss (Kohl, Miller and Barton 1990). This US policy is wide-ranging and includes rules for dealing with personnel issues, a comprehensive education programme and direct assistance to non-profit agencies dealing with AIDS issues. In the UK, much of the US experience has been used in formulating model policy outlines. One useful summary is provided by the National AIDS Trust:

- The policy must address both HIV and AIDS separately, and the company's response to each should acknowledge they are separate conditions. HIV and

AIDS can be integrated into existing policies, such as those concerning equal opportunities, sickness leave, etc.

- In an integrated policy, mention must be made of HIV and AIDS, to ensure that staff can obtain the information they need on company practice without having to ask specific questions.
- Any policy must clearly state that discrimination, in any aspect of company activity, against anyone who is HIV positive or who has AIDS will not be tolerated.
- The policy should state clearly that AIDS will be treated in the same manner as any other progressive or debilitating illness.
- The policy must contain a clear statement on confidentiality, explaining the way in which confidential information will be treated.
- The policy must make clear, by outlining or referring to discipline and grievance procedures, what action will be taken if staff breach the terms laid down.
- The best model policy will cover areas such as opportunities for redeployment, retraining, flexible working, compassionate leave, etc.. Where possible these should apply not only to those infected with HIV but also to carers.

In many key respects, therefore, policy based on these principles should exhibit a significantly different emphasis from the defensive approach. Again this can be illustrated by reference to UK policies. Consider first the unconditional statements about the treatment of employees with HIV/AIDS:

> There will be no discrimination in recruitment against applicants on the grounds that the applicant has HIV or AIDS. Applicants will not be refused an offer of work because they have AIDS *or* are anti-body positive.

> Applicants who are deemed to be medically fit at the time of recruitment will not be refused an offer of work because they have AIDS *or* HIV infection. Medical fitness will be determined through the usual process of consideration by the Organization's medical advisers.

Likewise regarding exclusion, this policy stance makes disclosure of HIV status a matter for individual discretion and emphasizes the need to avoid unilateral management decisions regarding redeployment (this usually being conditional only upon ability to do the job on medical grounds), placing a heavy emphasis on mutual decision-making and respect for individual wishes:

> The Organization has no right to require an individual to disclose that he or she has AIDS or to submit to medical tests for the virus.

> If it becomes known that an employee has AIDS the organization will ensure that resources are available to provide adequate support and any reasonable arrangements to enable work to be continued, on the grounds that to continue working may enable the person to maintain confidence and social contact and fight AIDS with more dignity.

Thus, where differentiation is necessary on medical grounds, care is taken that this is handled in a way which does not result in unfavourable treatment and which minimizes the risk of stigmatisation. The emphasis is on treating HIV/AIDS as an issue which, in one way or another, involves all employees, requiring positive procedures aimed at encouraging mutual responsibility and support. Indeed, most humanitarian policies acknowledge explicitly the assistance of trade unions and/or AIDS agencies in their construction and implementation.

A final distinguishing feature is the role of training and education. Although there is a reliance on 'information-providing' techniques (which tend to be factual, 'scientific' and didactic) these are often supplemented by forms of education akin to a 'community-oriented' model involving participatory learning and group work around shared experience. One such seminar run by a private sector organization includes the following issues:

> an understanding of epidemics, sexually transmitted diseases, death, dying, grief, drug use, loss, fear, sexuality, homophobia, prejudice, and the politics and economics of AIDS. Often people have negative attitudes about presumed lifestyles and behaviours.

> **Clearly, although there is virtually no risk of contracting HIV through normal work-related activity, the moral and social meanings which attach to this particular disease have important implications for the management of human resources. These implications involve the careful planning of policy levers designed to protect the interests of organizations and individuals – the balancing of which may be extremely difficult** (Banas 1992).

However, despite these challenges the need for development in this area has probably never been greater and there are many benefits to be gained from approaching this issue proactively:

- Prevention of new infections among employees by helping everyone understand how HIV is and is not transmitted.
- Alerting managers and supervisors to the legal issues raised by HIV infection in the workplace. The overwhelming majority of AIDS-related law suits in the US are linked to the workplace and involve discrimination and violation of confidentiality.
- Preventing discrimination by fearful or misinformed employees. Through education, the same employees are equally capable of creating a humane, supportive (and healthy) working environment.
- Preparing managers and supervisors to consider reasonable accommodation requests from people disabled by HIV infection.
- Raising morale and preventing fear and anxiety. Many US companies report positive effects on morale after employee training.

Substance abuse

There are many formal similarities between the issues posed by the abuse of substances such as alcohol and drugs and those posed by HIV/AIDS. As with those affected by HIV/AIDS, the majority of people with alcohol problems, and a considerable proportion of drug users, are in, or looking to be in, employment: according to O'Brien and Dufficy (1988), some 75 per cent of problem drinkers and 25 per cent of problem drug users are employees.

The implications for organizations of individual performance impaired by drink and drug problems are now better understood than those associated with HIV/AIDS. According to O'Brien and Dufficy, there are numerous benefits to be obtained from adopting a systematic approach to the issue:

> For employers it should show results in economic terms. Fewer accidents, less time off from alcohol and drug-related sickness, better relationships, more co-operation, improved judgement and surer decision-making will all pay dividends in the form of greater quantity and quality of production. Costs can be saved by avoiding the need to replace expensively recruited and trained staff, especially in key positions
>
> (O'Brien and Dufficy 1988: 22)

McDonnel and Maynard (1985), in fact, estimated the 'social costs to industry' in the UK at around £1,396 million at 1983 prices. The development of a policy response can, according to Means (1990), take one of two approaches:

1 A disease model driven by considerations of organizational performance: alcohol abuse leads to deteriorating performance, hence the need for a policy emphasizing prevention and treatment.
2 An approach which, while concerned with disease and performance, is influenced strongly by a legalistic rationale which emphasizes notions of legal and social responsibility towards the health and safety of employees in general: poor performance may be an indicator of alcohol abuse, requiring remedy to prevent legal problems and to promote 'social good'.

In many respects, these two approaches relate back to the earlier discussion of 'tough love'. The first approach, while accepting the necessity to remain within health and safety legislation and to provide treatment for the individual, ties this deliberately to performance objectives. In short, 'social responsibility' is strictly contingent upon organizational need. This is illustrated by guidelines to such an approach, cited by Means:

• The company should have a written policy dealing specifically with alcoholism alone – a policy which is known to all employees and which clearly delineates a positive procedure aimed at helping alcoholics to recover
• The company has developed specific procedures in regard to the *handling and referral of employees experiencing job performance problems, and line man-*

agement accomplishes compliance with these procedures as a job responsibility of supervisors at all levels.

- The programme has an effective referral system, ie procedures, qualified alcoholism diagnostic facilities, and personnel with the qualifications necessary to assure that alcoholics will be referred to the appropriate rehabilitative agencies.
- The programme has an effective medical record-keeping system which assures confidentiality to the individual employee, while furnishing evidence of programme effectiveness through reports on numbers of alcoholics identified and successfully motivated to accept treatment. *The data in these reports should permit comparison with results of other operating programmes, so as to obtain meaningful measures of programme effectiveness. These records should provide some acceptable measure of the programme's cost effectiveness.*

(Means 1990:27–8 emphasis added)

Approaches which tie welfare provision tightly to organizational performance objectives, however, make explicit a tension between corporate interests and those of the individual employee, although this is not necessarily an issue of rigid opposition, but rather of psychological and behavioural compliance: assistance can be provided, but only on the organization's terms. The 'discipline' that is sought here is not that of the deferential subordination associated with paternalism, nor of simple legal responsibility; rather it is a self-discipline which demands that the individual recognizes his or her 'failing' in the eyes of the organization and commits him or herself to a change of attitude and behaviour as a condition of continued employment.

This approach can be illustrated by reference to approaches to testing for controlled drugs which are developing in the US. Such testing is mandatory for federal employment and is becoming increasingly common in the private sector, especially among large companies (67 per cent of those with over 5,000 employees are estimated to be using drug tests, according to Brookler (1992)). The basic guidelines for federal testing include the following:

- An employee who tests positive should be referred to the employee assistance programme (EAP).
- If the employee occupies a sensitive position, the individual may be removed immediately from the position; and, at the employer's discretion, may be returned to duty in that position if it is determined that such return wouldn't endanger the safety and security of others.
- The employer may or may not take disciplinary action that could include removal or termination.
- The severity of action taken should depend on the circumstances of each case.

(Brookler 1992:130)

Clearly such guidelines allow a considerable degree of discretion to employers, although accepted 'good practice' suggests that testing positive should not normally result in dismissal on the first 'offence'. It is here that the notion of individual commitment appears to play a crucial role, as one proponent of testing explains:

> We believe in a two-strikes-you're-out approach. On the first positive, put the employee on a two week suspension without pay – you must get the individual's attention. Then refer the individual to the EAP or to a local rehabilitation program for evaluation and treatment. Before returning to work the employee must agree to abstain from drug use, to complete successfully the initial rehabilitation program and all ongoing treatment, and to undergo increased random drug testing. Have the employee sign a contract to this effect with the understanding that missing a single rehabilitation meeting or failing another drug test will mean termination.
>
> (Quoted in Brookler 1992:130)

Although on nothing like the scale practised in the USA, the use of screening for controlled drugs is spreading in the UK, with companies such as Esso, Texaco and, more recently, British Rail being in the forefront.

Stress

According to Cooper (1981), job-generated stress has damaging consequences for both individuals and organizations. It is the recent recognition of this which has placed stress on the agenda as an issue with implications for business strategy and human resource policy. The effects of stress are experienced in a number of ways:

- **Absenteeism**   Stress can account for significant levels of absenteeism, short-term absence being particularly prevalent in occupations with high levels of emotional and physical strain (e.g nursing). In this respect, absence may represent either a simple need temporarily to 'escape' from stressful situations, or be the direct result of stress-induced illness.
- **Turnover**   Stress is also thought to influence levels of turnover, quitting being a permanent means of 'escape'. Given that many high-stress occupations often involve considerable training, the costs of turnover in terms of replacement and retraining will be significant. Notwithstanding such training requirements, many stressful jobs are also relatively poorly paid, a fact which may exacerbate the turnover problem.
- **Health**   The link between stress and various health disorders (such as heart disease and mental illness) is now well established (around 111 million days lost from work in Britain in 1985 – with no reason to think this will have declined in subsequent years; although days lost from all illness declined over this period, that attributable to stress-related conditions increased for both men and women).
- **Litigation**   Although not a significant issue in the UK, there are numerous cases of US workers successfully suing their employer for damages resulting from work-induced stress. A US government report pointed to the growth in claims relating to 'gradual mental stress' resulting from 'cumulative emotional

problems stemming mainly from adverse psychosocial conditions at work', these accounting for some 11 per cent of all occupational disease claims.

- **Productivity** The link between stress and productivity is not a straightforward one. As stated in the 'Yerkes-Dodson law', there is a tendency initially for performance to rise as pressure (the sum total of demands) on a person increases, until an optimum level is reached. However, if pressure continues to rise beyond that level, performance shows a rapid decrease.

Often the sources of work-related stress are crucially linked to the nature of the work process itself (Smith *et al.* 1982), as shown in Figure 7.1.

To counter these problems, Arroba and James (1990) suggest the development of an organizational stress management programme involving four (normally) sequential stages intended to provide a manageable and methodical technique through which the 'pressure' level within the organization can be kept at an optimum level, thereby contributing to enhanced performance. Thus, there is the following progression:

1 Raising awareness of stress problems
2 Individual training to cope with stress
3 Provision of specialist skills (e.g., dedicated stress counselling services)
4 Stress audit (sources of stress within the organization are identified and changes implemented to reduce these to acceptable levels).

COUNSELLING

A common feature of all the welfare policy approaches outlined above is their reliance, to a greater or lesser extent, upon some form of counselling provision (IDS 1992b:1). The issues covered by counselling schemes vary and, in addition to matters related to stress and health, can also cover financial worries, bereavement, legal problems, and, in particular, redundancy. In the recessional climate of the early 1990s, the latter appears to have shown a particular increase. In broad terms there are two forms of counselling which are offered to employees being made redundant:

1 Support (or welfare) counselling
2 Outplacement counselling.

Support counselling is often made available not only to those being made redundant, but also to employees left behind and, significantly, to managers who have to make redundancy decisions. The usual function is to allow employees (and/or ex-employees) to 'talk-through' their feelings and experiences with experienced counsellors and not to affect in any way the personnel decision about the need for redundancy. In addition, counsellors may be trained to provide redundant employees with information about the benefits to which they are entitled and with advice about coping with the pressures and problems of unemployment. In some cases this may extend to more detailed financial advice and guidance.

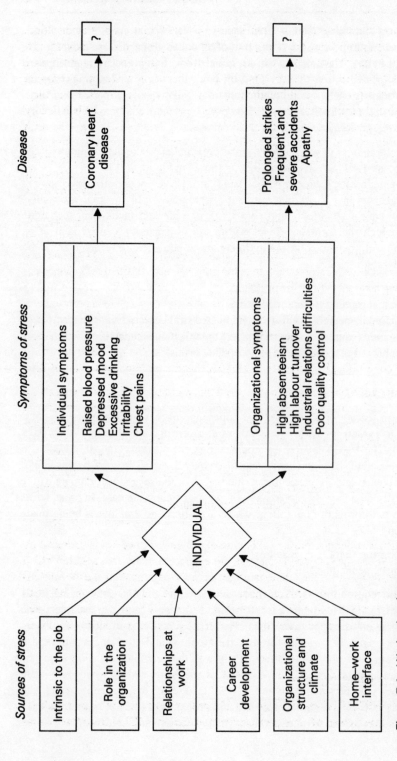

Figure 7.1 Work-related stress
(*Source*: Smith *et al.* 1982)

Outplacement counselling is significantly different from support counselling. Here the emphasis is upon providing redundant employees with the resources and skills to get themselves back into the job market. Traditionally regarded as a management or executive perk, outplacement services are now becoming common further down organizations, although the quality of the service provided may vary. It seems that at senior management level outplacement is likely to be handled by external consultants (of which there are now many hundreds in the UK, with business estimated to be worth £50 million – perhaps a case of 'an ill wind...'?) and may also involve the organization providing facilities such as office space, telephone, secretarial support and library resources. At lower levels, counselling is more likely to be provided in-house and to involve group sessions covering basic skills such as writing a CV, interview technique and presentation skills.

A recent assessment of outplacement provision in the UK (Crofts 1992) is interestingly subtitled 'A way of never having to say you're sorry', pointing to the role of counselling as a process through which individual 'worries' or problems are put into a context which, in effect, tries to neutralize any destructive or damaging potential they may have for the organization. Indeed, the significance attached to this practice as a means of bridging actual or potential gaps between personal and organizational lives is reflected in the title of a recent book aimed at practitioners: *One-to-one management: counselling to improve job performance* (Sidney and Phillips 1991). These authors explain one of the rationales for the provision of company counselling by reference to Mayo's Hawthorne initiatives of the 1930s:

> One outcome of the [Hawthorne] experiments was the setting up of a counselling service staffed by external consultants offering an opportunity for confidential discussion of personal concerns. The service was introduced in the belief that an individual's worries, from whatever source they arose, were likely to impede his or her work performance and could often be alleviated by counselling. Perhaps the strongest evidence of its effectiveness in reducing stress was provided by the unions, whose officials came to object that employees receiving counselling lost their commitment to union causes!
>
> (Sidney and Phillips 1991: V)

A very different interpretation of this type of employer 'concern' is provided by Grenier (1988 – see Chapter 8). Indeed, the expansion of welfare policies which emphasize the nature of the relationship between the organization and the individual employee points towards a wider debate about the tendency of HRM to individualize the employment relationship, a debate which has focused most explicitly on industrial relations, the role of trade unions and collective organization.

KEY LEARNING POINTS

- **Within HRM thinking the role of welfare has not received as much attention as other areas, often due to a concern to distance HRM from traditional** personnel management which has often been caricatured as having a 'welfarist' orientation and lacking a 'real' business focus.

- This dismissive view of welfare is usually a response to the nature of many traditional approaches to welfare provision – legalistic–reactive, corporate conscience, company paternalism – which have limited the potential to connect with wider organizational issues.
- From the perspective of 'tough love', welfare is about the provision of benefits and services which employees want and value and which simultaneously link strategically with the needs of the organization by enhancing performance.
- The welfare agenda for HRM in the 1990s is likely to focus on the following issues: health promotion; alcohol and drug abuse; stress; and counselling.
- Proponents claim that initiatives in all these areas can have direct benefits to the organization in terms of cost savings and performance enhancement. Others point to the potential of HRM-inspired welfare policies to 'individualize' workforces and undermine workplace trade unionism.

EXERCISES

1   Consider the following:

In many respects the HRM approach to welfare which defines employee 'problems' in terms of individual commitment to the organization sits uneasily with the culture of universal welfare provision by the State (and trade unions) common in much of western Europe where treatment of illness (including substance abuse) is regarded as a largely unconditional and secular 'right' rather than as part of an individual's obligation to an employer. Under these conditions it is more likely that employees will view the treatment of illness as something which is essentially between them and the State, impinging upon work behaviour only in terms of the provisions of sick leave and job protection. Thus any attempt by an employer to impose conditions on extra-work behaviour regarded as the provenance of State health treatment is more likely to be regarded as an infringement of rights than a legitimate organizational concern.

Will HRM approaches to welfare ever take root in societies with well-developed welfare systems?

2   Consider the moral, ethical and practical issues involved in the following account:

The oil company Texaco has a policy of random drug testing for all employees and routinely tests job applicants. The managing director, Roger Colomb confirmed that a number of applicants had tested positive and were rejected. As for confidentiality of test results, Mr Colomb said it was highly unlikely that information would be passed to police, unless evidence of a drugs ring emerged.

What if an employee was a recreational user of cannabis who tested positively and did not agree that he or she had a drugs problem? 'We treat cannabis as a controlled substance. They would have failed the test.'

It is this attitude which provokes John Marsden of the charity Turning Point, to accuse employers of using screening as an agent of social control.... 'Testing is defensible when it is post-event or post-accident, but I become troubled when it's beginning to be used for all employees. It's an invasive technique.'

(Sharrock 1992)

Chapter 8

Trade unions and the New Industrial Relations

THE NEW INDUSTRIAL RELATIONS

There has been considerable speculation *conjecture* about the emergence of a 'New Industrial Relations' (NIR) in which management has seized the initiative to change working practices and unions have become less confrontational, more flexible, more accommodating to 'local' conditions, and generally more 'realistic'. According to Beardwell (1992), debates about the NIR have taken two forms: those which emphasize the 'adaptation' of established industrial relations practices; and those which associate it with the emergence of 'new' developments in HRM. The latter position will be discussed in detail below. For the present, attention will be focused on the former. From this perspective, NIR is about making the existing system work in a slightly different way 'so that persistent problems with union job control, bargained wage systems and managerial workplace authority are mitigated or overcome', in line with the general restructuring of industries and economies (Beardwell 1992:1).

> **Thus, the key issues for unions have been the substantive ones of responding to declining membership and rising unemployment, a hostile political and legal environment, and a more assertive management, while attempting to retain a credible role at workplace level.**

Trade union adaptation

One of the major challenges facing the trade union movement in the 1980s and 1990s has been the steady erosion of membership. This decline, after the steady growth of the 1960s and 1970s, has reflected the drastic contraction of manufacturing employment, with the loss of highly concentrated pockets of membership, and the greater 'acceptability' of unemployment and job instability (both of which make unionization difficult). Where employment growth has taken place, it has often been in industrial sectors with weak traditions of unionization (e.g., services) and among groups of employees with a low propensity to join unions (e.g., women part-time workers). In summary then, it is generally agreed that the 1980s have confronted [the British trade union movement] with the most serious and sustained difficulties it has experienced since the 1920s. Union membership peaked at almost 13.3 million in 1979 and has fallen each year since then. In 1990 it stood at approximately 9.9 million, about 25 per cent below the 1979 level. Trade union density... declined in the process from its peak level of 55.4 per cent in 1979 to 40 per cent in 1990. The number of trade union members affiliated to the TUC fell even more sharply than total membership; affiliated membership at the end of 1990 was 8.2 million compared to 12.1 million in 1979, a decline of over 30 per cent.

(Marsh and Cox 1992:3)

Coupled to this membership crisis, however, has been more than a decade of legislation aimed specifically at restricting the power of trade unions. The Thatcher government rose to power in 1979 on, among other things, a wave of public disaffection with trade union power as exercised in the so-called 'winter of discontent'. The free-market philosophy of this government dictated that restrictions on product and labour markets be kept to a minimum and, on the grounds of curbing a growing abuse of power, identified the unions as a key target for 'reform'. The concern, according to the government, was to limit the excessive power of the unions politically and industrially and to return the 'right to manage' to employers, a view which was expressed with characteristic candour by (then) government minister Norman Tebbit: 'I use the word "neuter" because I've been told I must not use the vernacular when describing what I'm doing to the unions'.

In practice, this programme of 'reform' was spearheaded by a succession of pieces of legislation aimed at restricting the control which unions could exercise in the industrial arena, and introducing greater measures to ensure accountability to members. This legislation included, among many other measures, the following changes to trade union activity:

- Greater protection was given to workers who were sacked or victimized for non-membership of a trade union under a closed-shop agreement and to workers refusing to join a union on grounds of conscience or deeply held personal conviction.
- Protection was given to pickets only when picketing at their own place of work (not at or near a place of work, as before). A code of practice on picketing limited the number of pickets to six at any entrance.
- Secondary industrial action was limited to situations where there was a contractual relationship between the employers concerned and the purpose of the action was related to the trade dispute (i. e., not solidarity).
- The definition of a trade dispute was made more restrictive, referring to that between workers and *their* employer (previously employers *and* workers); and relating *wholly or mainly* (previously *connected with*) to one or more specific matters (i.e., terms and conditions, engagement or termination, allocation of duties, discipline, negotiation, etc.).
- Industrial action, including strikes and such things as overtime bans or work-

ing-to-rule, were to require a prior ballot. This should be secret, involve marking a paper, and be conducted by post.

It was against this backdrop of unprecedented challenge that NIR was worked out. Reduced membership, legal restraint, and economic uncertainty among employed members markedly reduced the bargaining power of unions *vis-à-vis* employers, conditions which simultaneously enhanced the power of managements to pursue wide-ranging change with or without union agreement.

In this unfriendly environment NIR can be seen as an attempt by the unions to retain that power and control which they still held in organizations by adapting to and/or accommodating the assertiveness of an increasingly self-confident management.

Two particularly noteworthy manifestations of this so-called 'new agenda' are single union agreements (i.e., where one union rather than a multiplicity, is given sole negotiating rights for employees or groups of employees within an organization) and no-strike deals.

Much of the debate among trade unions surrounding the establishment of single union agreements (SUAs) in the 1980s tended to focus on two sets of issues. The first is an issue of principle which asserts that a SUA binds a union too closely to the interests of a single organization (or plant) and encourages the emergence of so-called 'company unionism' whereby the wider issues of 'solidarity' and 'social justice' are submerged beneath an inward-looking local instrumentalism. This charge was repeatedly levelled against (and hotly denied by) the electricians' union EETPU which, in the 1980s, was thought by many in the union movement to have sold out' the principles of independence by being too accommodating towards management initiatives (contributing to its expulsion from the TUC in 1988).

The second issue was more practical and related to disputes over membership 'poaching' resulting from the derecognition of 'non-selected' unions, although this is an area now covered by TUC guidelines on membership transfers. Overall, however, the inter-union hostility surrounding the EETPU's public approval of this type of initiative tended to disguise the fact that SUAs were neither wholly new nor restricted to any particular union. In fact, throughout the 1980s such agreements were entered into, more or less willingly, by all the major unions, often on terms little different from those agreed by EETPU. Indeed, there is now a clear tendency for managements to resist 'first time recognition' except to a single union (Marsh and Cox 1992:21) and in this respect it is a situation with which unions appear to be coming to terms.

The other focus of the NIR debate has been that of 'no-strike agreements' (often, but not necessarily, associated with SUAs). These somewhat misleadingly named policies are usually based on pendulum arbitration' (or 'final offer arbitration' as it is sometimes called) as a mechanism for resolving (pay) disputes without recourse to strike action. Pendulum arbitration involves an independent arbitrator making a choice between the last offer of the company and the last claim of the union, with no option for a compromise solution. During this process it is agreed that there should be no concurrent industrial action (IDS 1988a:1). However, as the commitment to refrain from industrial action is normally morally rather than legally binding, there is no guarantee that no-strike agreements will always result in no strikes, either before, during or after the arbitration process (Wickens 1987:153). Thus, in reality, this type of agreement is better viewed as a mechanism intended to make industrial action unnecessary rather than impossible. The claimed benefits of this type of deal are that it makes both parties adopt a more 'realistic' stance in relation to bargaining: no side is going to be outlandish in its demands, as this will make more likely the prospect of the arbitrator deciding against them. On the validity of this point, however, opinion on both management and union sides is divided. Although favoured by several UK-based Japanese companies, other employers have rejected it, apparently in the belief that binding arbitration weakens managerial prerogative (Burrows 1986:56). On the union side, the EETPU has led the way in establishing such agreements, arguing that among other things they are 'recession-proof', capable of delivering good agreements even when bargaining power is weak. Other unions though, have resisted any mention of no-strike deals on the grounds that they smack of 'sweetheart deals' and represent a betrayal of a fundamental principle of independent unionism: the power to withdraw labour.

Thus, in relation to the practical responses which trade unions have adopted under these conditions, Lucio and Weston (1992) point to at least three possible patterns.

1 Concessionary and conciliatory union responses

These are seen as stemming from a mixture of managerial pressure associated with emerging high technology industries established on greenfield sites and the hostile political and legislative climate ushered in by the Thatcher administration. As such this resulted in a 'strategy of embracing much of these managerially led developments, and... negotiating agreements such as single union deals and no-strike agreements (often with pendulum arbitration) which conceded much of the autonomy of trade union influence with respect to worker representation *vis-à-vis* management'. This approach, frequently referred to as 'new realism' is also characterized as 'market unionism' on account of the tendency to perceive the union as providing a 'service' or package of services which must be 'sold' both to members and to management (Lucio and Weston 1992:219).

2 Institutional strategies and the extension of collective bargaining

This is an approach which Lucio and Weston associate with the GMB's 'New Agenda' policy. It too can involve single union deals and no-strike agreements, but treats these in a more proactive way:

At the heart of the New Agenda is the intention of extending the scope of collective bargaining into such areas as training, careers and recruitment issues... the GMB's approach envisages bargaining and the union's role being extended into areas such as the quality of production – 'talking to Britain's employers about how to achieve quality performance, cost and price competitiveness and a fairer society.' – and the company's preparation for the Single European Market – 'to ensure that their company is prepared for what lies ahead'... GMB's approach ultimately differs from that of market unionism through its emphasis on the social objectives of trade unionism, manifested in the approach to, and use of, collective bargaining.

(Lucio and Weston 1992:222).

3 Independent workplace strategies

These are responses facilitated by the decentralized structure of the unions involved, and appear similar to what Beaumont (1992) refers to as 'decentralized policy with national union guidelines' which can be characterized thus:

1   British unions are concerned about HRM developments as potentially undermining union organization and collective bargaining arrangements;
2   product and labour market circumstances will inevitably lead some employers to favour such initiatives;
3   the case for membership involvement (or not) must be made at the individual organizational level on a situation-by-situation basis;
4   hopefully local level negotiators will be wary about such involvement through the inclusion of safeguards and the obtaining of certain quid pro quos.

(Beaumont 1992:123–4)

There would seem to be little doubt that the developments in the so-called NIR which have taken place are attributable in no small part to the environmental conditions which faced the trade union movement in the 1980s: recession leading to loss of membership and reduced bargaining power, the latter exacerbated by government policy designed to limit the scope for industrial action. Less clear cut, however, is the specific contribution of HRM policy and practice to this process of change.

The impact of HRM

There are those who argue that a personnel regime informed by HRM ideas does not sit comfortably with active and independent trade unionism and may be used, in some cases, explicitly to undermine existing union membership and prevent new unionization. Grenier's (1988) study of Johnson and Johnson's new Albuquerque plant (Ethicon) in the USA, for example, details what he claims to be the use of HRM techniques as a tool for 'union-busting':

> My data strongly suggests that Ethicon-Albuquerque, as a self-proclaimed enlightened employer using the latest [HRM] approach to dealing with the workforce, victimized workers who did not accept the anti-union position of the corporation... rather than being used as a method to increase worker control over the working environment, the production team, a quality circle derivative, was used by management to increase its control over workers' attitudes and behaviour during an anti-union campaign... this was done consciously and deliberately, with the realization that the team had great potential, under the expert guidance of the social psychologist, to be an effective union-busting tool.
>
> (Grenier 1988:158)

This suspicion is reflected in the comments of the general secretary of Britain's largest general union, quoted by Lucio and Weston:

> a new era of crafty Rambo managers has come into existence which seek to ignore or deliberately disrupt union organization and collective bargaining procedures, by bringing in their own schemes based on fake committees and centred on the individual worker, not the organized worker, with the aim of undermining established working practices and bargaining methods.
>
> (Lucio and Weston 1992:215)

The evidence to support the widespread use of HRM techniques and policy levers as a means of deliberately attacking unionization is not strong, although there are a handful of cases where the 'phasing out' of collective bargaining and the derecognition of trade unions do appear to have been linked to policies of a HRM nature. The chemical company Tioxide, for instance, negotiated out trade union recognition in exchange for enhanced pension arrangements and harmonized conditions as part of a drive to gain 'unfettered flexibility'. The Unipart company adopted a more autocratic approach:

> employees and unions were informed of the company's decision to end recognition in the context of a wholesale programme of change – teamworking and the elimination of supervision, staff-status, skill-based pay, etc. The unions were simply told that the company saw 'no role in the business for third parties who do not have the same level of commitment' and were given six months' notice that the company would no longer negotiate or consult.
>
> (IDS 1993b)

In general, however, the relationship between non-union companies and HRM in the UK is more complex and variable. McLoughlin and Gourlay (1992), for instance, report the findings of a study of high technology firms in the South East which found evidence of HRM approaches existing in both unionized and non-union settings. In the former cases there were examples of unions having been apparently weakened by this, but also of them having been strengthened. Equally, they were unable to demonstrate that non-unionism was the product of a 'HRM-derived sophisticated "substitution" strategy designed to obviate a perceived need for union representation on the part of employees'(1992:685). It seemed as likely that non-unionism was the result of 'straightforward avoidance', opportunism, and a low propensity to join unions on the part of the particular workforces (which were largely white-collar, technical and professional, resident in an area with, at the time of the study, many alternative employment opportunities).

Thus, although the consolidation of HRM may well pose a challenge to unionization, this may be less of a frontal assault than a process of *ad hoc* attrition. This is summed up by Guest (1989):

> Since HRM seeks to produce a positive working climate, it need not appear overtly anti-union. However, it poses a threat in three ways. Firstly, in organizations where unions are already established HRM goals are likely to be pursued through policies that tend to by-pass the union. For example, management is likely to prefer its own channels of communication, to foster individualised forms of incentive and reward schemes, and to control socialisation of new recruits very carefully. Secondly, by practising high-quality management, the need for the union as a protective device against arbitrary management behaviour is likely to be reduced. The industrial relations system will still be used to negotiate annual wages, but if a policy of paying above-average rates is pursued, individualised incentive schemes are increasingly operating and longer-term pay deals are concluded, even this central trade union role may be diminished. The risk is that after a while the union will gradually wither and die. The third threat arises in non-union plants and at new sites where HRM policies should obviate any felt need for a union.
>
> (Guest 1989:44)

It would be a mistake, therefore, to view HRM as necessarily a part of a conspiratorial strategy on the part of management to control and manipulate workers against their collective interests.

One of the most robust assertions of this view is to be found in Storey's (1992) analysis of large 'mainstream' UK organizations. These companies, he argues, have established 'dual arrangements' whereby new HRM initiatives run in parallel with existing union institutions and procedures. Storey supports his conclusions with data relating to four key questions:

1   The stance taken by managements towards trade unions in terms of recognition and representation
2   The role of collective bargaining
3   The extent to which unions are treated as 'partners' in the change management process
4   The impact of new initiatives in the area of communication and participation.

Recognition

In Storey's case companies there were few examples of outright attacks on union recognition. Where this had occurred it had been directed at particular groups of employees, usually in managerial grades. The introduction of individual contracts for certain managers at British Rail, for instance, was accompanied by a withdrawal of collective negotiation from these groups (see also Pendleton 1992). In only one case was there a definite plan to withdraw all recognition for all employees, this being in an organization where levels of unionization were low and the unions relatively weak (Storey 1992:245–6). The general response to unions appeared to be the adoption of a more aggressive stance on the part of management but without any real plan to displace them. Thus, union–management relations tended to be conflictual, with management being happy to let this state of affairs stand, and to keep pressure on unions by wresting control from shop stewards' committees. Storey, however, is reluctant to view this aggressive stance as directly linked to new 'alternative' HRM measures, pointing to the separation in many of the companies between managers dealing with industrial relations and those responsible for the HRM initiatives, and to the pressures emanating from highly competitive product markets which would have existed with or without HRM (1992:247).

Collective bargaining

In this area Storey reports widespread moves to decentralize collective bargaining, both to take more account of local labour market conditions and to fit with the development of profit centres. In some cases this appeared to have undermined the ability of union representatives to identify and act on behalf of clear constituencies, a fact coupled to a general move away from detailed productivity bargaining and towards a wider span of initiatives extending beyond traditional pay bargaining concerns (1992:250).

Change partners

Here too, Storey provides details of union leaders being 'sidelined'. This he attributes to the fact that major change initiatives were generally formulated outside the industrial relations (IR) and personnel function. The case of Austin Rover is illustrative:

> In consequence, by the time this branch of management [i.e., IR/personnel] got a hold on the change package its shape was pretty well settled. As personnel were still widely regarded as the chief mediators with the unions, this inevitably meant late involvement by the unions.
>
> (Storey 1992:251)

In other cases, however, some attempts had been made by management to involve unions. In the case of Ford, for example, a range of change measures were initiated but were never 'tied together and presented as a coherent package with which to frighten or impress the unions', thereby allowing the unions to take each proposal in turn without feeling 'embroiled by an overarching plan':

> Furthermore, the company for its part saw an advantage in getting the unions on board for most if not all of these changes. Hence, it invested time in building and maintaining constructive relations with the unions. This did not mean of course that it did not drive hard bargains on the separate issues, but it did mean that the unions perceived at least that they were faced by a company ready to do business with them – now and in the future.
>
> (Storey 1992:252)

The overall picture of partnership painted by Storey is one of ambivalence and contradiction both in terms of management and unions and, frequently, between union representatives in different units and local and national leaders.

New HRM initiatives

Storey argues that measures relating to selection, appraisal, direct communication, task level participation, training, performance-related pay and culture change campaigns have, in general, had an adverse impact upon unions. The comments of one respondent, a personnel/IR specialist at Plessey Naval Systems, are significant:

> If I look at my list of priorities now and compare them with the list I would have had say, five years ago, there is a significant difference which is observable. Now, I am tasked with installing a sophisticated and modern system of communications so that we can get the message across to all our employees. I'm into management development in a big way and I'm monitoring change across the board – not just in this company but in others here and abroad. To be perfectly frank with you, the trade unions just do not figure in this list of priorities. But if I go back just a few years... then the situation could be reversed. In fact, then and for a period extending way back, because I was dealing so much with trade union issues, I had little time for anything else. We, like many other managers at the time were caught in the situation of simply reacting to their agenda. Today, we set the agenda and it is very different to the one we used to dance to.
>
> (1992: 256)

As Storey points out, however, the extent of this adverse impact should not be exaggerated. It seems to have been primarily in the areas of communication and job-level involvement, with relatively little impact in areas of pay review, which seemed to have been little affected, still leading, periodically, to outbreaks of industrial action. Nevertheless, there was a feeling among some managers that the new HRM techniques were leading to a greater measure of patience by shopfloor-workers, even in relation to pay.

Taking these four points together, Storey's conclusions point not towards a full frontal attack upon trade unionism within the case companies but, rather, a situation of 'general neglect' in which the existence of 'alternative' HRM practices plays a relatively minor and somewhat indirect part:

> the new neglect of trade unions and industrial relations was a studied neglect. It carried a symbolic message: managers are in the driving seat, unions and industrial relations have to be demonstrated as relatively secondary and incidental to meeting market priorities, and secondary to the newly discovered alternative ways of managing the labour (human) resource.... It seems likely that even without the new initiatives, trade unions would have experienced a hard time during this period. But the existence – or promise – of an 'alternative' (from a managerial viewpoint) rendered the situation rather more precarious. The marginalisation of the unions took on a greater significance than it might otherwise have been seen to carry.
>
> (1992:261)

An additional factor in this apparent decline in the centrality of trade unionism is often claimed to be the moderating influence of 'popular aspirations' on the part of 'rank and file' employees towards a new mood of realism. This has been widely hailed by the political right as an ideological shift on the part of employees towards a more unitarist view of employment relations. Such claims, however, require careful qualification, for although workers may decide that unionization is not in their interests, and may resist or ignore attempts by unions to organize their workplaces, this does not necessarily mean that they have been 'duped' by managerial cunning (a common view on the left), nor that their hearts and minds have been won by new HRM practices and ideas (as the right maintains). On the contrary, workers may conclude for essentially pragmatic reasons that non-unionism is in their interests, without developing any strong psychological attachment to managerial philosophy or any innate hostility to unionism (see Goss 1988; 1991: ch. 4).

This type of 'calculative' response is described in Dickson et al.'s (1988) account of IBM's manufacturing plant in Scotland. IBM, according to Dickson, has traditionally been a non-union employer.

> The company does not recognise trade unions as official negotiating bodies in its British plants. The company, however, argues that they are not proselytisers with regard to their attitudes on trade unionism. Their view is that they are a non-union rather than an anti-union firm; they consider that, *given their particular set-up*, for instance, their management policies, selection procedures and training schemes, IBM functions more efficiently to the benefit of all employees than it would if there were recognised trade unions.... The last attempt to secure the recognition of unions in the main IBM manufacturing facility in Scotland... in the latter part of the 1970s, resulted in an ACAS-organised referendum of the plant's employees and a vote *of over 90 per cent* against the proposal.
>
> (Dickson et al. 1988: 507; emphasis in original)

To explain this situation, Dickson *et al.* point to the structuring of employment relations in such a way as to discourage the formulation of complaints on a collective basis and to emphasize the individual relationship between the employee and the company. This includes the process where each employee 'negotiates' his or her annual pay rise with his or her immediate manager, and the avoidance of a belief in a rigid wage rate for a particular job. Coupled to this is a policy of easy and immediate access to each employee's direct manager and an 'open door' policy whereby a complaint can be taken to a higher manager if the immediate manager is not felt to have dealt with it satisfactorily. There are also measures aimed at encouraging identification with the company, including above-average wages and conditions, its (then) commitment to life-time employment, and the strong emphasis on personal development, internal promotion and retraining. Finally, there are collective forums such as quality circles and a plant Advisory Council (the latter consisting of elected delegates) which, although not having formal decision-making powers, allow the tackling of problems and the airing of grievances which cannot easily be handled by the individualized mechanisms.

Additionally this account explores the views of employees working under this system, revealing that the majority of workers responded positively to these individualized conditions and felt that under them, trade union representation was unnecessary. Indeed, many appeared to view the IBM system favourably in the light of their previous experiences in highly unionized workplaces, where they felt work practices were overly rigid, and dispute-ridden. In coming to these positive conclusions, Dickson *et al.* make clear that their respondents were neither naively manipulated nor unaware of the company's individualizing strategy but, in the light of their previous experiences, regarded it as a better system. However, these attitudes were tied strongly to the HRM policies of IBM rather than to any absolute sense of moral individualism or ideological opposition to the principal of trade unionism. Thus:

> The responses of the IBM workers suggest that it is dangerous to assume a simple relationship between one kind of individualism and the wider behaviour and attitudes of individuals. For example, despite the responses about unions... and the company's attempt to create an environment in which trade unionism is seen as unnecessary, our respondents displayed no generalised antipathy towards trade unions. On the contrary, during the detailed interviews a number of people went out of their way to stress their support for the *principle* of trade unionism.
>
> (Dickson *et al.* 1988:518)

Not even such a pragmatic rejection of trade unionism means that HRM could ever banish unions for good. It seems likely that complex forces are in play and that if HRM does not 'deliver the goods' a return to unionization is a distinct possibility. In short, workers' commitment to 'playing the HRM game' may often be calculative/instrumental (see Chapter 6) rather than absolute and, in this respect, any observed relationship between non-unionism and HRM can easily be both over-stated and, where it does exist, contingent rather than necessary.

It must be remembered, therefore, that for HRM the attachment to individualism is seldom absolute. However, where there is a strong notion of the collective within HRM thinking, it is an organic notion, the locus of which is the organization. Thus, activity which demonstrates or expresses commitment to the organization as a collective enterprise is encouraged, whereas that which challenges or fractures this unity is treated as pathological.

In this respect, 'traditional' trade union activity, based upon the assumed conflict of interests of employers and employees, and calling for loyalty and commitment to an extra-organizational body, will sit uneasily with strong notions of HRM. But it is not collectivism *per se* which is problematic, only those forms which are perceived to be anti-organizational. As such, collective forums such as works councils or company advisory committees can be supported (as can a trade unionism which accepts the primacy of the employee's bond to the organization, an understanding which is implicit in some SUAs).

Advisory boards and company councils

Advisory boards or company councils, according to Oliver and Wilkinson (1992), can exhibit significant differences from the Joint Consultative Committees (JCC) of traditional unionized plants. First, the elected employee membership of the advisory board is not restricted to union shop stewards and is chosen by all employees, rather than just union members (in some cases, however, advisory boards may reserve some places for union representatives). Second, advisory boards, unlike JCCs, are frequently not confined to dealing with issues of a non-collective bargaining nature and may be involved in discussion, and sometimes 'negotiation', of pay and conditions. Because advisory boards are formally inde-pendent of trade unions they are not restricted to workplaces where unions are recognized; indeed, in many instances they can be intended to serve as a substitute for, or alternative to, union representation for the collective workforce. According to an IDS Study (1989a), for instance, such councils are generally found in three types of company:

- those with a tradition of non-unionism
- Japanese-owned organizations with single union agreements
- unionized companies where they are part of a change in employee relations.

Non-union companies

In these companies, the rationale behind company councils is the belief that they 'fill a union gap', allowing the company to run more smoothly by giving employees a collective voice. In some of the cases studied by IDS (1989a) this approach was chosen in the context of a claimed lack of 'unionateness' amongst employees, while in others it was adopted to forestall the threat of unionization (instances were found of companies in this position subsequently rejecting union requests for recognition).

Japanese companies with SUAs

Advisory Councils have usually been established in these companies as part of moves to a 'new industrial relations' regime (see above). At Toshiba Consumer Products, for instance, the Advisory Board was established as part of the single union agreement with EETPU and serves as 'the sole forum for the discussion of collective issues, including pay and conditions'. In an interesting reversal of the traditional company–union stance, this agreement commits union representatives to supporting the resolution of all collective issues at the advisory board, and defines the union's role as being that of representing individual workers in, for example, disciplinary or grievance procedures (IDS 1989a:23).

Changing employee relations

Companies affected by major change situations, such as restructuring, relocation, take-overs and substantial technological development, often under crisis conditions, have tended to develop company councils as part of a major realignment of traditional industrial relations practices. In some of the cases covered by IDS (1989a), for example, councils were set up in the context of establishing single union deals; in others they were established in the wake of full derecognition.

In terms of impact both upon employees and unions, the effect of company councils appears variable. Garrahan and Stewart (1992), for instance, present a critical perspective on both the operation and effects of the Company Council at Nissan's Sunderland plant, quoting the words of one employee:

> The Company Council! That is a complete shambles that thing – it always just gives you the company line. You just get what the company wants – the odd bit of change here and there maybe
>
> (Garrahan and Stewart 1992:92–3)

However, Dickson et al.'s (1988) account of employees' responses to the Advisory Council at IBM's Greenock plant, while apparently characterizing it primarily as a 'talking shop', are more positive:

> I think that although we've got good management in here, management decisions should always be questioned and that, in my view, is the object of the Advisory Council. They're really there to question management decisions. And I think, as long as you're questioning management they'll maybe have a rethink

about a decision they've made and in certain instances, they'll change it. Maybe not change them at all, but then they'll give a fuller explanation about why they made that decision. And if the explanation seems okay, then that should be acceptable.

(Dickson *et al.* 1988:516)

Although these types of measure cannot be regarded as completely undermining the role of trade unions, it is easy to understand why even their limited success represents a concern to many trade unionists. Garrahan and Stewart, for instance, represent the single union agreement between Nissan UK and the AEU as a deliberate attempt by the company to emasculate the power of the union within the plant, not by direct challenge, but by the more subtle process of incorporation:

Nissan can say with all honesty and with hands on heart that it is in favour of the union (on its terms) and that Nissan wants individuals to join one. But arguably the union has no authentic role to play in any aspect of organizational life.... It is accurate to say the union does not play a significant part in what goes on at Nissan presently because it has no really independent role... the union itself is not even allowed to communicate with workers about recruitment.... It was hardly any surprise that union membership levels were low, since the AEU retained virtually no negotiating powers... such powers as the AEU might have are secondary to the role of the Company Council which is the real forum for 'involvement'. Half the members of the Company Council are management nominees, therefore the role of the union is dependent on patronage by the company. There is little sense in which an independent union operates within Nissan. The Company Council delivers participation without power, whilst the union achieves recognition but is marginalised from participation in procedures. The AEU has largely subordinated itself to the company's philosophy.

(Garrahan and Stewart 1992:68–9)

It seems, therefore, that HRM presents trade unions with a dilemma. On the one hand, where management is seeking to establish a flexible and highly committed workforce, the organization, through a variety of HRM policies (e.g., reward policy, communication, welfare, training and development, etc.) may effectively 'compete' with independent trade unions for the role of guardian of employee interests. To survive under these conditions, unions may be forced to develop closer and more co-operative links with companies, at the risk of losing their status as independent third parties. On the other hand, rejecting the legitimacy of this type of HRM approach places unions in a position where they may have to deal mainly with a growing number of employers concerned solely with cost-minimization and unambiguously opposed to any form of collective representation for employees (Purcell 1993).

The choice, then, may be that of embracing a new approach to organizational industrial relations and becoming incorporated into the

HRM project, even seeking its extension as a means of retaining a union presence, or risking being excluded from HRM initiatives and facing even more difficult battles for recognition with employers committed to low-wage 'secondary sector' employment regimes.

KEY LEARNING POINTS

- The emergence of the NIR, although having occurred at the same time as the rise of HRM, does not imply a definite causal connection. Indeed, it seems likely that the factors which have stimulated NIR have had more to do with the effects of recession and party politics than those of managerial initiative in the field of HRM. The growth in the number of non-union companies is not necessarily a barometer for the spread of HRM: often such situations arise from a concern with cost-cutting, pragmatism and opportunity, rather than strategic positioning.
- It can be suggested that the ease with which many managements have been able to introduce and experiment with HRM-inspired policy levers was greatly facilitated by the relative weakness of trade unions during the 1980s. In this respect, however, the relationship is probably contingent rather than necessary.
- HRM is not necessarily incompatible with all forms of collective workforce organization, although it is more comfortable with measures which link this as closely as possible to organizational interests, hence the preference for 'internal' company councils or, failing this, single union agreements.
- The rejection of trade union membership by workers in companies where HRM is predominant does not mean that there has been a fundamental and irreversible shift in employee opinion against the principle of independent unionism.

EXERCISES

1 Although HRM practices such as performance pay, individual development, participation, etc., can deliver the goods while the economic situation is buoyant, they may be less viable in times of recession. When pay cuts or stand-stills are involved, and redundancy and cut-backs are frequent, will there be a return to the union fold in a search for protection in the face of HRM practices which leave employees more exposed to the effects of economic down-turn?

2 Garrahan and Stewart (1992:69; see page 153 above) cite the following letter regarding union membership sent to employees by Nissan management:

> As you will know the level of union membership is lower than originally anticipated – although it is now growing. We enjoy excellent relationships within Nissan and these are greatly assisted by the formal Agreement we

have with the AEU which we know is committed to the success of both the Company and the staff. AEU representatives greatly support the Company, particularly in many external forums. We genuinely believe that with this joint commitment to success there are considerable advantages to everyone if the membership level increases. Direct benefits to employees include: 1. there may be many times when you need representation; 2. the union offers legal representation free of charge; 3. the union can provide a whole range of advice to your Company Council negotiators; 4. it can provide a comprehensive financial package arranged in conjunction with the Midland Bank; 5. the AEU has set up a Nissan branch which means you can have direct control of your affairs.

We attach a membership application form and would ask that you complete this and return it to the Personnel Department who will attend to the formalities. Please remember that the long-term success of the Company, employees and the Union are tied together and we would urge your assistance to make this a three-way success.

How close can union–company relations get before they become vulnerable to the charge of being 'sweetheart' or 'company unions'?

Chapter 9

Equal opportunities

Challenge and change

EQUAL OPPORTUNITIES: HUMAN CAPITAL AND SOCIAL JUSTICE

There are two ways in which equal opportunities issues are located within the HRM debate. The first relates to concerns about human capital: where opportunities to develop and progress are 'artificially' blocked for any particular group, this will result in the sub-optimal use of human resources; hence, it is economically rational to ensure that all those who have ability also have the opportunity to exercise it on behalf of the organization.

From this perspective, equal opportunities is a purely practical matter of outcomes that need not be concerned with the nature or origins of inequalities; what is important is the resource value of the employee, not their social status.

Clearly there will be an affinity between this perspective and the 'instrumental' approach to HRM identified in Chapter 1.

The second link between HRM and equal opportunities, in contrast, emphasizes the importance of social justice.

In this respect, equal opportunities is primarily a moral or ethical project that focuses on the processes giving rise to inequalities and seeks to address these in a qualitative sense, not by reducing social difference to a common economic currency, but by promoting its acceptance and understanding.

Thus, promoting equal opportunities is first and foremost a social duty for an employer, although economic benefits may subsequently flow from this. Here, then, the affinity is more with humanistic traditions of HRM.

While these approaches are not mutually exclusive, there is, nevertheless, a clear tension between them. The human capital perspective is essentially amoral and may, therefore, fluctuate in its commitment to equal opportunities in line with economic expediency. During the recessional climate of early 1993, for example, members of the CBI's employment policy committee are reported to have been circulated with a confidential paper arguing that rising unemployment had reduced the need for employers to concern themselves with supporting equal opportunities (which does not imply that such a paper represented official CBI policy). Such a fluctuating commitment does not sit easily with the social justice perspective, which is 'principled' in its stance on equal opportunities. Given this potential for tension between approaches to equal opportunities, its appearance as an issue within HRM frameworks is likely to be variable, depending, on the one hand, on the nature of management commitment and, on the other, on the ability of under-represented groups to influence employment policy. One way of describing the ways in which equal opportunities may appear as 'agendas' for HRM is shown in Figure 9.1. Both axes reflect the aforementioned balance of forces and represent the extent to which equal opportunities concerns are integrated into organizational practice. Thus, where an instrumental approach to HRM predominates, the commitment to equal opportunities is likely to be 'shallow' (i.e., capable of being adopted or abandoned, in line with legal or economic expediency) and 'narrow' (i.e., restricted only to those measures required by law or demanded by short-term labour market conditions). Where humanistic HRM predominates, in contrast, the tendency is likely to be towards a 'deep' commitment based upon principle and a 'wide' coverage beyond minimum legal requirements.

		Commitment	
		Shallow	*Deep*
Focus	*Broad*	Token agenda	Long agenda
	Narrow	Short agenda	Focused agenda

Figure 9.1   Equal opportunities agendas

The key distinction is that between the long and short agendas, the others being, in effect, variants of these. Thus, the 'token agenda' covers inequalities other than those specified in employment legislation, but treats these in a generally superficial way which owes more to public relations and short-term economic pressure than to a commitment to fundamental change. In this respect its approach, while broad, is essentially the same as the short agenda. Similarly, the 'focused agenda' approaches equal opportunities with the same concern for real change as the long agenda, but concentrates attention on a limited range of issues.

The short agenda

The short agenda is concerned merely with those policy measures which are necessary to ensure compliance with legal requirements (although where economic expediency becomes an issue, e.g., a shortage of 'conventional' employees, this may translate into a 'token' agenda to relieve immediate labour requirements). It is, thus, a static response concerned with protecting organizational interests (or those of certain organization members) rather than contributing to social change through positive action. In this respect it can be seen principally as a response to the following equal opportunities legislation:

- Race Relations Act 1976
- Equal Pay Act 1970 (amended 1983)
- Sex Discrimination Acts 1975 and 1986
- Disabled Persons Acts 1944 and 1958.

Both the Race Relations Act and the Sex Discrimination Act outlaw direct and indirect discrimination: direct discrimination takes place when a person is treated differently from others simply because of their race, colour, ethnic origins or sex; indirect discrimination occurs when people are treated the same, but conditions are applied to a job such that a considerably smaller proportion of women than men, or one racial group than another, can comply with the requirements (e.g., requiring applicants to be at least six feet tall will indirectly discriminate against women). Such conditions are allowed only if they can be shown to be a genuine occupational requirement.

The Disabled Persons Act puts employers of twenty or more people under a duty to employ as a proportion of their workforce 3 per cent of registered disabled people. Although it is not an offence to be below quota, it is an offence to employ a person who is not registered disabled while below quota unless a permit has been obtained from an office of the Secretary of State. Prosecutions under this law are extremely rare and it seems that many employers are either unaware of its existence or are prepared to ignore it.

The long agenda

Despite the prevalence of short agenda approaches, it is possible to identify in some areas, especially the public sector and larger businesses, the development of what may be the beginnings of a 'long agenda' (Cockburn 1991). The basis of the long agenda is an approach to equal opportunities which is both broad in its coverage and geared towards positive action to equalize employment opportunities. This sort of approach is characterized by Coussey and Jackson:

Achieving equality of opportunity essentially means changing how we do things, how we behave and how one's organization looks. It means that more women, ethnic minority and disabled applicants and employees will be given the same chances to take part, progress and succeed as white males. The basic premise is that talent and ability is evenly spread throughout all groups and between men and women. However, women and ethnic minorities are unevenly distributed in employment and concentrated in lower grade jobs because of the effects of past and present discriminatory practices, and of social and educational disadvantages. People with a disability are also most likely to be found in lower level jobs and this is unlikely to be entirely because of limited capacity. The long term of an equal opportunity programme is to remove any barriers which prevent these groups fully taking part in an organization, and thereby achieve a random distribution; that is, a workforce which fully reflects the population at all levels.

(Coussey and Jackson 1991:4)

In terms of coverage, therefore, the long agenda is likely to include not only inequalities based on sex, race (and derivatives of these, such as nationality and marital status) and disability but also those associated with, for example, age and sexual orientation. Similarly, the approach to these issues is not one of 'equal chance' but of (at least) 'equal share'. The distinction between 'equal chance', 'equal share' and the intermediate notion of 'equal access' is elaborated by Straw (1989) in terms of 'levels' of equal opportunities provision:

- **Equal chance**   This means that everyone has the same chance. In a society where opportunities are not legally regulated according to social status, this condition obviously applies. However, although all citizens may be formally the same, this does not mean that some will not encounter informal barriers (lawful or unlawful) which, because of some characteristic such as sex or race, prevent them from taking their equal chance. For example, it has been suggested that some organizations disregard job applications from people who have addresses in areas known to be inhabited by ethnic minorities.
- **Equal access**   Here, equal chance operates effectively to the extent that under-represented groups are not prevented from gaining access to employment at the first hurdle. The question now is, 'Access to what?' Are formerly under-represented groups locked into low-status or 'backstage' jobs and, if so, is this because they are not given the chance to progress higher in the organization?
- **Equal share**   According to Straw (1989:64–5) this is 'the ideal... not only is access and representation gained, but there is representation at every level. Account is taken of the history of particular groups, and particular measures taken to provide opportunities previously not available.... The only criteria against which people discriminate are lawful, justifiable and necessary'.

Thus, organizations aiming at 'equal share' provision will require policies going beyond those necessary merely to comply with legal responsibilities. The most widely recognized approach in this area is that of 'positive action'. At the outset it is important to be clear that positive action is not the same as positive discrimination. In the latter, steps are taken to ensure that predetermined 'quotas' of under-represented groups are present in specified organizational positions; meeting these quotas may (if all else fails) mean appointing members of such groups on the basis of their social status rather than their ability *per se*. (With the exception of Northern Ireland, where employers are legally required by the Fair Employment (NI) Act 1989 to take 'affirmative action' to remedy workforce imbalances between Protestants and Catholics, such positive discrimination is unlawful in the UK.) Positive action, in contrast, does not involve meeting quotas by positive discrimination at the appointment stage; rather it aims to provide members of under-represented groups with the skills/credentials necessary to reach the selection-pool and to be able, once there, to compete equally on merit alone. In short, it is a pre-selection device intended to level the playing field (not tilt it in favour of the under-represented). In this way, positive action programmes can have goals for the representation levels of certain groups, but these have to be met by fair competition rather than 'favouritism'. In broad terms, positive action covers four areas:

1　Policy and practice
2　Behaviour and attitude
3　Training and development
4　Positive provision.

Two of these areas, training and resource provision, address the needs of under-represented groups directly (e.g., by ensuring they have the skills the organization requires, and providing the resources necessary to enable full participation). The other areas focus on the behaviour of 'dominant' groups and on organizational practice (e.g., discouraging prejudicial or intimidatory behaviour; and ensuring that policies are neither directly nor indirectly discriminatory).

POLICY AND PRACTICE

The normal basis for the development of equal opportunities is a corporate policy. Such policies generally include a mission statement setting out the organization's commitment to furthering equal opportunities and specify, in varying degrees of detail, what action the organization will take to further this objective. The following example from Leicester City Council is illustrative:

• The City Council is committed to: (i) positive action to promote equality of opportunity in employment; and (ii) regular, comprehensive monitoring of the results of this commitment.
• All employees and applicants for employment will be given equal opportunity in recruitment, in training and in promotion to more senior jobs, irrespective of their racial origins, sex, disability, marital status, religious beliefs, social background or sexual orientation.
• All other policies and practices associated with the Council's role as an employer must be applied with strict observance of the equal opportunity policy and philosophy....

- Employees are expected to behave in a non-racist and non-sexist way towards both the public and fellow employees. Any breach of the policy may result in the disciplinary procedure being invoked. Where circumstances are appropriate disciplinary action, up to, and including dismissal may result.

(Cited in Coussey and Jackson 1991:18–19)

It is commonly recommended that policies should make only statements that are realistic and sustainable (thereby retaining credibility) and that they should be supported by clear procedures, training and awareness education. One means of furthering equal opportunities policy has been by the appointment of a specialist manager/officer. Barclays Bank, for instance, has an Equal Opportunities Manager within its central personnel section whose job includes implementing policies and initiating any necessary changes, co-ordinating equal opportunities training, and liaising with outside bodies to exchange ideas and promote the extension of good practice (IDS 1987:21). British Telecom, on the other hand, provides a network of Equal Opportunities Advisors to promote its policy. Clearly the option of a dedicated post will be more feasible within large organizations, although where equal opportunities is a fundamental component of organizational strategy it may also be important for smaller organizations. In particular, it may be crucial to the success of such posts for holders to keep in touch with personnel managers at operational/unit level. Research by Collinson (1991), for example, suggests that where personnel managers at local level have been appointed without proper professional training (usually from line management positions – 'poachers turned game-keepers', in his terms), there may be a tendency for them to ignore or undermine equal opportunities policy in the interests of local short-term financial expediency, regardless of corporate level intentions. This may lead to a situation where corporate intentions to develop a long agenda are thwarted at ground level as the 'practical agenda' is progressively and pragmatically shortened.

Another key component of the policy process is evaluation and monitoring. In practice this is the linchpin upon which equal opportunities initiatives will pivot and without which such a policy can easily be marginalized; where effective data is not available, no effective remedial action can be planned. As with most other forms of social research, equal opportunities monitoring involves three sets of decisions:

1 Conceptualization
2 Sampling
3 Timing.

Conceptualization

This covers the definition of under-represented groups on the one hand, and the definition of organizational positions and processes on the other. It is severely limiting, for instance, to have detailed breakdowns of a workforce's ethnic origins if these cannot be related to organizational position or, more importantly, to career development patterns. In this respect, the design of any monitoring instrument needs to be compatible with longitudinal analysis (e.g., tracking cohorts over time). Within the definition process, consideration needs to be given to the relevance and necessity of the information requested. The collection of data on ethnicity, for example, is often treated with suspicion and even hostility, usually on the grounds that it is an invasion of privacy, that (in a supposedly multi-cultural society) it is irrelevant, or that it will lead either to positive or negative discrimination. Similarly, sensitivity is necessary in the definition of categories (e.g., in the case of ethnicity it is important to be clear that ethnic origin is not a matter of nationality, right of abode or place of birth (Fowler 1991:23)), as is the need to be sure that all the data collected can be fully justified in positive equal opportunity terms (see Coussey and Jackson 1991:38).

Sampling

Sampling decisions involve choices between a census (all employees/potential employees of the organization), a random sample, or a non-random sample on the one hand, and between self-administered questionnaires or manager/supervisor reporting. The advantages of each approach are summarized in Table 9.1.

A further concern in this area is how to deal with non-response. Although this can be dealt with statistically, it may be appropriate, especially in the cases of censuses or non-random samples, to take steps to minimize non-response as far as

Table 9.1 Monitoring equal opportunities

	Manager reporting	Self-classification
Advantages	• Quick and cheap to administer • High response rate • Encourages managerial responsibility for success • Encourages managerial understanding of EO issues	• Seen as more open • Self-definition is more acceptable to most people • Involves all staff directly in the exercise
Disadvantages	• May be seen as being less open • May be less accurate (especially in relation to ethnicity) • Managers may be reluctant to get involved	• Can be costly and time-consuming • May result in low levels of response

Source: Adapted from Cousey and Jackson (1991:40–1)

possible. This will usually involve some form of 'follow-up', as was the case, for example, in the case of Austin Rover:

> Employees who did not carry out the exercise [a self-administered questionnaire sent to their home] were then sent a reminder, and if this failed to elicit a response, the line manager and union representative encouraged completion. Failing this, in the case of white-collar workers only, the manager and representative completed the form on the employee's behalf.
>
> (IDS 1987:18)

Timing

This concerns the points at which the monitoring process is undertaken. In general, all new recruits will be subject to monitoring, but there are various options for existing employees. One important source of information will be exit interviews for leavers, although this may involve a separate methodology from initial monitoring; additionally it may be desirable to monitor internal 'movement' after promotion rounds or performance reviews. In this respect, there is clearly a need for equal opportunities monitoring procedures to be tightly coupled with other human resource processes such as appraisal, career breaks and development activity.

Pervading each of the areas above are two further concerns which need to be addressed in the monitoring process:

1   The 'politics' of evaluation (see Chapter 4)
2   Research ethics.

Politics

Any form of research or monitoring has a political dimension. The findings have the potential to 'expose' individual and organizational failings and, as such, may be perceived by some as being threatening or dangerous. This problem can be alleviated (although never removed) by securing clear 'ground rules' for the exercise, open communication about its purpose, and commitment to its success from all key organizational stake-holders (e.g., under-represented groups, top managers, and union representatives).

Ethical issues

These concern not only the accuracy and integrity of the data collected, but also the use to which this is put and the way in which questions of confidentiality and openness surrounding the data are handled. It may be desirable, for example, to give individual employees details of all equal opportunities monitoring information which is held about them and how this will be used. Alternatively, this sort of explanatory information may be given as part of the introduction to the monitoring process.

BEHAVIOUR AND ATTITUDE

It is usually accepted that to get an equal opportunities culture established within an organization, it is not sufficient to rely on policy exhortations or the threat of disciplinary action in cases of unacceptable behaviour. These steps need to be complemented by awareness training to change (rather than merely suppress) 'hostile' attitudes towards under-represented groups wherever possible.

As defined by Straw (1989:86), such training 'aims to make one set of people aware of the needs and abilities of another set of people'. She goes on to add that 'Awareness training... can have a secondary function: to enable a particular group to understand the basis of their own conditioning and actions and, if necessary, to attempt to redress them'. These issues can be addressed through the examples of disability and sexual harassment, respectively.

IDS (1992d), for example, point to the growth of 'disability equality training' provided for managers and those responsible for recruitment and interviewing:

The aim of disability equality training is to make non-disabled people more aware of the practical, social and political issues surrounding disability and to help free them of traditional, negative and discriminatory thinking. It encourages participants to examine how it is not necessarily an individual's physical impairments, but attitude and environment which cause barriers to ability.

(IDS 1992d:3)

In the case of disability, there is good evidence to suggest that such training is widely needed. A study to measure the level of discrimination against people with physical disabilities in France (Ravaud, Madiot and Ville 1992) based on success in obtaining a favourable employer response from an unsolicited job application (controlled for both disability and level of qualification), showed that highly qualified able-bodied applicants were 1.78 times more likely to receive a favourable response than their disabled counterparts, and modestly qualified able-bodied applicants 3.2 times more likely to receive a favourable response. Similar findings are reported for the UK by Barnes:

a recent survey of the employment policies of 26 Health Authorities found that a third discriminated against disabled job-seekers. Employers claimed they could not meet the criteria necessary for work in the health service. These criteria included: lifting of patients and general heavy work; the need for a professional qualification or 'a range of physical and intellectual skills'; and the need for staff to be medically and/or scientifically trained 'in addition to having all their faculties'.

(Barnes 1992:57)

Barnes, however, is sceptical of the extent to which isolated workplace initiatives of the sort outlined by IDS (1992d) above, can change the institutionalized discrimination against disabled people and advocates instead a societal programme of social rights and a strengthening and enforcing of the employment quota scheme as the only effective way of producing meaningful change. Indeed, there is an important distinction to be made between 'awareness' and actually taking action that results in positive outcomes for disabled employees. In particular, this may mean that the very design of jobs has to be considered: rather than looking for jobs that a disabled person can do now, it might be necessary to ask 'Which jobs could we restructure – by team working maybe – to make it feasible for a person with this or that disability to do them?' (Cockburn 1991:206). Such an approach calls for far more commitment than simply providing 'token' or 'dead-end' jobs often in 'backstage' areas, that confirm rather than challenge disability.

This recognition of the need for extra-organizational direction is reflected in initiatives to combat sexual harassment. Thus, in 1991 the European Commission adopted a recommendation for the protection of the dignity of men and women at work, incorporating a code of practice on sexual harassment which has served as a basis for a code published by the Department of Employment in 1992. The definition of sexual harassment in this code is as follows:

[Sexual harassment can be defined as] conduct of a sexual nature, or other conduct based on sex affecting the dignity of women and men at work, including conduct of superiors and colleagues, if

(a) such conduct is unwanted, unreasonable and offensive to the recipient;
(b) a person's rejection of or submission to such conduct... is used explicitly or implicitly as a basis for a decision which affects that person's access to vocational training, access to employment, continued employment, promotion, salary or any other employment decisions; and/or
(c) such conduct creates an intimidating, hostile or humiliating work environment for the recipient.

(Cited in Coussey and Jackson 1991: 171–2)

Although the public profile of sexual harassment tends to reflect media interest in 'sensational' incidents, there is now a growing body of evidence to suggest that it is a pervasive and persistent feature of work experience for many employees, most of them women.

A 1991 survey of temporary workers used by the Alfred Marks employment agency, for instance, reported 61 per cent of respondents as having been subjected to some form of sexual harassment by a member of the opposite sex, and a further 10 per cent by someone of the same sex (the most common pattern being harassment of a younger woman by an older man of the same or more senior status;

one-third of respondents said they were harassed by their immediate boss). Fifty-four per cent of this sample felt that this harassment was a very serious or quite serious problem. An NOP survey of the same year found that 66 per cent of women agreed or strongly agreed that sexual harassment was now a big problem for working women (IDS 1992e:2). In 1993 the results of a Home Office study of sexual harassment in the police force were revealed. Based on responses from 1,800 policewomen, this showed that one in ten had considered leaving the service because of sexual harassment; six per cent had experienced serious sexual assaults and 30 per cent had been pinched or touched; 'nearly all policewomen experienced some form of sexual harassment from policemen' (Campbell 1993)

In terms of organizational responses to sexual harassment, a study of 132 employers (IRS 1992e) revealed that:

- 55 per cent of respondents said that cases of sexual harassment had been reported amongst their employees; 46 per cent had cases reported in the previous twelve months.
- Almost 90 per cent of employers reported that sexual harassment was a disciplinary offence.
- Of those cases reported to an employer, almost 90 per cent were claimed to be upheld.
- Where cases were upheld, formal warnings or disciplinary action against the harasser were used by 57 per cent of employers; 48 per cent mentioned dismissal as an outcome; informal warnings were reported by 40 per cent.

The distinction which these findings indicate between formal and informal means of dealing with cases of sexual harassment reflects a wider debate concerning the nature of harassment and the most effective means of dealing with it. Thus, those who favour an informal approach as a first step argue that this is more likely to encourage the victim to report the offence and has more chance of providing a means to change the harasser's behaviour. A formal procedure, it is claimed, discourages reporting because it requires what will usually be an embarrassing or emotionally difficult issue to be made public. There are, in addition, several reported cases of reprisals having been made against people who make formal harassment complaints (Campbell 1993). By taking the mechanism for dealing with harassment out of the 'formal' reporting chain, for example by establishing a specialist counsellor or designated manager outside the line relationship and guaranteeing confidentiality, harassed employees may feel more confident to complain. In some cases this approach may primarily be concerned with providing the victim with support and advice, with no direct contact with the harasser; in others, however, complaints through this mechanism may lead to an informal confrontation with the harasser by the counsellor or manager. The rationale for this is the belief that most (male) harassers do not understand that their behaviour is offensive. Under these conditions, it is suggested, an informal approach may be the most effective remedy.

While this may be a pragmatic solution, it does depend on a high level of commitment from the organization to ensure that informality does not become an apology for sexist/racist behaviour, or an encouragement for management to avoid tackling what they may regard as a 'sensitive' issue. Cockburn makes this point forcefully in her case studies of the practice of equal opportunity policy:

[In the retail and service industry cases] there were more instances where women's claims were considered unsubstantiated or 'over-reactive'. There was a noticeable preference for dealing with sexual harassment informally, hushing things up, 'having a talk with the fellow' and warning him that 'he's making a fool of himself'. The preferred treatment was to move the man quietly to some new office where he can 'make a fresh start'.... Many individual men, of course, respect women and behave courteously towards them. Such men are often pained by other men's obscenities and 'pranks'.... It is almost unthinkable, however, among men, to take issue directly and personally with other men's sexist behaviour.... Women too, though they think they are standing up to abuse, seldom do more than fall silent, turn their back or respond with mild sarcasm. Men who are habitually sexist very often get away with it unchallenged.

(Cockburn 1991:146–7)

Cockburn's (1991) argument points out that sexual harassment is not only about sexuality but also about power, in particular men's attempts to exert power over women, and that this 'gender power' is inherent in organizational hierarchies (see also Hearn and Parkin 1987).

Such an understanding broadens the notion of sexual harassment away from the narrow view that it is 'simply' about sexual desire (Kremer and Marks 1992) towards the realization that such harassment may be directed at individuals because of 'what they are'; an attempt to reassert in the workplace relations of social superiority and inferiority characteristic of wider society.

Such a broadening of the harassment issue extends its coverage more clearly to both racism and homophobia, a recognition which in the USA has led to the emergence of awareness programmes targeted at the 'promotion of diversity' and the control of 'hatred' in the workplace (Solomon 1992). There is a growing move in this field to devise organizational responses that go beyond simply policy prescriptions and, additionally, directly confront the attitudes of employees towards diversity, using 'focus groups' (which bring together members of different social groups), for instance, as vehicles through which people can discuss and reflect upon their own 'areas of bias and ignorance, and then build empathy'.

TRAINING AND DEVELOPMENT

If awareness training is targeted primarily at 'dominant' organizational groups, an equally important aspect of positive equal opportunity initiatives focuses on the members of under-represented groups themselves. The rationale for this type of programme is explained by Coussey and Jackson in relation to gender:

> Known as the 'glass ceiling', it appears that organizational cultures at the top of the pyramid, the effect of stereotyped attitudes about who 'fits' at senior level and the consequences of domestic pressures on women mean that senior levels are overwhelmingly white and male.... One major reason for this is the tendency for us all to select people who look and think like us. But if more women... had the skills, experience and confidence to compete equally, this would begin to change decision-making.
>
> (Coussey and Jackson 1991:123)

This can also, of course, apply to members of ethnic minorities. Dyer reports a report into racial discrimination in the Bar law school:

> whites have a far better chance of passing the one-year course and qualifying as barristers. The analysis [conducted by Birkbeck College, University of London]... found that blacks had a failure rate of 45 per cent, compared with 16 per cent for whites.... the disparity in failure rates is very unlikely to be due to systematic differences in academic potential.... The [Society of Black Lawyers] claims that the [Bar] council's use of practising barristers to assess students' videotaped performance in advocacy, conferencing and negotiation skills allows enormous scope for individual bias. The report found that ethnic minority students were up to five times as likely as whites to fail their advocacy assessment.
>
> (Dyer 1992:4)

One means of attacking this tendency is through the use of 'accelerated development programmes' which are designed to meet the needs of under-represented groups. An instance of this type of training is provided to ethnic minorities in BR as a device to enable them to compete effectively in tests to become train drivers. For example:

> In early 1991 several ethnic minority guards at Paddington Station took British Rail to an industrial tribunal, alleging that the selection process for train drivers discriminated against applicants from ethnic minorities.... BR agreed to... make the selection process fairer. One element of this was a workshop with the Paddington guards to explore their test-taking behaviour. It became apparent that they were not test-wise. As a result, BR commissioned an open-learning pack which the guards could work on in their own time before retaking the test.... The pack gave advice and tips on how to develop successful test-taking behaviour.... The result? Five of the seven guards passed the tests and have gone forward for training.
>
> (Wood and Baron 1992:35)

Possibly a more common form of positive action training is the development of 'women only' management courses. These are generally used when an organization identifies an imbalance in its managerial profile and in the take-up of management development opportunities. This situation is likely to constitute a vicious circle, whereby women see few other women in management and become resigned to accepting their current position or, when they do attend management development courses, find they are usually in a very small minority and feel that their needs and experiences are 'submerged' by those of male participants, thereby discouraging further development. In this respect, single sex courses may be the only way of breaking this circle.

POSITIVE PROVISION

Although there are many men who care for dependants – either children or parents – this role is overwhelmingly taken by women. In consequence the domestic responsibilities which women continue to shoulder have a direct impact on their employment experiences. In particular, this has been claimed to contribute to the high proportion of part-time women workers in the UK: because of poor state and employer provision for dependant care and the non-availability of flexible working and career patterns in many employment areas, women are forced into areas where part-time work is available, usually in low skill and low wage jobs. According to figures cited by Weston:

> The UK... comes second after Luxembourg in the league table of the widest earnings differentials between men and women. In 1990 women received 69 per cent of the male gross hourly earnings for manual workers and 55 per cent of the gross monthly earnings for male non-manual workers. Yet the UK has the second highest female participation in the workforce, after Denmark, 52 per cent compared with 61 per cent and against an EC average of 42 per cent. In 1990 the UK had nearly a third of the total female part-time workforce in the EC – five of the 15 million – putting the UK top of the league when it comes to the number of part-timers – and 86 per cent of part-timers are women.... Although the UK has the second highest proportion of women in the banking, insurance and finance sector (48 per cent), females in the non-manual occupations in the sector earn only 53 per cent of men's pay.
>
> (Weston 1992:2)

Similarly, it is argued that women are disadvantaged in many senior and professional careers where continuity of service has traditionally been the norm. According to Gillian Shepherd (Employment Secretary in 1992): 'The simple fact is that in many professions and at many levels women are not taking a fair share of the opportunities available. There are no-go areas, occupations which are automatically assumed to be the province of men, and there are areas where women make up the majority of the workforce but are segregated at the bottom' (cited in Milne 1992:4)

However, during the mid-1980s it was widely predicted that economic growth, coupled with demographic and social change, would make women 'returners' the principal source of available labour. As employers faced a recruitment shortage they would, it was claimed, attempt to attract women by offering improved dependant-care provisions (IDS 1990f) and more effective options to integrate childbearing with career development, such as career-break schemes. But although the issue of workplace nurseries in particular attracted attention, there is little evidence to suggest that any but a minority of employers rushed to establish these, and the onset of recession in 1990 effectively removed the economic 'push' which had motivated most employers in this direction. Thus, a 1992 survey of 175 private-sector companies found that only 4 per cent had crèche facilities, 4 per cent provided childcare vouchers or an allowance, and only 1 per cent had taken part in a holiday play scheme (Allan Jones and Associates 1992). In general, it seems that employers' contributions to childcare provision are extremely limited: based on the 1991 General Household Survey, workplace nurseries represent only 1 per cent of all pre-school childcare arrangements made by parents, and workplace facilities only 1 per cent of childcare arrangements during school holidays (IDS 1993:4). This situation, coupled to one of the lowest levels of state provisions of pre-school childcare in Europe, is held to contribute significantly to the fact that in the UK less than one-third of women with children under five are in employment compared with well over half in France, Belgium and Denmark, although it has been estimated that around 1 million women not in employment would enter if adequate childcare was available (Newell 1992:37). Similarly, it has been found that over half of women returning to work after childbirth return to work in a different occupational category from that which they held before childbirth, 37 per cent going into an occupational category well below that of their last job (Newell 1992:38; see also Dale 1987).

A common response to this situation has been to advocate that employers adopt more flexible employment policies and career programmes that accept the reality of most women's 'dual responsibilities', both in terms of 'social justice' (it is unfair that social pressures upon women should disadvantage them in the workplace) and 'human capital' (women employees possess necessary and often expensively acquired skills and it is economically unsound for employers to let these decay because of lack of suitable working arrangements) (Vaughan and Lasky 1991).

Structured career-break provision is now more common in large organizations, most notably in the public sector, but it is still rare in small and medium-sized companies, and even where it does exist there can be considerable differences in the interpretation of what a 'career break' will involve – for example:

• Guaranteed return to work after several years' absence but on condition that contact (either training, updating or part-time work) has been maintained with the employer.
• Guaranteed return to work on a part-time or job-share basis at the same level as before, or the opportunity of working from home (see Chapter 2).
• Extended maternity leave beyond the statutory allowance and return at the same level as before.

• Re-recruitment after absence depending on the availability of a suitable vacancy, but no guarantee that it will be at the same level as before.

(Hobsons 1992:9)

Developments in job-sharing are seen as another means of allowing access to higher level jobs in particular, on a less than full-time basis: 'it involves dividing one established full-time post between two (or possibly more) people. Each sharer does a proportion of the work... which can be divided by specific duties or areas of responsibility, or merely apportioned as time' (IDS 1987:10). Both job-sharing and career breaks have met with resistance in some quarters on the grounds that they disrupt the acquisition of experience which needs to be continuous in more senior positions. Such arguments have been heavily criticized as both sexist and myopic:

The hitherto unquestioned assumption that senior positions can only be held on a full-time basis has been shown for the nonsense it always was. For many years there has been little, if any, questioning of men being able to sit effectively on boards, commissions and tribunals in combination with their main jobs. Why should different criteria be applied to women, the champion time and task jugglers?... Parenthood is often seen as the only reason for employees to take a career break. This is nonsense. There are secondments to take courses, or to undertake a short-term task, being laid off temporarily and lengthy sick leave.

(Hobsons 1992: 8–10)

Hakim (1991), however, suggests that such provision may not necessarily make a significant impact on the tendency for women returners to take casual or low-paid 'secondary sector' part-time jobs. She questions the assumptions made by many commentators that either most women really would want full-time work in preference to part-time if it were available, or that most women exhibit an orientation to work essentially similar to that of men – albeit commonly frustrated – and are thus dissatisfied with part-time work. Her conclusions from a detailed study of survey research are as follows:

The paradox of women's high satisfaction with comparatively poor jobs can be explained by their having different life-goals from men. Most women's preference has been for the home-maker role, with paid employment regarded as a secondary activity, to be fitted in as and when homemaker activities allow it. Only a one-third minority of women dispute... [the] explanation for enduring job segregation and the continued sex differential in earnings: that 'most' married women seek less demanding jobs and invest less in paid work, due to the competing priority of their family responsibilities. The key questions are how many is 'most',? and is that percentage changing? The evidence is that less than half of adult women give priority to their workplans, compared with a two-thirds majority of adult men.... Women who have chosen a homemaker career often have some paid work as well, but their job preferences emphasise

convenience factors over the high pay and security of employment conventionally valued by men.

(Hakim 1991: 131)

Hakim's 'radical' suggestion is that it is no longer sustainable to treat women in
the labour market as a homogeneous group, but, rather, to recognize that they
comprise at least two qualitatively different groups: one is composed of women
who have chosen to adopt a work commitment similar to that of men, leading to
long-term workplans and usually continuous full-time work, often in higher status
jobs; the other group includes women with little or no commitment to paid work
and a clear preference for the homemaker role, for whom paid employment is a
secondary activity often in low-skilled, low-paid, part-time jobs. Although Hakim
points out that there is no firm boundary line between these two groups and that
women may often cross between groups at different times in their lives, she also
argues that many women do make a firm choice between these 'careers' before
entry into the labour market. Thus, Hakim's position is that it is unsatisfactory to
explain the persistence of job-segregation by gender simply in terms of constraints
upon women; there must be a recognition that women are 'active' in this process
and can and do make choices regarding career and employment. This leads her to
the following conclusion:

> policy measures to facilitate women's return to work after childbearing, such as
> improved childcare services, could well result in an increase in job segregation
> and sex differentials in earnings rather than the reverse, because their main effect
> is to increase the labour force participation of secondary workers with little or
> no work commitment and an insignificant investment in paid employment.

(Hakim 1991:115)

There may be some evidence, however, that the dominance of the homemaker role
may be changing. A survey of 1,011 women aged 16–70 has reported that 'Getting
on in a job' was more important than having children for nearly 80 per cent of
women aged under 35, that 76 per cent of mothers of working age said they wanted
to get on in their jobs or get a job, but 40 per cent were doubtful of achieving their
career goals. Thirty-two per cent of working women said their job was very
satisfying but less than half were satisfied with their career prospects. Nearly
three-quarters of the women wanted more education and many felt under-appreci-
ated and under-used at work, 49 per cent saying managers were not interested in
their careers, and a third of those aged 35–44 believing they had skills which were
not being used (Bunting 1992:7; cf. Newell 1992:38).

Hakim's position can certainly be criticized for minimizing the significance of
institutionalized sexism both in terms of sex role stereotyping and within the
education system (Cockburn 1985) whereby the 'choices' which women are
asserted freely to enter into may, in fact, be severely constrained by gender role
conditioning (as Hakim does in fact admit, women's choices may be greatly
affected by the attitudes and interests of men, in particular of husbands). Similarly,

even if the notion of the paid employee/homemaker roles is accepted, this does little to explain the discrimination and harassment faced by many women seeking to further their career development. As Kennedy reports:

> Women in management are still seen by their male peers as not quite up to the job, according to a survey of 1,500 women and 800 men in industry, which found old prejudices firmly entrenched. The survey concludes that the 'old boy network' operates as strongly as ever to keep women in their place, and that having children and maintaining a management career are still incompatible. 'Men are the prime barrier to women in management', said Roger Young, director general of the Institute of Management.... One in five men said it was difficult to work for a woman, and one in three women said they did not receive adequate respect for their work from male superiors.... Having children proved a disaster for women. Almost half said their careers had been damaged, compared with 16 per cent of men.
>
> (Kennedy 1992:4)

This brings the discussion back to the distinction between the short and the long agendas. Hakim's analysis is convincing within the former but can only be a building block towards the latter.

If HRM is to be serious in its commitment to the development of all human resources, it may need to face the challenge of wider patterns of social inequality. This means looking not only at disadvantage, but also addressing the issue of who benefits from the status quo.

Such a recognition means that equal opportunities initiatives are essentially a political project, as much concerned with deep organizational change as with simple personnel administration.

KEY LEARNING POINTS

- **Equal opportunities issues feature in HRM debate in two main ways: as a function of 'human capital' concerns (which have an affinity with 'instrumental' approaches to HRM), and/or as a concern with 'social justice' (here the affinity is with humanistic traditions of HRM).**
- **These concerns lead to different equal opportunities agendas, the most important of which are the 'short' and 'long' agendas. The short agenda is concerned merely with policy measures which meet short-term economic and legal requirements. The long agenda is both broad in its coverage and geared towards positive action to equalize employment opportunities beyond the level required by law or economic expediency.**
- **The long agenda approach is one of 'equal share', which goes beyond simple 'equal chance', usually involving some form of positive action.**
- **Positive action does not involve meeting quotas by positive discrimination;**

rather it provides members of under-represented groups with the skills necessary to reach the selection-pool and to be able, once there, to compete equally on merit alone.

• In broad terms, positive action covers four areas: policies and practices; behaviour and attitudes; training and development; and resource provision.

EXERCISE

To what extent does the following view of equal opportunities reflect the situation in your organization, and what are the implications for the future? :

equal opportunity initiatives... involve a struggle. Different people have different purposes for them.... The average man in Britain is paid for more than forty-three hours of work per week, the average woman for less than thirty. Yet women work as many or more weekly hours than men. The difference is that much of women's work is unpaid. For the paid work, hour for hour, a woman earns less than three-quarters of what a man earns. The average man thus has considerably more income at his disposal than the average woman, and more leisure time. It is a privilege enjoyed by most men that food, clothing, cleaning and other contributions to comfort and the quality of life are organized for them by women – their wives, mothers and daughters. Men benefit too from having their dependants (children, aged relatives) looked after by women. Such advantages accrue to men of all social classes and ethnic groups in Britain.... We should not expect men to relinquish their privileged position voluntarily.

(Cockburn 1991:17)

Chapter 10

Towards a European HRM?

A EUROPEAN HRM?

The prospect of the Single European Market has focused attention on the development of a European HRM. At present, however, such a project would seem to be subject to two countervailing pressures: on the one hand, patterns of diversity in economic, cultural and industrial practices among European states remain clear; and on the other, the attempt by the European Commission to establish a common 'floor' of social/employment rights and duties via the Social Charter initiative is facing severe challenge in the wake of the Maastricht Treaty ratification problems.

HRM in Europe

The basic contours of the European human resource management landscape have been mapped out by Brewster and Bournois (1991) on the basis of the Price Waterhouse Cranfield Project data. This analysis concentrates on three elements which the authors claim are core components of most models of HRM:

1 Close involvement of HRM and corporate strategy.
2 Organizational independence to take personnel decisions, including *inter alia* an independent remuneration policy and minimal influence from trade unions.
3 Preference for carefully controlled or internal labour market, including *inter alia* freedom to recruit, absence of limitation on employment contracts, and a substantial degree of training.

Some of the key findings are given in Table 10.1.

In terms of the link between HRM and business strategy, Brewster and Bournois (1991) find 'limited encouragement' for closer connections, with only between a third and a half of organizations involving a senior personnel specialist in strategy formulation in most countries, with many senior personnel staff involved at only the implementation stage, or not at all.

Enterprise autonomy reveals a picture of generally high trade union influence (albeit with significant variations between countries), increasing consultation with employees, growing levels of information provision and a continuing influence of

Table 10.1　HRM in Europe

	CH	D	DK	E	F	I	N	NL	S	UK
Involvement in corporate strategy (% of organizations)										
From outset	48	55	42	46	50	32	54	48	59	43
Consultative	20	19	30	21	22	23	24	31	28	27
Implementation	6	6	9	8	12	17	6	8	4	8
Not consulted	14	8	4	2	2	3	4	3	5	7
Don't know	12	13	15	23	13	25	11	12	6	15
Level of determination of basic pay (% of organizations)										
National/industry wide collective bargaining	na	na	62	41	31	59	77	78	68	37
Regional collective bargaining	na	na	17	18	10	2	22	na	8	8
Company/division	38	na	13	22	46	45	16	22	32	31
Establishment/site	na	na	9	15	24	12	13	6	11	32
Individual	50	na	10	8	14	9	13	8	13	6
(na = question not asked)										
Change in influence of trade unions over previous 3 years (% of organizations)										
Increase	18	25	18	44	7	8	38	34	20	4
Decrease	13	10	12	12	46	38	6	9	21	52
Same	69	65	70	44	47	54	56	57	59	44
Use of atypical contracts (% of orgs. with more than 10% of employees on terms shown)										
Part-time	37	20	37	3	13	6	41	35	44	24
Temporary	4	1	4	23	9	3	8	18	14	7
Fixed term	10	12	8	26	15	10	11	3	1	5
Days training p.a. per manual employee, average (valid %)										
Less than one	36	38	25	14	13	22	20	14	73	21
One to three	36	35	31	20	37	41	28	32	20	37
Three to five	17	15	27	25	25	19	28	29	5	24
Five to ten	5	9	12	22	20	14	17	17	2	13
Ten plus	2	4	5	19	6	5	8	8	0	6

Source:　Adapted from Brewster and Bournois (1992)

extra-firm wage determination and legal labour market regulation, leaving European managers with considerable restrictions on their autonomy.

In the area of labour market control there is some evidence of a move towards the use of external markets for atypical workers, although a reliance on internal labour market recruitment remains predominant in some countries.

On the basis of this data base, Brewster and Bournois conclude that the evidence suggests that two paradoxical trends run through HRM in Europe. First there are 'clear country differences' which can only be understood and explained in the context of national cultures and associated histories, laws and industrial relations traditions. Against this, however, there is 'an identifiable difference' between the way in which HRM is conducted in Europe and the situation in the USA. On the last issue they point to a greater degree of influence from the 'social partners' (i.e., trade unions and employers) and from government than in the USA.

A similar paradox is identified by Grahl and Teague, who characterize European HRM in terms of a continuum ranging from 'competitive flexibility' to 'constructive flexibility'. The former approach is closely associated with the US-inspired 'ideal-type' of HRM:

> [HRM] concerns establishing a delicate *quid pro quo* in which progressive workplace policies and conditions are introduced as a trade-off and as a facilitator for the unrestrained use of employees for the enterprise's commercial objectives.
>
> (Grahl and Teague 1991: 82)

Such a regime is premised on the belief that European economies have suffered because of a loss of competitiveness which can be restored only by minimizing the restrictions placed upon managers and employers and by removing labour market impediments to flexibility. If this approach becomes institutionalized, however, it is deemed likely to increase social divisions and inequalities in the wider community, as the dominant logic of competitiveness and deregulation encourages a core–periphery division in which 'a majority of the population enjoy a relatively good standard of living at the expense of a large underclass' (Grahl and Teague 1991:84). Britain, it is claimed, is the European economy in which competitive flexibility is most pronounced.

Constructive flexibility, in contrast, aims to achieve greater adaptability across the economy without increasing social divisions. Under this regime, governmental influence over labour markets and social protection is modified, updated or replaced to match the needs of greater flexibility, but not removed or lessened. In particular, this is likely to involve improved legal rights and protection for the new atypical workforce of part-time and casual employees and an enhanced role for the state in the fields of training and labour market regulation. At the enterprise level the relationship between capital and labour is seen as one of exchange (as opposed to one of putative common interest under HRM), based on a 'productivity coalition' between employers and, in particular, trade unions whereby the latter agree to compromise and co-operate with the former to improve levels of accumulation on the basis of protected skill-based employment and the avoidance of gross social inequalities. Germany and Sweden are the economies held to be closest to this model. Thus, according to Grahl and Teague:

> The majority of European countries lie somewhere between these two extremes, introducing aspects of both competitive and constructive flexibility in an *ad hoc* and hybrid manner. In most of these countries, economic policy as well as wider political thinking have been heavily influenced by the neo-liberal ideas which underpin the competitive flexibility approach, but the institutions and structures of welfare capitalism and widespread social and political opposition have limited the extent to which these ideas have been put into effect.
>
> (Grahl and Teague 1991:89)

The Social Charter

In many respects this tension is apparent in the debates and conflicts which have surrounded the development of the EC's 'Social Dimension' and, in particular, the so-called Social Charter, which has been seen by commentators such as Grahl and Teague (1991) and Thurley (1990) as an instrument designed to foster 'consultative flexibility'. The UK Conservative government, however, has consistently opposed moves to implement measures derived from the Charter in the UK, on precisely the grounds that it countermands labour market deregulation, which is seen to be a precondition for the UK's competitive regeneration. Against this the French and German governments, especially, have pointed to the social divisions that could result in a European market which was based only on free-market principles; indeed, a particular concern behind the development of the Charter was the growth in 'flexible' atypical (i.e., part-time and temporary) contracts and the need to regulate these to prevent exploitation and the development of an extensive secondary labour market (either within particular member states or between states in the form of 'social dumping' – the movement of capital to countries where labour is relatively cheap and social responsibilities of employers are low).

Since its inception, the EC has always had aspirations to develop the so-called 'Social Dimension'. Key aspects of this have always been the organization of the workplace and the provision of benefits and legal rights to safeguard citizens from poverty and exploitation. Early moves in the 1970s involved attempts by the European Commission to introduce EC Regulations imposing common conditions across all member states. This ambitious plan was abandoned in the face of fierce resistance from virtually all quarters of the Community and the realization that the practical difficulties in such a universal scheme were just too vast to handle. In its place came a more limited and piecemeal approach which restricted itself to the introduction of relatively uncontentious pieces of legislation in areas of common concern (e.g. the management of collective redundancies and sexual equality). By the 1980s, however, the idea of a more embracing approach to social policy had re-emerged. This was stimulated by concern for public welfare at a time of recession and by the growth of atypical working patterns. A special concern was the fact that such conditions appeared more acute in some member states than in others. Indeed, as the prospect of the Single European Market drew ever closer, there was a growing fear of 'social dumping', whereby employers would relocate their enterprises from member states where they had to pay high wages and contribute heavily to social protection, to those where labour was cheap and unregulated. Out of this concern came the notion of a 'floor' of basic social rights. In effect this would act as a uniform minimum standard governing terms and conditions of employment and forms of benefit provision in all member states. This floor would act only as a minimum, and individual states would be free to build upon it according to national custom and practice, thereby retaining the principle of subsidiarity.

The 1989 Social Charter is the statement setting out these basic rights. Contrary to widely held belief, it is neither a legal document nor a set of laws. It is, as its introduction states, merely a 'solemn declaration' that the signatories will work towards the goals contained therein. These goals are listed under twelve headings, thus:

1 Freedom of Movement
2 Employment and Remuneration
3 Improvement of Living and Working Conditions
4 Social Protection
5 Freedom of Association and Collective Bargaining
6 Vocational Training
7 Equal Treatment of Men and Women
8 Information, Consultation and Participation of Workers
9 Health Protection and Safety at the Workplace
10 Protection of Children and Adolescents
11 Protection of Elderly Persons
12 Protection of Disabled Persons.

Again contrary to widespread belief, the Charter makes no reference to an EC-wide minimum wage (only to the desirability of an 'equitable wage' allowing a 'decent standard of living', neither of which is defined), nor to an EC-wide 'right to strike'. Indeed, matters relating to collective bargaining and industrial action are not to be the subject of EC legislation, but to be left to the two sides of industry (the 'social partners') in accordance with national regulations and agreements. Thus, the objectives of the Charter remain very general (some would say vague) and are to be achieved by a combination of voluntary action by member states (presumably with the exception of the UK, which has refused to sign) and, more importantly, a series of legislative measures aimed at selected areas of the Charter. The latter is termed the Social Action Programme (SAP) of the Social Charter and consists of a number of Directives intended to be in place by the 1992/3. Thus, although the UK failed to sign the Charter, it is still bound by any of the directives in SAP which are passed by the Council of Ministers, as these are part of the normal EC legislative process.

It is here, however, that controversy starts. Although many SAP directives are concerned with health and safety and, in this area at least, have not been opposed by the UK, others attempt to regulate wider areas of working practice. Such attempts have been viewed by the Conservative government as economically damaging and contrary to their philosophy of labour-market deregulation. It is worth noting, however, that many of the most controversial directives are not as inflexible as has sometimes been claimed; most contain clauses which allow for national differences and for adaptations to suit particular industrial/organizational exigencies (derogation). Indeed, the conditional nature of much of the SAP legislation has been a source of annoyance to those who favour a strong regulatory role for governments.

In the wake of the Single European Act, certain areas of EC law-making are now governed by qualified majority voting (QMV). This means that no one state can block the passage of a law with which it alone disagrees (as is the case with unanimous voting). Under the Treaty of Rome (the nearest thing to an EC constitution) issues relating to employment are mostly dealt with under Article 118. Directives developed under this Article are normally dealt with by unanimous vote, except for health and safety matters (which come under Article 118A and are governed by QMV. This state of affairs means that the UK has been able to block progress on any SAP measures not concerned directly with health and safety. In an attempt to circumvent this blocking, the Commission has attempted to introduce measures relating to employment under QMV Articles by using somewhat contentious definitions. For example, a directive regulating part-time and temporary workers' conditions of employment was introduced under Article 100A which covers matters relating to Distortions of Competition. Similarly, the directive on working time (which proposes regulation of hours of work, night work, holiday entitlement, and rest periods – the much-publicized 48-hour week and four weeks' annual paid holiday) was introduced under Article 118A on the grounds that unregulated night work could have an adverse effect on health and was therefore a matter of health and safety – the health and safety effects of the other objects of the directive, such as daily and weekly rest periods and holiday entitlement, have also been hotly disputed by the UK government. Thus, in this way it seemed that many of the SAP measures would find their way into UK legislation sooner or later, despite the Conservative government's opposition. This was certainly the consensus before the Maastricht Summit.

The Maastricht Summit was held (in December 1991) to produce a new Treaty establishing closer European Union. Part of this new Treaty was the so-called Social Chapter, containing details of a new Social Protocol intended to speed up progress towards the goals of the Social Charter. Basically, the intention was to extend QMV to *all* Article 118 areas (i.e., improvement in the working environment and working conditions, information and consultation of workers, and labour market discrimination of various sorts). Not surprisingly the UK opposed such developments; more surprising was John Major's claim to have secured for the UK exemption from the Social Chapter of the Treaty. This was claimed to have resulted in the establishment of a 'twin-track' approach, whereby the UK would be excluded from discussion of, and being affected by, measures taken under the QMV Article 118 of the new Treaty. The eleven other states would deal with such matters by QMV but without the UK. On the face of it this seemed a very significant revision of the EC process but, in practice, the exemption is by no means as far-reaching as it at first appeared.

According to IDS (1992f), a number of points about the Maastricht Agreement need to be borne in mind. First, the UK will remain explicitly bound by its existing obligations under the present Treaty. Second, the present treaty provisions remain the only basis for action covering all twelve member states. Third, proposals currently in the pipeline under the Social Action Programme may continue to be brought forward. And finally, new social policy proposals can still be introduced on the present Treaty basis beyond 1992.

This means that all the directives presently being proposed under SAP will stand, including that on working time, if they are accepted by a majority of the Council of Europe. Also it will still be possible for the European Commission to bring through wide-ranging employment measures under existing QMV Articles which continue to bind the UK (e.g., 118A). It seems that the Maastricht Agreement merely means that the UK has lost its veto, or, alternatively, will be marginalized and excluded if its agreement is not forthcoming.

At the time of writing the future of the Maastricht Treaty itself is in doubt, and with it the Social Protocol, and possibly the entire social dimension of the EC project. In this respect, the outcome of the political turmoil which has arisen in the wake of Maastricht may have implications which go beyond the Social Chapter *per se*, even influencing whether or not the UK sees the spread of Human Resource Management based on principles of competitive flexibility, or the development of a Management of Human Resources informed by consultative flexibility. With regard to the possibility of the former developments, Purcell points to the findings of the UK Workplace Industrial Relations Survey which:

> paint a compelling, and depressing, picture of the emergence of the non-union sector based firmly around the principle of cost-minimisation.... These non-union, private sector establishments reported better industrial relations than in the union sector; experienced virtually no strikes or other forms of industrial conflict; had higher labour turnover and a higher rate of industrial injuries; more often used performance-related or merit pay;... had higher pay differentials between the bottom and top earners; had a higher proportion of employees earning low pay... ; were more likely to use freelance or temporary labour; were more likely to use compulsory redundancy as a means of labour force reduction; had a dismissal rate twice that of union firms; were less likely to have formal grievance procedures, consultative committees, or employee health and safety

representatives; and, finally, as many as half of managements in these firms gave no regular information to their employees.

(Purcell 1993:22)

As the UK's Conservative government is likely to continue to oppose the extension of labour market regulation based on the principles of the Social Charter and consultative flexibility, and, under conditions of continuing economic uncertainty and faltering recovery, it seems that if competitive flexibility is encouraging a form of HRM, then it is one based less on the 'humanistic' variant of HRM and more on the 'instrumental' pattern. If this is the case then it may be worth asking how long the HRM phenomenon will continue to enjoy favour with personnel professionals and academics as a 'progressive', 'enlightened' and 'future-oriented' system of people management.

References

Adam-Smith, D. and Goss, D. (1993) 'HIV/AIDS and hotel and catering employment: some implications of perceived risk', *Employee Relations* 15(2): 25–32.

Adam-Smith, D., Goss, D., Sinclair, A., Rees, G., Meudell, K. (1992) 'AIDS and employment: diagnosis and prognosis', *Employee Relations* 14(3): 29–40.

Allan Jones and Associates (1992) *Maternity and Childcare Survey Report*, Monmouth: Apex House.

Anderson, G. (1992a) 'Performance Appraisal' in Towers, B. (ed.) *The Handbook of Human Resource Management*, Oxford: Blackwell.

—— (1992b) 'Selection' in Towers, B. (ed.) *The Handbook of Human Resource Management*, Oxford: Blackwell.

Anon. (1988) 'Graphoanalysis', *Personnel Today* March 1988:18.

Ansoff, I. and McDonnel, E. (1990) *Implanting Strategic Management*, Hemel Hempstead: Prentice Hall.

Applebaum, S. and Shappiro, B. (1991) 'Pay for performance: implementation of individual and group plans', *Journal of Management Development*, 10(7): 30–40.

Armstrong, M. (1989) *Personnel and the Bottom Line*, London: IPM.

Armstrong, M. and Murlis, H. (1991) *Reward Management: a Handbook of Remuneration Strategy and Practice*, London: Kogan Page.

Arroba, T. and James, K. (1990) 'Reducing the cost of stress', *Personnel Review* 19(1): 21–7.

Ashton, D., Maguire, M. and Splisbury, M. (1990) *Restructuring the Labour Market: Implications for Youth*, Basingstoke: Macmillan.

Atkinson, J. (1984) 'Manpower strategies for the flexible firm', *Personnel Management*, August: 28–31.

Banas, G. (1992) 'Nothing prepared me to manage AIDS', *Harvard Business Review* July–August: 26–33.

Barnes, C. (1992) 'Disability and employment', *Personnel Review* 21(6): 55–73.

Bartram, D. 1991 'Addressing the abuse of psychological tests', *Personnel Management* April: 34–9.

Bateman, T. and Zeithaml, C. (1989) 'The psychological context of strategic decisions', *Strategic Management Journal* 10: 59–74.

Beardwell, I. (1992) 'The new industrial relations? A review of the debate', *Human Resource Management Journal* 2(2): 1–7.

Beaumont, P. (1992) 'Trade unions and HRM', in Towers, B. (ed.) *The Handbook of Human Resource Management*, Oxford: Blackwell.

Beer, M., Spector, B., Lawrence, P., Quinn Mills, D. and Walton, R. (eds) (1984) *Managing Human Assets*, New York: The Free Press.

Bennison, M. (1984) *The Manpower Planning Handbook*, London: McGraw-Hill.

Best, M. (1990) *The New Competition*, Cambridge: Polity Press.

Beynon, H. (1975) *Working for Ford*, Wakefield: EP Publishing.

Blanksby, M. and Iles, P. (1990) 'Recent developments in assessment centre theory, practice and operation,' *Personnel Review* 19(6): 33–44.

Blinkhorn, S. and Johnson, C. (1990) 'The insignificance of personality testing', *Nature* 348: 671–2.

—— (1991) 'Personality tests: the great debate', *Personnel Management* September: 38–42.

Blyton, P. and Morris, J. (1992) 'HRM and the limits of flexibility', in Blyton, P. and Turnbull, P. (eds) *Reassessing Human Resource Management*, London: Sage.

Blyton, P. and Turnbull, P. (eds) (1992) *Reassessing Human Resource Management*, London: Sage.

Boxall, P. (1992) 'Strategic human resource management: beginnings of a new theoretical sophistication', *Human Resource Management Journal* 2(3): 60–79.

Brewster, C. and Bournois, F. (1991) 'HRM: a European Perspective', *Personnel Review*, 20(6): 4–13.

Brindle, D. (1992) 'NHS told to put women on shortlists', *Guardian* 9.1.92.

Brookler, R. (1992) 'Industry standards in workplace drug testing', *Personnel Journal*, April: 128–32.

Bunting, M. (1992) 'Women aspire first to getting on in their job', *Guardian* 27.11.92.

Burrows, G. (1986) *No Strike Agreements and Pendulum Arbitration*, London: IPM.

Butler, R. (1991) *Designing Organizations*, London: Routledge.

Campbell, D. (1993) 'Nine in ten policewomen harassed', *Guardian*, 12.2.93.

Carlton, I. and Sloman, M. (1991) 'Performance appraisal in practice', *Human Resource Management Journal* 2(3): 80–94.

Casey, D. and Pearce, D. (1977) *More than Management Development*, Aldershot: Gower.

CBI (1989) *Managing the Skills Gap*, London: Confederation of British Industry.

Chandler, A. (1962) *Strategy and Structure*, Cambridge, Mass: MIT Press.

Cockburn, C. (1985) *Machinery of Dominance*, London: Pluto.

—— (1991) *In the Way of Women*, Basingstoke: Macmillan.

Collin, A. (1992) 'The role of the mentor in transforming the organization', paper presented at the *Employment Research Unit Annual Conference*, University of Cardiff Business School, September.

Collinson, D. (1991) 'Poachers turned gamekeepers: are personnel managers one of the barriers to equal opportunities?', *Human Resource Management Journal* 1(3): 58–76.

Constable, J. and McCormick, R. (1987) *The Making of British Managers*, London: BIM/CBI.

Cooper, C. (1981) *The Stress Check*, Englewood Cliffs, NJ: Prentice Hall.

Coopers and Lybrand and Associates (1985) *A Challenge to Complacency*, London: MSC and NEDO.

Coopey, J. and Hartley, J. (1991) 'Reconsidering the case for organisational commitment'. *Human Resource Management Journal* 1(3): 18–31.

Coussey, M. and Jackson, H. (1991) *Making Equal Opportunities Work*, London: Pitman.

Crofts, P. (1992) 'Outplacement: a way of never having to say you're sorry', *Personnel Management* May: 46–50.

Dale, A. (1987) 'Occupational inequality, gender and life cycle' *Work Employment and Society* 1(3): 326–51.

Dawson, C. (1988) 'Costing labour turnover through simulation processes: a tool for management', *Personnel Review* 17(4): 29–37.

Dawson, C. (1989) 'The moving frontiers of personnel management: human resource management or human resource accounting', *Personnel Review* 18(3): 3–12.

Deal, T. and Kennedy, A. (1988) *Corporate Cultures*, London: Penguin.

Dickson, T., McLachlan, P., Prior, P. and Swales, K. (1988) 'Big Blue and the unions: IBM, individualism and trade union strategy', *Work, Employment and Society* 2(4): 506–20.

DOE (1990) *Aids and the Workplace*. London: Department of Employment/Health and Safety Executive.

Drucker, P. (1986) *Innovation and Entrepreneurship*, London: Pan.

Dulewicz, V. (1991) 'Personality testing: the great debate', *Personnel Management* September: 38–42.

Dyer, C. (1992) 'Blacks three times more likely to fail Bar exams', *Guardian*, 17.11.92:4.

Easterby-Smith, M. (1986) *Evaluation of Management Education, Training and Development*, Aldershot: Gower.

Easterby-Smith, M. and Mackness, J. (1992) 'Completing the cycle of evaluation', *Personnel Management* May: 22–45.

Easterby-Smith, M. and Tanton, M. (1985) 'Training course evaluation: from an end to a means', *Personnel Management*, April.

Elliott, J. (1989) *Training Needs and Corporate Strategy* (IMS Report 164), Brighton: IMS.

Employment Department (1991) *Investors in People: A Brief for Top Managers*, Sheffield: Employment Department.

Evans, P., Doz, Y. and Laurent, A. (eds) (1989) *Human Resource Management in International Firms*. Basingstoke: Macmillan.

Eysenck, H. (1968) *Sense and Nonsense in Psychology*, London: Pelican.

Fevre, R. (1992) *The Sociology of Labour Markets*, Brighton: Wheatsheaf.

Flamholtz, E. and Lacey, J. (1981) *Personnel Management: Human Capital Theory and Human Resource Accounting*, Los Angeles: UCLA Press.

Fletcher, C. (1982) 'Assessment centres', in Mackenzie Davey and Harris (eds) *Judging People*, London: McGraw Hill.

Fombrun, C., Tichy, N. and Devanna, M. (1984) *Strategic Human Resource Management*, New York: Wiley.

Fowler, A. (1991) 'How to monitor equal opportunities', *Personnel Management Plus* April: 22–3.

Garrahan, P. and Stewart, P. (1992) *The Nissan Enigma*, London: Cassell.

Geary, J. (1992) 'Employment flexibility and HRM: the case of three American electronics plants', *Work, Employment and Society* 6, (2): 251–70.

Giles, W. and Robinson, D. (1972) *Human Asset Accounting*, London: IPM.

Goss, D. (1988) 'Social harmony and the small firm', *Sociological Review* 36(1): 114–32.

—— (1991) *Small Business and Society*, London: Routledge.

Goss, D. and Jones, R. (1992) 'Pathways to progress', *MEAD* 23(1): 65–74.

Goss, D., Adam-Smith, D., Sinclair, A., Rees, G. (1993) 'Corporate AIDS policies as data: possibilities and precautions', *Sociology* 27(2) forthcoming.

Grahl, J. and Teague, P. (1991) 'Industrial relations trajectories and European human resource management' in Brewster, C. and Tyson, S. (eds) *International Comparisons in Human Resource Management*, London: Pitman.

Graves, D. (1986) *Corporate Culture*, London: Francis Pinter.

Gray, R. and Maunders, K. (1987) *Corporate Social Reporting*, London: Prentice Hall.

Grenier, G. (1988) *Inhuman Relation*, Philadelphia: Temple University Press.

Grummitt, J. (1983) *Team Briefing*, London: Industrial Society Press.

Guest, D. (1989) 'HRM: implications for industrial relations', in Storey, J. (ed.) *New Perspectives on HRM*, London: Routledge.

—— (1992) 'HRM in the United Kingdom', in Towers, B. (ed.) *The Handbook of HRM*, Oxford: Blackwell.

Guest, D. and Peccei, R. (1992) 'Employee involvement: redundancy as a critical case', *Human Resource Management Journal* 2(3): 34–59.

Gullan-Whur, M. (1991) 'Research papers relating to the validity and reliability of graphology', British Institute of Graphologists.

Gulliford, A. (1991) 'The role of personality in assessing managerial performance', *Personnel Review* 20(1): 55–31.

Hakim, C. (1990) 'Core and periphery in employers' workforce strategies: evidence from the 1987 ELUS survey', *Work, Employment and Society* 4(2): 157–88.

—— (1991) 'Grateful slaves and self-made women: fact and fantasy in women's work orientations' *European Sociological Review* 2(2): 101–16.

Hammer, T. (1991) 'Gainsharing', in Steers and Porter (eds) (1991) *Motivation and Work Behaviour*, New York: McGraw-Hill.

Handy, C. (1985) *Understanding Organizations*, London: Penguin.

Hanson, C. and Watson, R. (1990) 'Profit sharing and company performance', in Jenkins, G. and Poole, M. (eds) *New forms of Ownership*, London: Routledge.

Hearn, J. and Parkin, W. (1987) *Sex at Work*, Brighton: Wheatsheaf.

Hendry, C. and Pettigrew, A. (1990) 'Human resource management: an agenda for the 1990s'. *International Human Resource Management Journal* 1(1): 17–43.

Hermanson, R. (1964) 'Accounting for human assets', *Occasional Paper no. 14*, E. Lancing, Michigan: Bureau of Business and Economic Research.

Hill, S. (1991) 'Why quality circles failed but total quality management might succeed', *British Journal of Industrial Relations* 29(4): 541–68.

Hilton, P. (1992) 'Shepherd defends training policy', *Personnel Management*, December.

Hobsons (1992) *Working Women*, London: Hobsons Publishing.

Holdsworth, R. (1991) 'Appraisal', in Neale, F. (ed.) *The Handbook of Performance Management*, London: IPM.

Hollway, W. (1991) *Work Psychology and Organizational Behaviour*, London: Sage.

Holmes, L. (1990) 'Trainer Competences: turning back the clock', *Training and Development* April: 17–20.

Honey, P. (1986) 'Styles of Learning' in Mumford, A. (ed.) *Handbook of Management Development*, Aldershot: Gower.

Howe, W. (1986) *Corporate Strategy*, Basingstoke: Macmillan.

IDS (1987) *IDS Study 392* 'Equal rights or empty rites', August.

—— (1988a) *IDS Study 409* 'One or the other', May.

—— (1988b) *IDS Study 411* 'Uniting the Workers', June.

—— (1989a) *IDS Study 437* 'Round Table Discussions', July.

—— (1989b) *IDS Study 442* 'Common to all', December.

—— (1990a) *IDS Study 462* 'Why Use Attitude Surveys' July.

—— (1990b) *IDS Study 468* 'A Testing Time for Financial Participation', October.

—— (1990c) *IDS Focus 57* 'The politics of production'.

—— (1990d) *IDS Study 454* 'Flexibility in the 1990s', March.

—— (1990e) *IDS Study 457* 'A total approach to quality', May.

—— (1990f) *IDS Study 472* 'Caring for the kids', December.

—— (1991a) *IDS Study 481* 'DIY Benefits for the 1990s', May.

—— (1991b) *IDS Study 487* 'Healthier attitudes', August.

—— (1991c) *IDS Study 495* 'Rewarding Ideas', December.

—— (1991d) *IDS Focus 61* 'Performance Pay'.

—— (1991e) *IDS Study 486* 'Reshaping working time', July.

—— (1992a) *IDS Study 500* 'Skilling Up', February.

—— (1992b) *IDS Study 503* 'Can I help you?', April.

—— (1992c) *IDS Study 507* 'Brief and to the Point', June.

—— (1992d) *IDS Study 508* 'Cancelling out disability', July.

—— (1992e) *IDS Study 513* 'Protecting employees dignity at work', September.

—— (1992f) *IDS European Special*, 'Social Europe after the Summit', February.

—— (1993a) *IDS Study 521* 'Still in its infancy', January.

—— (1993b) *IDS Focus 65* 'De-recognition: how much of a trend?'

Iles, P. (1992) 'Centres of excellence? Assessment and development centres, managerial competence, and human resource strategies', *British Journal of Management* 3: 79–90.

Iles, P., Mabey, C. and Robertson, I. (1990) 'HRM practices and employee commitment', *British Journal of Management* 1: 147–57.

IMS (1992) *Introducing Flexible Benefits: the Other Side of the Coin*, Brighton: IMS.

IPM/IMS (1991) *Computers in Personnel 1991 Conference Book*, Brighton: IMS.

IRS (1990a) *IRS Recruitment and Development Report 1* 'Widening the pool of recruits'; 'Rethinking manual worker recruitment at Ealing'; 'Biodata', January.

—— (1990b) *IRS Recruitment and Development Report 3* 'Links with schools', March.

—— (1990c) *IRS Recruitment and Development Report 5* 'Developing potential – Triplex Lloyd's Centurion Programme'; 'Recruitment News', May.

—— (1991a) *IRS Recruitment and Development Report 13*, Corporate relocation', January.

—— (1991b) *IRS Recruitment and Development Report 14*, 'Developing managers in the great outdoors', February.

—— (1991c) *IRS Recruitment and Development Report 17* 'The state of selection 2', May.

—— (1991d) *IRS Recruitment and Development Report 19* 'The state of selection 3', July.

—— (1991e) *Employment Trends 495* 'BT managers hostile to PRP', September.

—— (1991f) *IRS Recruitment and Development Report 23* 'NVQs: what are they?'; 'Managerial capabilities and self-development at Brooke Bond foods', November.

—— (1991g) *IRS Employment Trends 502* 'Going to the polls: employee opinion surveys', December.

—— (1991h) *IRS Health and Safety Information Bulletin 187/8* 'AIDS at the workplace 1/2'.

—— (1992a) *IRS Recruitment and Development Report 25* 'NVQs: NVQs at work', January.

—— (1992b) *IRS Recruitment and Development Report 27* 'Employee development', March.

—— (1992c) *IRS Recruitment and Development Report 28*, 'Auditing the management of human resources in the NHS', April.

—— (1992d) *IRS Employee Development Bulletin 31* 'Skills-based pay: the new training incentive', July.

—— (1992e) *IRS Employment Trends 513*, 'Sexual harassment in the workplace', June.

Jones, R. and Goss, D. (1991) 'The role of training strategy in reducing skill shortages', *Personnel Review* 20(2): 24–30.

Keenoy, T. (1990) 'HRM: a case of the wolf in sheep's clothing', *Personnel Review* 19(2): 3–9.

Keep, E. (1989) 'A training scandal?' in Sisson, K. (ed.) *Personnel Management in Britain*, Oxford: Blackwell.

Kennedy, M. (1992) 'Sex bias still hinders women managers'. *Guardian*, 17.11.92.

Kenney, J., Reid, M. and Donnelly, E. (1990) *Manpower Training & Development*, London: IPM.

Kerr, S. (1991) 'On the folly of rewarding A while hoping for B', in Steers and Porter (eds) (1991) *Motivation and Work Behaviour*, New York: McGraw-Hill.

Kessler, I. and Purcell, J. 1992 'Performance related pay: objectives and application', *Human Resource Management Journal* 2(3): 16–33.

Kohl, J. Miller, A. and Barton, L. (1990) 'Levi's corporate AIDS programme' *Long Range Planning* 23(6): 31–4.

Kolb, D. (1984) *Experiential Learning* New York: Prentice Hall.

Kremer, J. and Marks, J. (1992) 'Sexual harassment: management and trade union responses', *Journal of Occupational and Organizational Psychology* 65: 5–15.

Krulis-Randa, J. (1990) 'Strategic human resource management in Europe after 1992', *International Journal of Human Resource Management* 1(2) 131–39.

Laabs, J. (1992) 'Surveillance: tool or trap', *Personnel Journal* June: 96–104.

Lawler, E. (1991) 'The design of effective reward systems' in Steers and Porter (eds) (1991) *Motivation and Work Behaviour*. New York: McGraw-Hill.

Lawler, E. and Mohrman, S. (1991) 'High-involvement management' in Steers and Porter (eds) (1991) *Motivation and Work Behaviour*, New York: McGraw-Hill.

Lawrence, J. (1986) in Mumford, A. (ed.), *Handbook of Management Development* Aldershot: Gower.

Legge, K. (1989) 'Human resource management: a critical analysis', in Storey, J. (ed.) *New Developments in Human Resource Management*, London: Routledge.

Leighton, P. and Syrett, M. (1989) *New Work Patterns*, London: Pitman.

Lewis, C. (1991) 'Personality tests: the great debate', *Personnel Management* September: 38–42.

Likert, R. (1967) *The Human Organization*, London: McGraw Hill.

Lockyer, C. (1992) 'Pay, performance and reward' in Towers, B. (ed.) *The Handbook of Human Resource Management*, Oxford: Blackwell.

Long, P. (1986) *Performance Appraisal Revisited*, London: IPM.

Lowe, J. (1991) 'Teambuilding via outdoor training: experiences from a UK automotive plant', *Human Resource Management Journal* 2(1): 42–59.

Lucio, M. and Weston, S. (1992) 'HRM and trade union responses: bringing the politics of the workplace back into the debate', in Blyton, P. and Turnbull, P. (eds) *Reassessing Human Resource Management*, London: Sage.

Lynch, P. (1991) 'Making time for productivity', *Personnel Management*, March: 30–5.

McDonnel, R. and Maynard, A. (1985) 'The costs of alcohol abuse', *British Journal of Addiction* 80: 27–35.

McEvoy, T. and Butler, R. (1990) *Training and Development Journal* August 1990.

McGregor, A. and Sproull, A. (1992) 'Employers and the flexible workforce', *Employment Gazette* May: 225–34.

Mackenzie Davey, D. (1991) 'Personality testing: the great debate', *Personnel Management* September: 38–42.

McLoughlin, I. and Gourlay, S. (1992) 'Enterprise without unions', *Journal of Management Studies* 29(5): 669–89.

Malloch, H. (1988) 'Evaluating strategies on a cost-based manpower planning model', *Personnel Review* 17(3): 22–28.

Marchington, M. and Parker, P. (1990) *Changing Patterns of Employee Relations in Britain*, Hemel Hempstead: Harvester.

Marchington, M., Goodman, J., Wilkinson, A. and Ackers, P. (1992) *New Developments in Employee Involvement*, EDG Research Paper 2, Sheffield: Employment Department.

Marsh, A. and Cox, B. (1992) *The Trade Union Movement in the UK 1992*, Oxford: Malthouse.

Means, R. (1990) 'Alcohol, alcohol problems and the workplace', in Doogan, K. and Means, R. (eds) *Alcohol and the Workplace*, Bristol: SAUS.

Miller, P. (1991) 'Strategic HRM: and assessment of progress', *Human Resource Management Journal* 1(4): 23–39.

Milne, S. (1992) 'Minister attacks slow progress for women', *Guardian* 18.11.92.

Mintzberg, H., Raisinghani, D. and Therot, A. (1976) 'The structure of unstructured decision processes', *Administrative Science Quarterly* 21(2): 246–75.

Moss, G. (1992) 'Different European perspectives on selection techniques: the case of graphology in business', in Vickerstaff, S. (ed.) *Human Resource Management in Europe*, London: Chapman Hall.

Muller, F. (1991) 'A new engine of change in employee relations', *Personnel Management* July: 30–3.

Mumford, A. (ed.) *Handbook of Management Development*, Aldershot: Gower.

Neale, M. and Northcraft, G. (1991) 'Factors influencing organizational commitment', in

Steers and Porter (eds) (1991). *Motivation and Work Behaviour*, New York: McGraw-Hill.

Newby, H. (1977) *The Deferential Worker*, London: Penguin.

Newell, S. (1992) 'The myth and destructiveness of equal opportunities: the continued dominance of the mothering role', *Personnel Review* 21(4): 37–47.

Norris, G. (1979) 'Industrial paternalist capitalism and local labour markets', *Sociology* 12(3).

O'Brien, O. and Dufficy, H. (1988) 'Alcohol and drugs policies', in Dickenson, F. (ed.) *Drink and Drugs at Work*, London: IPM.

Oliver, B. and Wilkinson, N. (1992) 'Human resource management in Japanese manufacturing companies in the UK and USA', in Towers, B. (ed.) *The Handbook of Human Resource Management*, Oxford: Blackwell.

Oliver, N. and Lowe, J. (1991) 'The high commitment workplace: two cases from a hi-tech industry', *Work Employment and Society* 5(3): 437–50.

O'Reilly, C. (1991) 'Corporations, control, and commitment', in Steers and Porter (eds) (1991).

Pearce, J. (1991) 'Why merit pay doesn't work' in Steers and Porter (1991) *Motivation and Work Behaviour*, New York: McGraw-Hill.

Pearson, R. (1991) *The Human Resource*, London: McGraw-Hill.

Pedler, M. (ed.) (1983) *Action learning in Practice*, Aldershot: Gower.

Pedler, M., Burgoyne, J. and Boydell, T. (1986) *A Manager's Guide to Self-Development*, London: McGraw-Hill.

Pendleton, A. (1992) 'PRP in BR', in Vickerstaff, S. (ed.) *HRM in Europe*, London: Chapman & Hall.

Pettigrew, A. (1985) *The Awakening Giant: Continuity and Change in ICI*, Oxford: Blackwell.

Pickard, J. (1991) 'Annual hours: a year of living dangerously?', *Personnel Management* August.

Porter, M. (1990) *The Competitive Advantage of Nations*, London: Collier-Macmillan.

Purcell, J. (1989) 'The impact of corporate strategy on human resource management', in Storey, J. (ed.) *New Developments in Human Resource Management*, London: Routledge.

Purcell, J. (1993) 'The end of institutional industrial relations', *Political Quarterly* 14: 6–23.

Quinn Mills, P. and Balbaky, S. (1985) 'Planning for morale and culture' in Walton and Lawrence (eds) *HRM Trends and Challenges*, Cambridge, Mass: Harvard Business School Press.

Ramsay, H. (1991) 'Reinventing the wheel? A review of the development and performance of employee involvement', *Human Resource Management Journal* 1(4): 1–22.

Ramsay, H., Hyman, J., Baddon, L., Hunter, L. and Leopold, J. (1990) 'Options for workers: owner or employee', in Jenkins, G. and Poole, M. (eds) *New Forms of Ownership*, London: Routledge.

Randall, D. (1987) 'Commitment and the organization: the Organization Man revisited', *Academy of Management Review* 12(3): 460–71.

Randell, G. (1989) 'Employee appraisal', in Sisson, K. (ed.) *Personnel Management in Britain*, Oxford: Blackwell.

Ravaud, J., Madiot, B., Ville, I. (1992) 'Discrimination towards disabled people seeking employment', *Social Science and Medicine* 35(8): 951–8.

Reichers, A. (1985) 'A review and reconceptualisation of organizational commitment', *Academy of Management Review* 10: 465–76.

Revans, R. (1980) *Action Learning: New techniques for Management*, London: Blond and Biggs.

Richards-Carpenter, C. (1992) 'Capitalizing on devolution', *Personnel Management* April.

Robertson, I. (1991) 'Personality tests: the great debate', *Personnel Management* September: 38–42.

Rocco, F. (1991) 'The write stuff to test recruits', *Independent on Sunday* 20.10.91: 12–13.

Rodger, D. and Mabey, C. (1987) 'BT's leap forward from assessment centres', *Personnel Management* July: 32–5.

Rose, M. (1975) *Industrial Behaviour*, London: Penguin.

Rowan, D. and Milner, M. (1992) 'Toyota gears up', *Guardian* 17.12.92.

Sadri, G., Cooper, C., and Allison, T. (1989) 'A Post Office initiative to stamp out stress', *Personnel Management* August: 40–5.

Salancik, G. (1977) 'Commitment' in Salancik, G. (ed.) *New Directions in Organizational Behaviour*, Chicago: St Clair Press.

Sapsed, G. (1991) 'Appraisal the IBM way', *Involvement and Participation* February: 8–14.

Saunders, G. (1984) *The Committed Organization*, Aldershot: Gower.

Schein, E. (1989) 'Organization culture: what it is and how it works', in Evans, P., Doz, Y., Laurent, A. (eds) *Human Resource Management in International Firms*, Basingstoke: Macmillan.

Seegers, J. (1992) 'Assessment centres for identifying long-term potential and for self-development', in Salaman, G. (ed.) *Human Resource Strategies*, London: Sage.

Selby, R. (1991) 'IT and assessment: Securicor', *Computers in Personnel 1991 Conference Book* Brighton: IPM/IMS.

Sewell, G. and Wilkinson, B. (1992) 'Empowerment or emasculation? Shopfloor surveill-ance in a total quality organization', in Blyton, P. and Turnbull, P. (eds) *Reassessing Human Resource Management*, London: Sage.

Sidney, E. and Phillips, N. (1991) *One-to-One Management: Counselling to improve job performance*, London: Pitman.

Sigman, A. (1992) 'The state of corporate health care', *Personnel Management*, February: 24–9.

Sisson, K. (1989) *Personnel Management in Britain*, Oxford: Blackwell.

Sharrock, D. (1992) 'Texaco forces random drug testing on staff', *Guardian*, December.

Slee Smith, P. (1983) *Employee Suggestion Schemes*, London: British Institute of Management.

Smith, I. (1992) 'Reward management and HRM', in Blyton, P. and Turnbull, P. (eds) *Reassessing Human Resource Management*, London: Sage.

Smith, M., Beck, J., Cooper, C., Cox, C., Ottaway, D. and Talbot, R. (1982) *Introducing Organizational Behaviour*, London: Macmillan.

Solomon, C. (1992) 'Keeping hate out of the workplace', *Personnel Journal* July: 30–6.

Spencer, S. (1990) 'Job evaluation: a modern day 'genie' for management information?', *Employment Gazette* June: 306–12.

Stanworth, J. and Stanworth, C. (1991) *Telework, The Human Resource Implications*, London: IPM.

Steers, R. and Porter, L. (eds) (1991) *Motivation and Work Behaviour*, New York: McGraw-Hill.

Storey, J. (ed.) (1989) *New Developments in Human Resource Management*, London: Routledge.

Storey, J. (1989) 'A literature review and implications for further research', *Personnel Review* 18(6): 3–19.

—— (1992a) *Developments in the Management of Human Resources*, Oxford: Blackwell.

—— (1992b) 'HRM in action: the truth is out at last' *Personnel Management* April: 28–31.

Straw, J. (1989) *Equal Opportunities: The Way Ahead*, London: IPM.

Stuart, D. (1986) 'Performance appraisal', in Mumford, A. (ed.) *Handbook of Management Development*, Aldershot: Gower.

Taylor, S. and Sackheim, K. (1988) 'Graphology', *Personnel Administrator* May: 71–6.

Thierry, H. (1992) 'Pay and payment systems', in Hartley, J. and Stephenson, G. (eds) *Employment Relations*, Oxford: Blackwell.

Thurley, K. (1990) 'Towards a European approach to personnel management', *Personnel Management* September: 54–7.

Tolley, K., Maynard, R. and Robinson, D. (1991) *HIV/AIDS and social care*, Discussion Paper 81, Centre for Health Economics Institute for Health Studies.

Torrington, D., Hall, L., Haylor, L. and Myers, J. (1991) *Employee Resourcing*, London: IPM.

Towers, B. (ed.) (1992) *The Handbook of Human Resource Management*, Oxford: Blackwell.

Townley, B. (1989) 'Selection and appraisal: reconstituting social relations?', in Storey, J. (ed.) (1989) *New Developments in Human Resource Management*, London: Routledge.

Training Agency (1989a) *Training in Britain: A Study of Funding, Activity and Attitudes* (Main Report), London: HMSO.

—— (1989b) *Training in Britain: Employees Perspectives* (Research Report), London: HMSO.

Turnbull, P. (ed.) *Reassessing Human Resource Management*, London: Sage, 169–84.

Tyson, S. (1985) 'Is this the very model of a modern personnel officer'. *Personnel Management* April.

Tyson, S. and Fell, A. (1986) *Evaluating the Personnel Function*, London: Hutchinson.

Vaughan, E. and Lasky, B. (1991) 'How will women manage? A speculation on the effects of equal opportunities in management training', *Journal of General Management* 16(4): 53–65.

Walton, R. (1991) 'From control to commitment in the workplace' in Steers and Porter (eds) (1991) *Motivation and Work Behaviour*, New York: McGraw-Hill.

Weston, C. (1992) 'EO? It is still a man's world in the UK', *Guardian* 20.11.92.

Whitaker, C. (1991) 'Measurement – the foundation of performance management', in Neale, F. (ed.) *The Handbook of Performance Management*, London: IPM.

Whyte, W. (1956) *The Organization Man*, New York: Doubleday.

Wickens, P. (1987) *The Road to Nissan: Flexibility, Quality, Teamwork*, Basingstoke: Macmillan.

Williams, S. (1991) 'Strategy and objectives' in Neale, F. (ed.) *The Handbook of Performance Management*, London: IPM.

Wilson, J., and Cole, G. (1990) 'A healthy approach to performance appraisal', *Personnel Management* June: 46–9.

Wilson, P. (1992) *HIV and AIDS in the Workplace*, London: National AIDS Trust.

Wood, R. and Baron, H. (1992) 'Psychological testing free from prejudice', *Personnel Management* December: 34–7.

Wood, S. Barrington, H. and Johnson, R. (1990) 'An introduction to continuous development' in Wood, S. (ed) *Continuous Development* London: IPM.

Woodley, C. (1990) 'The cafeteria route to compensation', *Personnel Management* May: 42–5.

Woodruffe, C. (1990) *Assessment Centres*, London: IPM.

Woodward, T. and Winchurch, R. (1991) 'Molecular human resourcing', *Computers in Personnel Conference*, Brighton: IMS/IPM: 77–84.

Index

Note. References are to the United Kingdom, except where otherwise indicated.

'ABCD' (A Boost for Continuous Development) 74–5
ability and aptitude tests 45–6, 48–9
absenteeism and stress 134
'accelerated development' 168
acceptance of appraisal 58
access, equal 159
accounting, human asset 20–2
accuracy of appraisal 58
ACs (assessment centres) 43, 57–60
action learning 76–7
Adam-Smith, D. 126, 127
adaptation by unions to NIR 140–4
administration of reward 98
ADST (Approved Deferred Share Trusts) 95
advantages: of appraisal 58; of flexibility 34–5; of training and development 63–4
advisory boards and NIR 151–3
AEU (union) 153, 155
'affective' commitment 108–9
'affirmative action' 160; *see also* positive action
AIDS 125–32
Alfred Marks Employment Agency 165–6
'alienative' commitment 109–10
Allison, T. 110
Anderson, G. 44–5, 53
Ansoff, I. 8
Applebaum, S. 94
application form 43
appraisal 39, 51–60; assessment centres 43, 57–60; characteristics 40; developmental 51, 55–7; interview

56–7; judgemental 51, 55
Approved Deferred Share Trusts 95
Armstrong, M. 26, 104
Arroba, T. 135
Ashton, D. 41
assessment 39–61; centres (ACs) 43, 57–60; recruitment 39, 40–2; *see also* appraisal; selection
assets, employees as 20–2
Atkinson, J. 9, 31, 32
attitude: continuous development as 75; and equal opportunities 164–7; surveys 115–16, 166
audits, human resourcing 20–2
Austin Rover 147, 163
awareness training 164, 167–9

Balbaky, S. 103, 104
Banas, G. 131
Barclays Bank 161
Barnes, C. 164–5
Baron, H. 48, 168
Barrington, H. 75
Barton, L. 127, 129
Bartram, D. 45, 47
Bateman, T. 9
Beardwell, I. 140
Beaumont, P. 144
Beer, M. 4, 12–13, 14, 99
behaviour: behavioural observation scales in appraisal 52; and commitment 105; and equal opportunities 164–7; and meaning 84–6
Bennison, M. 19, 20
Best, M. 4
Beynon, H. 123
biodata 49–50
biography 49

Blanksby, M. 58, 59
Blinkhorn, S. 46–7
Blyton, P. 14, 28, 32
Boston Consulting Group Matrix 8
Bournois, F. 175–7
Boxall, P. 11–12
Boydell, T. 74
Brewster, C. 175–7
Brindle, D. 41
British Petroleum 42, 116
British Psychological Society 47
British Rail 147, 168
British Telecom 93, 161
Brookler, R. 133–4
Bunting, M. 172
Burgoyne, J. 74
Burrows, G. 143
business ethics and pay 86
Butler, R. 9, 80

Cadbury Schweppes 59
cafeteria schemes 97–9
Campbell, D. 166
career-break provision 170–1
Carlton, I. 53–4
Casey, D. 77
CBI *see* Confederation of British Industry
CD (continuous development) 72–6
chance, equal 159
Chandler, A. 8
change: acceptance of 112; vs results
    objectives in training 80
Civil Service 49
Cockburn, C. 158, 165, 167, 172, 174
Cole, G. 56
collective bargaining 143–4, 147
Collin, A. 73
Collinson, D. 161
Colomb, R. 139
commitment 13, 102–11, 112; and equal
    opportunities 157
communication: and appraisal 58;
    improvement 112; IT 22–5, 37–8
company councils and NIR 151–3
compensation and reward 98
competence 13
competition: competitive flexibility 177;
    international 4
compliance: and appraisal 54;
    commitment 109
computers 37–8; computerized personnel
    information systems (CPIS) 22–5

concessionary response to NIR 143
conciliatory response to NIR 143
Confederation of British Industry (CBI)
    63–4, 71, 78, 157
conflict of principles and reward 98
Constable, J. 72
constructive flexibility 177–8
continuous development (CD) 72–6
control: controlling purpose in evaluation
    79; pay 84; *see also* power; reward
Cooper, C. 110, 134
Coopers and Lybrand and Associates 72
Coopey, J. 110
core and periphery distinction in firm 31–2
corporate conscience welfare rationale
    122–3
costs: of appraisal 58; cost effectiveness
    13; cost management and reward 97; of
    training and development 63, 65, 66,
    79; *see also* finance
counselling 135–7
County NatWest Bank 53
Coussey, M. 158–9, 161, 162, 165, 168
Cox, B. 141, 142
CPIS (computerized personnel
    information systems) 22–5
Crofts, P. 137
culture: cultural change and appraisal 58;
    organizational 54, 102

Dale, A. 170
Dawson, C. 10–11, 21–2
Deal, T. 103
deep commitment 157
defensive HIV/AIDS policy 128–9
Department of Employment: and equal
    opportunities 165; and training and
    development 63, 70–1; and welfare 127
Department of Health and Social Security
    79
development 71–8; action learning 76–7;
    'centres' 110; defined 62;
    developmental appraisal 51, 55–7;
    developmental appraisal 51, 55–7;
    outdoors 77–8; self-development and
    continuous development 72–6; *see also*
    training and development
Dickson, T. 149–50, 152–3
directly employed work pattern 33–4
disabled people and equal opportunities
    158, 159, 164–5
disadvantages: of appraisal 58; of
    flexibility 35

discrimination *see* equal opportunities
disease 125–32
Drucker, P. 36
drug abuse 132–4, 139
Dufficy, H. 132
Dulewicz, V. 47
Dyer, C. 168

Ealing Borough Council 42
EAP (employee assistance programme)
    133–4
earnings *see* reward
Easterby-Smith, M. 79
education *see* training and development
EETPU (union) 54, 142, 143, 152
effectiveness of appraisal 58
efficiency and health *see* welfare
EI *see* employee involvement
Elliott, J. 66
employee assistance programme (EAP)
    133–4
employee involvement 111–20; attitude
    surveys 115–16; quality circles and
    TQM 116–20; suggestion schemes
    113–15; team briefing 111–13
employee reaction to reward 98
employee–organization relationships and
    commitment 102
employees *see* human resource
    management
Employment Department *see* Department
    of Employment
equal opportunities 156–74; and appraisal
    58–9; human capital and social justice
    156–7; long agenda 157, 158–60;
    policy and practice *see* positive action;
    short agenda 157, 158
ethics: business 86; of equal opportunities
    action 163–4
ethnic minorities: and equal opportunities
    158, 159, 160–1, 162, 168; recruitment
    42
Europe 175–82; and competition 4; equal
    opportunities 164–5; and NIR 144;
Europe (continued): performance
    management system 27; selection 50;
    Social Charter 175, 178–82; training
    and development 63
evaluation and monitoring: equal
    opportunities 161–4; training and
    development 78–81
Evans, P. 2

explicitness and commitment 105
Express Foods 30
external: employment 34; vs internal
    objectives in training 80
extrinsic rewards 87
Exxon 77–8
Eysenck, H. 51

failure: and reward 94; and training 64
feedback and appraisal 58
Fell, A. 21
Fevre, R. 41
finance: human asset accounting 20–2;
    and training evaluation 79; *see also*
    costs
Flamholtz, E. 20, 21
Fletcher, C. 57
flexibility 9; and Europe 177–8; flexible
    firm 31–3; functional 9, 28; numerical
    9, 30–6; and reward 90; temporal
    28–30; and working practices 28–36
focused agenda and equal opportunities
    157
Fombrun, C. 12
Ford, H. 123
Ford Motor Company 38, 148
Fowler, A. 162
France 50, 164
functional flexibility 9, 28

Garrahan, P. 28, 152–3, 154–5
Geary, J. 33
gender *see* women
Germany 178; and competition 4;
    performance management system 27;
    training and development 63
Giles, W. 21
Glaxo Pharmaceuticals 42
GMB 143–4
Goss, D. 64, 67, 127, 149
Gourlay, S. 145–6
Grahl, J. 177–8
graphology 50–1
Graves, D. 103
Gray, R. 21
Grenier, G. 8, 48, 54–5, 119, 137, 144–5
group profit schemes 92, 94–6
Grummitt, J. 111–12
Guest, D. 2, 101, 146
Gullan-Whur, M. 51
Gulliford, A. 47

Hakim, C. 32–3, 171–3
Half, R. 44
Hammer, T. 95
handwriting tests 50–1
Handy, C. 72, 103
Hanson, C. 95
Harrold, C. 42
Hartley, J. 110
'Harvard School' 12–13
Harvard School 102–3
Hawthorne experiments 7, 137
health promotion policy 125–35; and
    efficiency see welfare; HIV/AIDS
    125–32; stress 134–5, 136; substance
    abuse 132–4, 139
health service: appraisal 50; and equal
    opportunities 164–5; human resource
    audit 21; performance management
    system 27; recruitment 41
Hearn, J. 167
Hendry, C. 12, 13–14, 66
Hermanson, R. 21
high commitment 107–8
Hill, S. 10, 67–8, 117–19
Hilton, P. 71
HIV/AIDS 125–32
Hobsons 171
Holdsworth, R. 55, 56
Hollway, W. 7
Holmes, L. 69, 75
Honey, P. 74
Howe, W. 8
HRM see human resource management
human asset accounting 20–2
human capital and social justice 156–7
human relations psychology 4, 7–8, 122
human resource management 1–18;
    analytical model 14–18; approaches to
    10–14; contemporary significance 1–6;
    see also assessment; commitment;
    employee involvement; equal
    opportunities; Europe; human
    resourcing; industrial relations; key
    themes; reward; training and
    development; welfare
human resourcing 19–38; flexibility and
    working practices 28–36; human asset
    accounting and audits 20–2; and
    information technology 22–5;
    manpower planning 19–20; systematic
    innovation 36–7
humanistic approaches 10, 12–14

humanitarian HIV/AIDS policy 129–32

IBM 56, 149–50, 152–3
ICL 25
IDS: on appraisal 51–2; on employee
    involvement 112, 114, 115–16; on
    equal opportunities 161, 164–6, 170,
    171; on flexibility 28, 29–30; on
    Maastricht 181; on NIR 143, 151–2; on
    performance management system 27,
    28; on reward 90, 95, 96–7; on training
    and development 67, 68; on welfare
    125, 135
IIP ('Investors in People') scheme 70–1
Iles, P. 58, 59, 108–10
improving purpose in evaluation 79
IMS: on IT 22; on reward 98; on training
    and development 66
independent union workplace strategies
    144
individual: biography 49; PRP 91–4
industrial relations and trade unions 3; and
    appraisal 54; Europe 181–2; and reward
    98; and training and development 63;
    see also New Industrial Relations
Industrial Society 111, 114
information: from others and commitment
    106; technology (IT) 22–5, 37–8
innovation, systematic 36–7
Institute of Personnel Management (IPM)
    22, 47, 74, 122
institutional response to NIR 143–4
instrumental approaches 10–12
'instrumental-calculative' commitment 109
integration of learning with work 75
inter-rater reliability of selection 44
internal: consistency and reliability of
    selection 44; vs external objectives in
    training 80
international competition 4
interviews 40, 43–5; appraisal 56–7
intrinsic rewards 87
'Investors in People' scheme 70–1
involvement see employee involvement
IPM see Institute of Personnel
    Management
IR see industrial relations
IRS: on appraisal 59; on equal
    opportunities 166; on human resource
    audit 21; on recruitment 42; on reward
    90; on selection 43–4, 45–7, 49; on
    training and development 67–9, 72,

77–8; on welfare 127
IT *see* information technology
ITN 30

Jackson, H. 158–9, 161, 162, 165, 168
Jaguar 43
James, K. 135
Japan and Japanese companies in UK: and
    commitment 104; competition from 4,
    117; and flexibility 28; and NIR 143,
    152, 153, 154–5; and reward 90; and
    selection 43, 60–1; and training and
    development 63; and welfare 124
JCC (Joint Consultative Committees) 151
job: design 102; evaluation 89–91;
    -sharing 171
Johnson, C. 46–7
Johnson and Johnson 144–5
Johnson, R. 75
Joint Consultative Committees 151
Jones, R. 64, 67
judgemental appraisal 51, 55

Kay 120
Keenoy, T. 11, 12
Keep, E. 63
Kennedy, A. 103
Kennedy, M. 173
Kenney, J. 63–4
Kerr, S. 85–6
Kessler, I. 91, 92
key themes of HRM 6–10; strategic
    management theory 8–9; *see also*
    flexibility; human relations
Kingston, A. 30
Kohl, J. 127, 129
Kolb, D. 74, 75–6, 77
Kremer, J. 167
Krulis-Randa, J. 1–2

Laabs, J. 38
Lacey, J. 21
Lasky, B. 170
law and legislation: and equal
    opportunities 158, 160; Europe 178,
    179–80; and unions 141–2
Lawler, E. 7
Lawrence, J. 76–7
learning 74–6; action 76–7; cycle 74–6,
    77; integrated with work 75; purpose in
    evaluation 79; *see also* training and
    development

legalistic–reactive welfare rationale 122
Legge, K. 25, 124
legislation *see* law and legislation
Leicester City Council 160
Leighton, P. 33, 35–6
Lewis, C. 47
Likert, R. 20
litigation and stress 134–5
Lockyer, C. 89
long agenda of equal opportunities 157,
    158–60
Long, P. 51
low commitment 107
Lowe, J. 77–8, 102, 103–4
Lucas Industries 65–6
Lucio, M. 143–4, 145
Lynch, P. 28, 29

Maastricht Treaty 175, 180–1
Mabey, C. 108–10
McCormick, R. 72
McDonnel, E. 8
McDonnel, R. 132
McEvoy, T. 80
McGregor, A. 33
Mackenzie Davey, D. 47
Mackness, J. 79
McLoughlin, I. 145–6
Madiot, B. 164
Maguire, M. 41
Major, J. 181
Malloch, H. 20
Management Charter Initiative (MCI) 72
manpower: planning 19–20; and training
    evaluation 79
'map of HRM territory' 13
Marchington, M. 101, 111, 113, 114
Marks, J. 167
Marks and Spencer 77–8
Marsden, J. 139
Marsh, A. 141, 142
Maunders, K. 21
Maynard, A. 132
Mayo, E. 7–8, 137
MCI (Management Charter Initiative) 72
meaning and behaviour 84–6
Means, R. 132–3
membership crisis of unions 140–1
mentoring 72–3
Miller, A. 127, 129
Miller, P. 11
Milne, S. 169

Milner, M. 61
Mintzberg, H. 9
'mismatch', pay 85–6
misunderstandings, preventing 112
Mohrman, S. 7
monitoring *see* evaluation and monitoring
MORI polls 115
Morris, J. 28, 32
Moss, G. 44, 51
motivation *see* reward
Muller, F. 65
multiple commitment 108
Murlis, H. 26

National Health Service *see* health service
National Opinion Polls (NOP) 115
National Vocational Qualifications
    (NVQs) 68–71, 72
Neale, M. 7, 26
networks 16–17
New Industrial Relations (NIR) 140–55;
    adaptation by unions 140–4; advisory
    boards and company councils 151–3;
    impact of HRM 144–51
new managerialism 5–6
Newby, H. 123
Newell, S. 170, 172
Nissan UK: flexibility 28; NIR 152, 153,
    154–5; reward 90; selection 43; welfare
    124
non-union companies 151–2
NOP (National Opinion Polls) 115, 166
Norris, G. 123
Northcraft, G. 7
Northern Ireland 160
no-strike agreements 142–3
Nuffield Hospitals 56
numerical flexibility 9, 30–6
NVQs (National Vocational
    Qualifications) 68–71

objective outcome measures in appraisal 52
O'Brien, O. 132
Oliver, B. 151
Oliver, N. 102, 103–4
openness of appraisal 55
operations and training evaluation 79
opinion polls 115–16, 166
O'Reilly, C. 105–7
organization: culture 54, 102;
    development *see* training and
    development; –employee relationships

and commitment 102; restructuring 5
outcome measures in appraisal 52
outdoors training and development 77–8
outplacement counselling 137
over-commitment 108
ownership and appraisal 55–6

Parker, P. 113
Parkin, W. 167
Parnaby (Lucas Industries) 65
participation: and commitment 106; and
    reward 88
partner change and NIR 147–8
part-time and temporary work 32–3,
    39–40, 171
paternalism welfare rationale 123
pay *see* reward
Pearce, D. 77
Pearce, J. 86, 93
Pearson, R. 11, 20, 22
Peccei, R. 101
Pedler, M. 74, 77
Pendleton, A. 147
perceived value and reward 97
performance *see* appraisal
performance-related pay (PRP) 83, 85, 88,
    97; individual 91–4
perk vs work objectives in training 80
personality tests 45–9
personnel management 3, 6; and welfare
    122–5; *see also* human resource
    management
Pettigrew, A. 8–9, 12, 13–14, 66
Phillips, N. 137
Pickard, J. 30
picketing 141
Plessey Naval Systems 54, 148
pluralist view of commitment 108
police force 166
policy and practice of equal opportunities
    see positive action
politics of equal opportunities action 163
Porter, L. 87
Porter, M. 4
positive action and equal
    opportunities 159, 160–73;
    behaviour and attitude 164–7;
    conceptualization 161–4; evaluation
    and monitoring 161–4; problem
    169–73; training and development 160,
    164, 167–9
Post Office 110

power: of unions curbed 141–42; *see also* control
Price Waterhouse Cranfield project 175
process not technique in learning 75
productivity and stress 135
proving purpose in evaluation 79
PRP *see* performance-related pay
psychology *see* human relations
psychometric tests 43, 45–9
publicity and commitment 105
Purcell, J. 11, 91, 92, 153, 181–2
purpose of appraisal 55

Quaker manufacturers 123
qualified majority voting (QMV) 180–1
qualitative assessment 55
quality: circles 116–20; management doctrines 9–10; *see also* total quality management
Quality of Work Life (QWL) 7
Quinn Mills, P. 103, 104

racism *see* ethnic minorities
Ramsay, H. 96, 101, 117
Randall, D. 107–8
Randell, G. 52–3, 55
Rank Xerox 34
rationality and 'rational outcome' view 8–9, 11–12
Ravaud, J. 164
recognition of NIR 147
recruitment 24, 39, 40–2
references 43
Reichers, A. 108
Reid, M. 63–4
reinforcement of management 112
relative positions first pay 84
reliability issues and selection 44
resource: people as *see* human resource management; provision and equal opportunities 160
restructuring, organizational 5
results vs change objectives in training 80
Revans, R. 77
revocability and commitment 105
reward (and pay) 83–100; and appraisal 53–5; and commitment 106–7; equal pay 158, 169, 174; and IT 24; nature of 83–8; skill-based 67; *see also* systems of reward
Richards-Carpenter, C. 23, 24
risk assessment model 35

Robertson, I. 47, 108–10
Robinson, D. 21
Rocco, F. 50
Rodger, D. 110
Rose, M. 7
Rover Group 65, 147, 163
Rowan, D. 61
Rucker, A. 95

Sackheim, K. 50
Sadri, G. 110
Salancik, G. 105
salaries *see* reward
salient motives pay 84
sampling and equal opportunities action 162–3
SAP (Social Action Programmes) 179–81
Sapsed, G. 56
Saunders, G. 104
Save As You Earn (SAYE) 95–6
Scanlon, J. 95
Schein, E. 103
Scotland 149–50, 152–3
Securicor 25
Seegers, J. 57, 58
Selby, R. 25
selection 39, 43–51; biodata 49–50; graphology 50–1; interviews 40, 43–5; psychometric tests 43, 45–9
self-classification and equal opportunities 162–3
self-development 72–6
self-directed learning 75
self-employment 32, 34
Sewell, G. 119–20
sexism *see* women
sexual harassment 165–7
shallow commitment 157
Shappiro, B. 94
share, equal 159
share schemes 92, 94–6
Sharrock, D. 139
Shepherd, G. 169
short agenda of equal opportunities 157, 158
Sidney, E. 137
Sigman, A. 125
simplicity and reward 90
simultaneous improvement of employees and organization 75
single union agreements (SUAs) 142, 151
Sisson, K. 123

skill-based pay 67
Slee Smith, P. 114
Sloman, M. 53–4
Smith, I. 83
Smith, M. 135
Social Action Programmes (SAP) 179–81
Social Charter 175, 178–82
social justice and human capital 156–7
Solomon, C. 167
Spencer, S. 25
Splisbury, M. 41
Sproull, A. 33
Stanworth, C. 34
Stanworth, J. 34
Steers, R. 87
Stewart, P. 28, 152–3, 154–5
Stochastic Rewards Valuation Model 21
Storey, J. 14; on appraisal 51, 54; on
    employee involvement 111, 112–13; on
    flexibility 28, 33; on 'hard' HRM 10;
    on NIR 146–9; on personnel
    management 2–3, 6; on selection 43,
    45; on training and development 66, 82
strategic change 15
strategic management theory 8–9
Strauss, L. 129
Straw, J. 159, 164
stress 134–5, 136
strikes and industrial action 141; no-strike
    agreements 142–3
structures and commitment 102
Stuart, D. 75–6
style of appraisal 55
SUAs (single union agreements) 142, 151
substance abuse 132–4, 139
substantive vs symbolic objectives in
    training 80
success: and reward 93–4; and training 64
succession planning 24
suggestion schemes 113–15
support counselling 135, 137
Sweden 178
Switzerland 50
symbolic action and commitment 106
symbolic vs substantive objectives in
    training 80
Syrett, M. 33, 35–6
systematic innovation 36–7
systems and commitment 102
systems of reward 88–99; cafeteria or
    flexible benefit schemes 96–9; group
    profit and share schemes 92, 94–6; job

evaluation 89–91; meaning and
    behaviour 84–6; system and function
    86–8; see also performance-related pay

Tanton, M. 79
tax implications of reward 98
Taylor, F.W. / Taylorism 4, 7, 69
Taylor, S. 50
Teague, P. 177–8
team briefing 111–13
Tebbit, N. 141
TECs (Training and Enterprise Councils)
    70–1
temporal flexibility 28–30
temporary work see part-time
test-retest reliability of selection 44
tests, psychometric 43, 45–9
Texaco 139
Texas Instruments 68
Thierry, H. 84–5, 89, 91
Thurley, K. 178
time: needed for appraisal 58; timing of
    equal opportunities action 163
Tioxide 145
token agenda and equal opportunities 157
Tolley, K. 126
Torrington, D. 24
Toshiba 152
total compensation and reward 98
total quality management (TQM) 10; and
    employee involvement 114, 116–20;
    and training 67–8
'tough love' 124
Towers, B. 14
Townley, B. 45, 48, 54–5
Toyota 60–1
TQM see total quality management
trade unions see industrial relations and
    trade unions
Trades Union Congress see TUC
training and development 62–82; appraisal
    58; definitions 62; development 71–8;
    and equal opportunities 160, 164,
    167–9; evaluation of 78–81; mentoring
    72–3; training 63–71
Training and Enterprise Councils (TECs)
    70–1
trait scales in appraisal 52
Triplex Lloyd 59
TUC (Trades Union Congress) 63, 141,
    142
Turnbull, P. 14

turnover and stress 134
Tyson, S. 11, 21

unions *see* industrial relations and trade
    unions
Unipart 145
'unitarism' 12
United States 177; appraisal 54, 57;
    competition 4; equal opportunities 167;
    humanistic approach 12–13; industrial
    restructuring 5; and NIR 144–5; reward
    83, 85, 97, 98–9; selection 48; training
    and development 63; welfare 123, 124,
    126–7

Vaughan, E. 170
Ville, I. 164
vocational education and training (VET)
    see training and development
volition and commitment 105

Walton, R. 7, 102–3
Warburg (SG) 50
Watson, R. 95
welfare 122–39; counselling 135–7; health
    promotion policy 125–35; personnel
    management 122–5
West Germany *see* Germany

Weston, C. 169
Weston, S. 143–4, 145
Whitaker, C. 11
Whyte, W. 48
Wickens, P. 28, 43, 89–90, 119, 124, 143
Wilkinson, B. 119–20
Wilkinson, N. 151
Williams, S. 25
Wilson, J. 56
Wilson, P. 126
Winchurch, R. 23–4
women: and equal opportunities 158, 159,
    160–1, 165–7, 168–73, 174; and
    flexibility 30; and recruitment 41
Wood, R. 48, 168
Wood, S. 75
Woodley, C. 97
Woodruffe, C. 57
Woodward, T. 23–4
work vs perk objectives in training 80
working practices and flexibility 28–36
workplace strategies 144

Young, Lord 63
Young, R. 173

Zeithaml, C. 9